DI'BIL B. 'ALĪ

LEON ZOLONDEK

Di'bil b. 'Alī

THE LIFE & WRITINGS OF AN EARLY 'ABBĀSID POET

UNIVERSITY OF KENTUCKY PRESS

Printed in the United States of America by the
Division of Printing, University of Kentucky
Library of Congress Catalog Card No.
61-6553

The publication of this book has been made possible partly through a grant from the Margaret Voorhies Haggin Trust, established in memory of her husband, James Ben Ali Haggin.

PREFACE

THIS BOOK WAS undertaken in order to add to our knowledge of the history of Arabic literature by a study of an early ʿAbbāsid poet, Diʿbil b. Alī al-Khuzāʿī. In addition to collecting and editing 229 fragments of his poetry, consisting of 778 verses, it was also possible to reconstruct the essential features of Diʿbil's long-lost yet widely quoted *Book of the Poets.* From this reconstruction, Diʿbil emerges as one of the great transmitters of Arabic poetry as well as a major figure in the formation of the specifically Arabic view of literary history. Ibn al-Jarrāh's (d. 296 A.H./908 A.D.) *Kitāb al-Waraqah* and other later sources reveal their dependence on Diʿbil's book, which forms a link between al-Jumahī's (d. 230/845) *Tabaqāt* and the *Kitāb ash-Shiʿr wa'sh-Shuʿarā'* of Diʿbil's pupil Ibn Qutaibah (d. 276/889), which up to the present have been our main sources for the literary history and criticism of the ninth century.

The author has also made a critical study of the sources for Diʿbil's biography. Schaade's short article in the *Encyclopedia of Islām* is based chiefly on one source, the *Kitāb al-Aghānī.* This is also true for the still shorter references to Diʿbil made by Brockelmann in the *Geschichte der arabischen Litteratur* and by Rescher in his *Abriss der arabischen Litteraturgeschichte.* Though the *Kitāb al-Aghānī* is perhaps our most important source of biographical material, it has to be studied critically and in conjunction with other historical and literary sources. By examining the reports of the *Kitāb al-Aghānī* and collating them with the related accounts in such works as the *Tabaqāt* of Ibn al-Muʿtazz (d. 296/908), the *Ta'rīkh Baghdād* of al-Khatīb al-Baghdādī (d. 463/1069), and the *Ta'rīkh Dimashq* of Ibn ʿAsākir (d. 571/1176), the writer hopes to have laid a foundation for the biography of Diʿbil and to have shown the necessity of altering significantly some of the previously held views regarding one of the major poets of the ʿAbbāsid Age.

My warmest thanks are due to Professor G. E. von Grunebaum, for the suggestion of this study and for his guidance in the field of Arabic metrics. I would also like to thank Professor N. Abbott for her criticisms and help in the utilization of the sources. My thanks are also extended to Professor J. A. Wilson for reading the original manuscript and for his corrections.

The abbreviations used in annotating the Arabic text, here reproduced photographically from the author's dissertation, have been retained in the footnotes and in the key to works cited. In the English text of the present volume, a different system of transliteration is used.

L. Z.

CONTENTS

PREFACE *page* v

1. THE POET AND HIS TIME 1
2. THE POETRY (ARABIC TEXT) 9
3. THE POETRY (ENGLISH TEXT) 92
4. THE POET AS A CRITIC 125
5. THE BOOK OF THE POETS 133

WORKS CITED 181

INDEX 185

1

THE POET AND HIS TIME

THE ARAB PERIOD of Islamic history came to an end in 132/750 with the rise of the 'Abbāsids. The center of the Islamic world moved from Syria to Irāq; the Syrians lost the power and influence which they had possessed under the Umayyads (40/661—132/750), and Persians now occupied the chief positions of the state. From 170/786 to 187/803 the Persian family of Khālid b. Barmak were the practical rulers of the 'Abbāsid state; after the fall of the Barmakids, the Persian family of Sahl played the major role, especially during the reign of the caliph al-Ma'mūn (198/813—218/833), who in 210/825 married Būrān, the daughter of al-Hasan b. Sahl.

Not only did the Arabs lose their political leadership with the rise of the 'Abbāsids, but their military dominance as well. Under the first caliphs the bodyguard was largely composed of Khurāsānid troops, to whom the 'Abbāsids owed their rise to power. But during the reign of al-Mu'tasim (218/833—227/842), whose mother was of Turkish origin, the army became dominated by Turks from central Asia. These forces, originally brought in to counterbalance the Persians and the Arabs, became the terror of Baghdād, and in 221/836 al-Mu'tasim built for himself and his Turks the new capital of Sāmmarā, which remained the seat of the government for fifty-six years.

Besides the struggle between Arabs, Persians, and Turks for the political and military domination of the caliphate, the 'Abbāsid regime was torn by strife over the succession, at times breaking into civil war, and by the politico-religious conflict between the Sunnites, or orthodox party, and the Shī'ites. The Shī'ites were partisans of 'Alī, Muhammad's cousin and husband of his daughter Fātimah. They claimed that Muhammad, before his death in 10/632, had appointed 'Alī as his successor. The Shī'ites regarded Abū Bakr, who was selected as the prophet's successor, and the two caliphs who followed him as usurpers. 'Alī himself became caliph in 35/656, but after his death five years later the office was wrested from his family—regarded by the Shī'ites as his legitimate successors—by the Umayyads, who remained in power until 132/750. During the period of the Umayyad caliphate the Shī'ite cause attracted many who were dissatisfied for political, social, economic, or religious reasons with the regime, including a number of groups who supported the descendants of various members of Muhammad's family. Among these were the 'Abbāsids, descendants of one of Muhammad's uncles. After two years of civil war, a coalition of Shī'ite, 'Abbāsid, and Khurāsānid forces succeeded in driving the Umayyads from power. But it was an 'Abbāsid caliph who now seized office, and to the irreconcilable Shī'ites he and his successors were also usurpers, having preempted the office which properly belonged to the descendants of 'Alī. Thus the politico-religious conflict continued during the reign of the 'Abbāsids, and in 144/762 an abortive revolt was led by Ibrāhīm and Muhammad, great-grandsons of al-Hasan, the older son of 'Alī, who became martyrs to the Shī'ite cause. In 198/813 a conflict over the succession between al-Amīn and al-Ma'mūn ended with the death of al-Amīn. The confusion following this fight induced various Shī'ite claimants, notably Ibn Tabātabā in Kūfah and Zaid b. Mūsā in Basrah, to rise against the 'Abbāsids, but these rebellions were quelled by al-Ma'-mūn's forces.

The early 'Abbāsids (ca. 132/750—247/861) were patrons of culture and attracted the most brilliant poets and scholars to their court. The new capital, Baghdād, became the center for literature and culture, the marketplace where intellectual wares were brought to be appraised. The caliphs of the Golden Age literally awarded thousands for an apt phrase or verse at the right time and place. Not only the caliphs but the notables of the realm as well, especially the Barmakids, bestowed fortunes on their panegyrists. This patronage of the poets was not motivated only by the personal literary tastes of the caliphs and their courts. The poets from the pre-Islamic period onward were the press of the times and the molders of public opinion. Each change in the affairs of state was reflected in poetry. Under such circumstances, it would be too much to expect that the poets would be completely unbiased in their verses. Since they were dependent upon the beneficence of their patrons, they regarded their loyalty and their verses as stock in trade. It is therefore not surprising to find that the poets are inconsistent ideologically and politically. The poetry of the Golden Age reflects the struggles of a period of violent religious and political conflict.

The most original literary development of the early 'Abbāsid period was the emergence of the "new style" in poetry. The classical ode of the pre-Islamic age, *qasīdah,* with its glorification of desert life and Bedouin ideals, begins with reflections on the traces of the deserted dwelling places of the tribe, to which is linked an erotic prelude bewailing the poet's separation from his beloved. The poet then professes to seek comfort by mounting his camel for a perilous ride through the desert. After depicting the danger and hardships of his journey, he concludes by addressing a request to a powerful personage. This form, which was still the model for the Umayyad poets, was not a suitable vehicle for the poetic tastes of the 'Abbāsids. The patronage of the court, the pietistic spirit fostered by the state, the needs of the governmental secretaries, the foreign influence coming mainly from Persia, and the change in social conditions all contributed to the popularity of the "new style," which was distinguished by the use of novel similes, praise and satire exceeding the limits of credibility, simplicity of expression, avoidance of strange words, and padding.

One of the earliest exponents of the "new style" was the blind Persian poet Bashshār b. Burd (d. 167/783), who was famous for his satires. Another representative was the half-Persian Abū Nuwās (d. 194/810), famous for his love and wine poems, who mocked the conventions of the classical ode. While Abū Nuwās portrayed the lighter side of life, his contemporary, Abū'l-'Atāhiyah (d. 213/828) composed religious poems expressing in simple language his pessimistic meditations on mortality.

The early critics, however, were philologians by profession, and held fast to the view that poetry of the pre-Islamic age had reached a perfection which no modern poet could hope to emulate. Those poets who desired their approval had to follow the traditions of the classical ode and its portrayal of Bedouin life. Such was their bias for the pre-Islamic poetry that to have been born after Islām was in itself proof of poetic inferiority. Not being of pure Arab stock or not to have learned Arabic in the pure atmosphere of the desert were charges often raised by the critics against the modern poets, many of whom had mixed ancestry.

The 'Abbāsid dynasty attained its most brilliant period of political and intellectual growth soon after its establishment. It reached its peak in the period between the reigns of the third caliph, al-Mahdī (158/775—169/785), and the ninth, al-Wāthiq (227/842—232/847), more particularly in the days of Hārūn ar-Rashīd (170/786—193/809) and his son, al-Ma'-mūn (198/813—218/833). After al-Wāthiq the state began on the downward course which ended with its destruction at the hands of the Mongols in 656/1258. The period of the Golden Age, which forms the background of Di'bil's life and work, was a time of ferment not only in literature but in every aspect of the national life.

THE POET Abū 'Alī Muhammad b. 'Alī b. Razīn al-Khuzā'ī was born in 148/765.[1] Through the meaning and origin of the nickname "Di'bil" are unknown, the poet became famous under this name, and all of the sources refer to him by his nickname rather than his personal name.

Di'bil's birthplace is uncertain, the two cities of Kūfah and Qarqīsiyā being mentioned by different authorities.[2] According to the *Kitāb al-Aghānī*, Di'bil spent his youth in Kūfah, where he is said to have associated with disreputable companions and to have been guilty of robbery and even, in some versions, of murder.[3] But these accounts are of questionable authenticity.[4] That Di'bil in his youth engaged in some mischievous activity is quite probable, but exactly what he did is open to question. That he was not alone in such behavior is attested by similar stories regarding Hammād ar-Rāwiyah (d. 156/772) and Di'bil's contemporary, the poet Bakr b. an-Nattāh.[5]

There is no reason to doubt that Di'bil was of the tribe of Khuzā'ah, though some of his contemporaries denied it, charging that he was not of pure Arab stock.[6] These statements cannot be taken seriously, since rival poets regularly indulged in such accusations. That there was a question as to which branch of the Khuzā'ah Di'bil belonged is apparent from the two genealogies listed for him.[7] The more frequently cited genealogy, which gives his descent through Budail b. Warqā', may be an attempt to link his family with the 'Alids and with Muhammad, for 'Abd Allāh b. Budail was a man of influence in Makkah before Islām and an early and influential follower of Muhammad.[8] In any case, Di'bil's family was famous, for it produced successive generations of poets. Di'bil's father, grandfather, and son, as well as his first and second cousins, are cited as poets.[9]

Di'bil's apprenticeship as a poet, according to Di'bil himself as well as to other sources, was under the tutelage of the poet Muslim b. al-Walīd (d. 208/823).[10] Following the common practice, the fledgling poet would present his product to Muslim

[1] *Ta'rīh Baghdād,* VIII, 385. This date is generally accepted by later historians: Ibn 'Asāk., *Tar.*, V, 241-42; Ibn Hallikān, Slane, I, 510; *Nujūm*, II, 322. *Lisān*, II, 430, gives his birth date as 142 A.H.

[2] *Ta'rīh Baghdād*, VIII, 382; Ibn 'Asāk., *Tar.*, V, 227; *Irshād*, IV, 194.

[3] Ag., XVIII, 31, 35, 36. See *Abriss*, II, 20-21.

[4] Ag., XVIII, 31.

[5] *Abriss*, I, 275; II, 34.

[6] Ag., XVIII, 31, 47, 56. See Ibn Hallikān, Slane, I, 510, where Di'bil's grandfather Razīn is confused with Tāhir b. al-Husain's grandfather Ruzaiq, thus making Razīn a client of Khuzā'ah. This error is continued in *Lisān*, II, 430; *Bidāyah*, X, 348; *EI*, I, 967. The source for the error is to be found in *Si'r*, pp. 539-40.

[7] Ag., XVIII, 29; *Ta'rīh Baghdād*, VIII, 382; Ibn 'Asāk., *Tar.*, V, 277. Cf. Ag., XV, 108. See *Genealogisches Handbuch*, p. 272.

[8] Ibn Sa'd, IV, part II, 31; *Genealogisches Handbuch*, p. 280. See *A'yān*, I, 263.

[9] *'Umdah*, II, 236; *Fihrist*, p. 161. See Ag., XVIII, 30, where Di'bil cites verses of his father. Ibn al-Mu'tazz, *Tab.*, pp. 193-94, devotes a section to the poetry of Di'bil's son al-Husain.

[10] Ag., XVIII, 46-47, 57; Ibn 'Asāk., *Tar.*, V, 233. See *Abriss*, I, 54, where al-Kumait presents his poetry before al-Farazdaq.

for approval. Di'bil relates, "I continued to compose poetry and to present it to Muslim. Muslim used to say, 'hide it,' until I recited the verse 'where is youth, where has it gone . . .?' Then Muslim said, 'Go and present your poems however and to whomever you desire.' "[11] This poem approved by Muslim appears to have been Di'bil's earliest published product. Sung before Hārūn ar-Rashīd, it caused Di'bil to be summoned before the caliph, who bestowed a pension on him. 'Abd Allāh b. Ṭāhir, the authority for the account of Di'bil's entry into the circle of the court, further asserts that Hārūn was the first to urge Di'bil to compose poems.[12] Di'bil probably entered the court during the later years of Hārūn's reign, *i.e.*, 179/795—193/809.

Like many another poet, Di'bil held public office. The first occasion was as a prefect for al-'Abbās b. Ja'far b. Muhammad b. al-Ash'ath in the town of Siminjān. The date of Di'bil's tenure of office is uncertain.[13] His second public office was that of prefect in Aswān for al-Muttalib b. 'Abd Allāh b. Mālik al-Khuzā'ī, who was governor of Egypt during 198/813—200/815. However, al-Muttalib soon removed Di'bil from office.[14]

There is a quaint anecdote describing the relationship between Di'bil and al-Muttalib which, whether true or not, illustrates the shrewdness of Di'bil and the forbearance of caliphs and men of power toward subordinates. Having been satirized by Di'bil, al-Muttalib states he is going to kill him. Di'bil replies that al-Muttalib should feed him first lest he be killed hungry. Al-Muttalib retorts that this is more satiric than his earlier attack, but he is really impressed by the reply and is again reconciled with Di'bil. Di'bil in return promises to praise him as long as he lives.[15]

Though Di'bil is spoken of as one of the most famous of Shī'ites, he apparently was not connected with any of the more extreme sects which by this time had arisen within the Shī'ah.[16] The author of the *Kitāb al-Aghānī* states merely that he was a famous partisan of 'Alī, whereas other Shī'ite poets are identified as adherents of the Kaisaniyyah.[17] It should be noted that attachment to 'Alī and to the 'Alids is not objectionable from the Sunnite point of view—it is the denunciation of 'Alī's predecessors in the caliphate, Abū Bakr and 'Umar, which is unacceptable to the orthodox of Islām. The extant fragments of Di'bil's poems contain no such denunciation. The concepts reflected in them are those which by his day had become the accepted doctrine of the Shī'ah as a whole, namely, the belief that 'Alī was the appointed executor of Muhammad and the belief in the future coming of an Imām, a divinely guided one who will restore true Islām.[18] If any partisanship is to be ascribed to Di'bil, it is his personal attachment to 'Alī ar-Riḍā, who came so close to becoming a Shī'ite caliph.

In 202/817 al-Ma'mūn appointed 'Alī ar-Riḍā as his heir, and soon after March, 817, Di'bil was in Khurāsān, reciting before 'Alī his famous poem praising the Family of the Prophet.[19] Di'bil and Ibrāhīm b. al-'Abbās as-Sūlī (d. 243/857) had gone to Khurāsān to recite their poems before 'Alī ar-Riḍā and al-Ma'mūn, both of whom rewarded

[11] *Ag.*, XVIII, 46-47; *Muslim*, p. 245. See poem CLV.

[12] *Ag.*, XVIII, 57; Ibn 'Asāk., *Tar.*, V, 233.

[13] *EI*, I, 967-68; *GAL Suppl.*, I, 121; Zambaur, p. 48.

[14] *Ag.*, XVIII, 48.

[15] Ibn 'Asāk., *Tar.*, V, 241.

[16] See Ibn Sharāshub, p. 139, where Di'bil is listed among the moderate Shī'ites.

[17] *Ag.*, XVIII, 29. Cf. XII, 142, for Abū'l-Faraj's opinion of Dīk al-Jinn, whose Shī'ism he regards as of the proper temper. The Kaisaniyyah poets are as-Sayyid al-Himyarī and Kuthayyir. See *Ag.*, VII, 5; VIII, 5.

[18] *Maqālat*, I, 5; *Vorlesungen*, p. 209; See Hodgson, p. 6. See poem XLI.

[19] Ibn al-Mu'tazz, *Tab.*, p. 125; *Ag.*, XVIII, 29, 42-43; *Faraj*, II, 115-17; Daulat-Shāh, p. 23; *A'yān*, XXX, 327-28.

Di'bil.[20] The revolt which erupted in Baghdād after al-Ma'mūn designated 'Alī ar-Riḍā as heir resulted in the election of Ibrāhīm b. al-Mahdī as counter caliph, and Di'bil may have witnessed the revolt of the counter caliph's troops in Baghdād.[21] After the death of 'Alī ar-Riḍā in 203/818 and the eclipse of the 'Alid hopes for the caliphate, Di'bil satirized al-Ma'mūn and his father, Hārūn;[22] later, however, probably before 207/822, he was reconciled to al-Ma'mūn. But Di'bil later satirized the 'Abbāsid caliphs al-Mu'tasim, al-Wāthiq, and al-Mutawakkil (232/847—247/861),[23] who earned the eternal hatred of the Shī'ah for his destruction of the tomb of 'Alī at Najaf and that of al-Husain at Karbalā.

The poets 'Alī b. al-Jahm (d. 249/863) and Abū'l-'Alā' al-Ma'arrī (d. 449/1057) impugned Di'bil's orthodoxy and his devotion to the 'Alids.[24] But 'Alī b. al-Jahm, who accused Di'bil of unbelief, was anti-'Alid and a close friend of Abū Tammām who was attacked by Di'bil.[25] Poets as a group were frequently thought of as heretics or freethinkers.[26] As to al-Ma'arrī's charge that Di'bil was motivated by worldly gain, it should be noted that other Shī'ite poets were not hindered by their beliefs from seeking rewards from anti-'Alid patrons.[27]

It would seem to be beyond mere coincidence that those poets with whom Di'bil had friendly relations were pro-Shī'ah, namely, Abū Nuwās, Muslim b. al-Walīd, Ibrāhīm b. al-'Abbās as-Sūlī, and Dīk al-Jinn (d. 236/849).[28] But the partisanship of the Shī'ite al-Kumait (d. 126/743) for the North Arabs against the South Arabs occasioned Di'bil's posthumous satire against him, and Di'bil's friendship with Muslim b. al-Walīd broke on financial grounds.[29]

The animosity between Abū Sa'd al-Makhzūmī and Di'bil, which continued through the reigns of al-Ma'mūn and al-Mu'tasim, resulted from an incident when the tribe of Banū Makhzūm were inhospitable to Di'bil and from Di'bil's attack on the North Arabs.[30] In addition, it appears that Abū Sa'd did not miss the opportunity to play on the hatred of those satirized by Di'bil, but the chief factor was the continual conflict between the two Arab factions. Di'bil's attack on the North Arabs, which was a rejoinder to al-Kumait's poem praising them, could not remain unchallenged. It appears that Di'bil, though he had the upper hand against Abū Sa'd, failed in his attack on al-Kumait and the North Arabs. Di'bil tells the story of seeing the Prophet Muhammad in his sleep. Muhammad asks him to explain what is going on between him and al-Kumait. Di'bil answers that there is nothing between them except that which usually goes on between poets. The Prophet then tells Di'bil to desist from maligning al-Kumait, for God has forgiven him by reason of one of his pro-Shī'ah verses. Di'bil concludes his story by stating that he thereafter has desisted from attacking al-Kumait.[31] This is further supported by the statement of Mihrawaihi, one of the principal authorities for Di'bil's biography, that Di'bil was held in high esteem by the people until he attacked al-Kumait, and that this was one of the factors in the decline of his popularity.[32]

[20] Ibn 'Asāk., *Tar.*, V, 231; Murtaḍā, II, 130.
[21] Abbott, pp. 224-26; see poem CXXVI.
[22] See poems LXV and XCV.
[23] See poems XIV, LIX, and CXCIX; LIX and CXCIX; LXI.
[24] Sūlī, *Abū Tammām*, p. 61; *Gufrān*, p. 352.
[25] Ibn Hallikān, Slane, II, 294-97.
[26] *Mutī' b. Iyās*, p. 172; *Salm al-Hāsir*, p. 54.
[27] See *Abriss*, I, 153, 299.
[28] Ibn Hallikān, Slane, II, 213; *MS*, I, 83; *Muslim*, pp. 241-42; *Ag.*, XII, 142; *'Umdah*, I, 147.
[29] See poem CCXIII. *Ag.*, XVIII, 47; *Muslim*, pp. 241-42.
[30] *Ag.*, XVIII, 29, 50.
[31] *Ag.*, XV, 124; XVIII, 21.
[32] *Ag.*, XVIII, 31. Brockelmann (*GAL Suppl.*, I, 121) mistranslates the Arabic texts and states: "Seinen ersten poetischen Ruhm hatte er durch einen Angriff auf al-Kumait erworben."

Apart from Abū Tammām's satire of Di'bil for his attack on al-Kumait and Abū Tammām's lukewarm allegiance to the Shī'ah,[33] Di'bil's criticism of Abū Tammām is chiefly based on his opinion of him as a poet. How little Di'bil thought of Abū Tammām's poetry is indicated by the fact that Di'bil did not include him in his *Book of the Poets.* According to Di'bil, Abū Tammām's poetry was closer to prose; and of this, only one third was sound, the rest being either worthless or the result of plagiarism.[34] The defenders of Abū Tammām charged Di'bil with envying Abū Tammam's success with the caliph al-Mu'tasim, for Di'bil's star was on the decline at this period.[35]

After Abū Tammām's death, however, Di'bil could find a good word for him. Di'bil visits al-Hasan b. Wahb seeking his help. He is then attacked by one of Abū Tammām's supporters for his unfair criticism of Abū Tammām; and when certain of Abū Tammām's verses are recited, Di'bil praises their merit.[36] This incident seems to indicate a change of heart, but Di'bil mav have praised Abū Tammām in order to mollify al-Hasan, who had been one of Abū Tammām's patrons.

Following the eclipse of the Shī'ite hopes with the death of 'Alī ar-Ridā in 203/818, Di'bil's relation with the 'Abbāsid caliphs is marked by extreme antagonism.[37] Flight, the forbearance of the caliphs, the intercession of influential friends, and the expedient of lying appear to have saved the life of the poet.[38] When Di'bil is brought before the caliph al-Mu'tasim, who orders his death for having satirized him, Ibrāhīm b. al-Mahdī unexpectedly comes forward and states that he composed the satire and attributed it to Di'bil, for he therewith wished to cause Di'bil's death. After freeing Di'bil, al-Mu'tasim asks Ibrāhīm whether he really did compose the poem. Ibrāhīm replies that he did not and that he only claimed its authorship in order to save Di'bil's life, though Di'bil was most hateful to him.[39] However near the end of al-Mutawakkil's reign, Di'bil finally met a violent death at the instigation of Mālik b. Tauq (d. 259/872).[40]

Apart from its historical interest, the determination of Di'bil's death date is of importance, since it involves the authorship of certain poems attributed to him. Yāqūt puts his death at the hands of al-Mu'tasim as early as 220/835, a dating which is followed by Blachère.[41] Brockelmann first gives as Di'bil's death date the year 246/860, but in his *Supplement* he cites various sources, including Yāqūt, which indicates that he felt some uncertainty in the matter.[42] However, the evidence tends to confirm the date of 246/860 given in the *Ta'rīkh Baghdād,* which is generally followed by the later historical sources.[43]

It is significant for an evaluation of Di'bil's technique and of the sincerity of his

. . . .

[33] Sūlī, *Abū Tammām,* pp. 267-69. Ibn Sharāshub, p. 139, lists Abū Tammām among the poets who exercised caution in their partisanship to the House of the Prophet. For Di'bil's relations with Abū Tammām, see *Ag.,* XVIII, 142; Ibn 'Asāk., *Tar.,* III, 19-20; *K. Baghdād,* p. 246.

[34] *Muwassah,* pp. 200-201, 237, 244; *Muwāzanah,* pp. 8-9, 29. See *Plagiarism,* pp. 234-53.

[35] Sūlī, *Abū Tammām,* p. 61, 201; *Muwāzanah,* p. 10. Ibn Rashīq points out that the success of Abū Tammām obscured such excellent poets as Abū Hiffān, Dīk al-Jinn, and Di'bil. *'Umdah,* I, 64.

[36] Sūlī, *Abū Tammām,* p. 202.

[37] See poems XIV, LIX, LXI, LXV, XCV, CXCIX, and CCXXI.

[38] *Ag.,* XVIII, 39, 41; Husrī, I, 297-98; *K. Baghdād,* pp. 193-94.

[39] Ibn 'Asāk., *Tar.,* V, 232-33.

[40] *Ag.,* XVIII, 60.

[41] *Buldān,* II, 960-61; Ibn 'Asāk., *Tar.,* V, 242; Blachère, p. 132.

[42] *GAL,* I, 78; *GAL Suppl.,* I, 122.

[43] Ibn al-Athīr, VII, 60; Abū'l-Fidā', II, 204; *Duwal,* I, 116; *Bidāyah,* X, 347. *Mir'āt,* II, 115, gives his death date as 244 or 246 A.H. For data supporting this date see *Ta'rīh Baghdād,* II, 342; Sūlī, *Abū Tammām,* pp. 202, 250, 274; *Nujūm,* II, 284.

satires that he at times composed them in advance as stock pieces, leaving out the name of the future victim.[44] Of course the statements regarding those whom he satirizes are not to be taken at their face value, nor were they so taken by his contemporaries. Like his predecessors Muslim b. al-Walīd and Bashshār b. Burd, Di'bil believed that satire provided a better living than the best panegyric, for in his view, men were most influenced by the fear that their defects be broadcast.[45] It is in this light that the charge of ingratitude against Di'bil must be viewed. His poems were the sole means of his livelihood. If the patron were remiss in his reward, the poet's loyalty, largely based on monetary considerations, ceased. The poet's loyalty, furthermore, usually returned upon the bestowal of the proper remuneration. From this viewpoint, Di'bil is no better nor worse than his contemporaries.

If Di'bil is most famous for his satires—at times of the vilest content—he is also capable of expressing a fine sentiment toward his patrons and an appreciation of nature.[46] Though he appears to follow the conventional diffuseness of the classical ode in his longer poems, he soon goes on to the heart of the matter.[47] The simplicity and directness of his expression are characteristic of the early 'Abbāsid age.[48] Though the greater part of his poetry is to us of little beauty and is limited to specific situations, it reflects the conditions of his time, and thereby gives added color to the accounts of the history of the period.

The *Fihrist* estimates Di'bil's *Dīwān*, which was compiled by as-Sūlī (d. 335/946), at around three hundred leaves.[49] An earlier selection of his poems was made by Ahmad b. abī Tāhir (d. 280/893) in his anthology *The Book of the Selections from the Poetry of the Poets.*[50] The *Dīwān*, according to the author of the *A'yān ash-Shī'ah*, was still in existence in the last century, but now is lost.[51]

Abū'l-Faraj considers Di'bil a natural poet and a malicious satirist, who spared neither the caliphs nor their grandees.[52] According to Ahmad b. al-Anbārī, Di'bil was the greatest satirist of his time, and in the opinion of Mihrawaihi, poetry came to an end with Di'bil.[53] Both Abū Nuwās and al-Mubarrad regard him as an eloquent poet.[54] The extreme partisanship of the Shī'ites for Di'bil can be seen in the opinion of Daulat-Shāh, who places him among the ten great Arabic poets.[55] An interesting and less biased view of his status is obtained from the account in which Ibn al-Kalbī regards Di'bil as "the whole of Khuzā'ah," an opinion which was shared by the caliph al-Ma'mūn.[56]

As regards his position among his contemporaries, Ibn Rashīq makes Di'bil bring up the rear of the class of Abū Nuwās.[57] Al-Buhturī rates him above Muslim b. al-Walīd, stating that Di'bil's language and outlook was closer to that of the desert Arabs.[58] However, al-Buhturī also states that "Di'bil put his hand into a bag but brought forth nothing," while he regards Abū Tam-

44 *Ag.*, XVIII, 33. Cf. *Salm al-Hāsir*, p. 61.
45 *Ag.*, XVIII, 31; *Abriss*, I, 294, II, 14.
46 See poems XIII, XLII, CCXVIII, and CCXXII; CXCVIII.
47 See poems XXXIV, XLI, and CCXIII.
48 See Von Grunebaum, p. 132.
49 *Fihrist*, p. 161. His Dīwān is mentioned in Ibn 'Asāk., *Tar.*, V, 227; Daulat-Shāh, p. 23, and *Kashf*, III, 279-80. *GAL Suppl.*, I, 940, cites a *Sharh Qasīdat Di'bil* by M. al-Qanawī al-Fārisī, Teheran, 1308/1890.
50 *Fihrist*, p. 146.
51 *A'yān*, XXX, 320.
52 *Ag.*, XVIII, 29. Ibn Rashīq calls him the devil of the poets (*shaitān ash-shū'arā'*). *'Umdah*, I, 73.
53 *As'ār*, p. 330; *Ag.*, XVIII, 30.
54 *Ta'rīh Baghdād*, VIII, 384-85; Ibn 'Asāk., *Tar.*, V, 230.
55 Daulat-Shāh, p. 16.
56 *Ag.*, XVIII, 39, 47.
57 *'Umdah*, I, 64.
58 *Ag.*, XVIII, 37.

mām as an admirable poet.[59] Adh-Dhahabī refers to Di'bil as the outstanding poet of his age.[60]

Undoubtedly because of his authorship of the *Kitāb ash-Shū'arā'* and the *Kitāb al-Wāhidah fī Mathālib al-'Arab wa Manāqibihā,* Di'bil is regarded as an authority on matters of poetry.[61] Ibn Sharaf al-Qairawānī considers him the "poet of the learned and the learned of the poets."[62] On a question regarding the identity of two poets, Ibn 'Asākir prefers Di'bil's opinion to that of al-Marzubānī, stating that Di'bil was earlier and more learned in these matters.[63]

59 *Muwassah,* p. 21.
60 *Duwal,* I, 116.
61 *Fihrist,* p. 161; A'*yān,* XXX, 265; Löfgren, II, 99-101; *Nujūm,* II, 372.
62 Ibn Sharaf, p. 38.
63 Ibn 'Asāk., *Tar,* VII, 46.

2

THE POETRY (ARABIC TEXT)

I

Ibn Šaj, Hamāsah, I, 234; Wāḥidī, p. 24.   Sarīʿ

مَا أَطْيَبَ ٱلْعَيْشَ فَأُمَّا عَلَى   أَنْ لَا أَرَى وَجْهَكِ يَوْمًا فَلَا

لَوْ أَنَّ يَوْمًا مِنْكِ أَوْ سَاعَةً   تُبَاعُ بِٱلدُّنْيَا إِذًا مَا غَلَا

la Wāḥidī   فإمّا

II

1-4 K. Baghdād, p. 281. 4 Murtaḍā, III, 65   Ramal

كَانَ يَنْهَى فَنَهَى حِينَ ٱنْتَهَى   وَٱنْجَلَتْ عَنْهُ غَيَابَاتُ ٱلصِّبَا

خَلَعَ ٱللَّهْوَ وَأَضْحَى مُسْبِلًا   لِلنُّهَى فَضْلَ قَمِيصٍ وَرِدَا

كَيْفَ يَرْجُو ٱلْبِيضَ مَنْ أَوَّلُهُ   فِي عُيُونِ ٱلْبِيضِ شَيْبٌ وَجَلَا

كَانَ كُحْلًا لِمَآقِيهَا فَقَدْ   صَارَ بِٱلشَّيْبِ لِعَيْنَيْهَا قَذًا

III

1-2 Tashbīhāt, p. 86; Amālī, I, 212 (n.e. I, 209). 2 MM, p. 207.
Kāmil

يَا رَبْعُ أَيْنَ تَوَجَّهَتْ سَلْمَى   أَمَضَتْ فَمُهْجَةُ نَفْسِهِ أَمْضَا

لَا أَبْتَغِي سُقْيَا السَّحَابِ لَهَا   فِي مُقْلَتِي خَلَفٌ مِنَ السُّقْيَا

1b <u>Tashbīhāt</u> لهجة   2a <u>Amālī</u>, I, 212 سقيى   2b <u>Amālī</u>, I, 209 عوض

IV

1-8 Ibn al-Muʿtazz, <u>Ṭab</u>, p. 126. 1 <u>Ǧufrān</u>, p. 467. 2 <u>Muḥāḍarāt</u>, I, 401   Ramal

عَلِّلَانِي بِسَمَاعٍ وَطِلَاءٍ   وَبِضَيْفٍ طَارِقٍ يَبْغِي ٱلْقِرَا

نَغَمَاتُ ٱلضَّيْفِ أَحْلَى عِنْدَنَا   مِنْ رُغَاءِ الشَّاءِ فِي ذَاتِ ٱلرُّغَا

نُنْزِلُ الضَّيْفَ إِذَا مَا حَلَّ فِي   حَبَّةِ ٱلْقَلْبِ وَأَلْوَاذِ ٱلْحَشَا

رُبَّ ضَيْفٍ تَاجِرٍ أَخْسَرْتُهُ   بِعْتُهُ ٱلْمَطْعَمَ وَٱبْتَعْتُ الثَّنَا

أَبْغَضُ ٱلْمَالَ إِذَا جَمَّعْتُهُ   إِنَّ بُغْضَ ٱلْمَالِ مِنْ حُبِّ ٱلْعُلَا

إِنَّمَا ٱلْعَيْشُ خِلَالٌ حَبَّذَا   حَبَّذَا تِلْكَ خِلَالًا حَبَّذَا

خِدْمَةُ ٱلضَّيْفِ وَكَأْسٌ لَذَّةٌ   وَنَدِيمٌ وَفَتَاةٌ وَغِنَا

وَإِذَا فَاتَكَ مِنْهَا وَاحِدٌ   نَقَصَ ٱلْعَيْشُ بِنُقْصَانِ ٱلْهَوَا

1b <u>Ǧufrān</u> ونصيف   <u>Ibid</u>., 176, 467 قرى ز جائع
2b <u>Muḥāḍarāt</u> من ثغاء الشاء او تلك الوغا

V

<u>Aǧ</u>, XVIII, 41   Ḫafīf

إِنَّ هٰذَا ٱلَّذِي دُؤَادُ أَبُوهُ   وَإِيَادٌ قَدْ أَكْثَرَ ٱلْأَنْبَاءَ

ساحقت أمه ولاط أبوه   ليت شعري عنه فمن أين جاء

جاء من بين صخرتين صلودين   ن عقامين ينبتان الهباء

لا سفاح ولا نكاح ولا ما   يوجب الأمهات والآباء

VI

<u>Muḥāḍarāt</u>, II, 121   Wāfir

فلا تنكح كريمك نهشليا   فتخلط صفو مائك بالغثاء

VII

<u>Kāmil</u>, p. 525   Ḫafīf

وابن عمران يبتغي عربيا   ليس يرضى البنات للأكفاء

إن بدت حاجة له ذكر الضيـ   ف وينساه عند وقت الغداء

VIII

Ibn ʿAsāk, <u>Tar.</u>, V, 241.   Mutaqārib

سألت الندى لا عدمت الندى   وقد كان منا زمانا غرب

فقلت له طال عهد اللقا   فقد غبت بالله أم لم تغب

فقال بلى لم أزل غائبا   ولكن قدمت مع المطلب

IX

<u>Rasāʾil</u>, p. 174; <u>Tirāz</u>, p. 88   Mutaqārib

لقطع الرمال ونقل الجبال   وشرب البحار التي تصطخب

وَكَشْفُ ٱلْغِطَاءِ عَنِ ٱلْجِنِّ أَوْ   صُعُودُ ٱلسَّمَاءِ لِمَنْ يَرْتَقِبْ

وَإِحْصَاءُ لُؤْمِ سَعِيدٍ لَنَا   أَوِ ٱلثُّكْلُ فِي وَلَدٍ مُنْتَخَبْ

أَخَفُّ عَلَى ٱلْمَرْءِ مِنْ حَاجَةٍ   تَكَلَّفَ غَشْيَانَهَا مُرْتَقِبْ

لَهُ حَاجِبٌ دُونَهُ حَاجِبٌ   وَحَاجِبُ حَاجِبِهِ مُحْتَجِبْ

4b Rasāʾil غَسَّانَهَا

X

Amālī, III, 97; Fuṣūl, p. 73   Basīṭ

أُذَكِّرُ أَبَا جَعْفَرٍ حَقًّا أَمُتُّ بِهِ   أَنِّي وَإِيَّاكَ مَشْغُوفَانِ بِٱلْأَدَبِ

وَأَنَّنَا قَدْ رَضَعْنَا ٱلْكَأْسَ دِرَّتَهَا   وَٱلْكَأْسُ دِرَّتُهَا حَظٌّ مِنَ ٱلنَّسَبِ

1a Fuṣūl امرت   2b Ibid. حرمتها حظ

XI

Ibn ʿAsāk, Tar., V, 237   Tawīl

فَلَا تُفْسِدَنْ خَمْسِينَ أَلْفًا وَهَبْتَهَا   وَعِشْرَةَ أَحْوَالٍ وَحَقٌّ تَنَاسُبْ

وَشُكْرًا تَهَادَاهُ ٱلرِّجَالُ تَهَادِيًا   إِلَى كُلِّ مِصْرٍ بَيْنَ جَاءٍ وَذَاهِبْ

بِلَا زَلَّةٍ كَانَتْ وَإِنْ تَكُ زَلَّةٌ   فَإِنَّ عَلَيْكَ ٱلْعَفْوَ ضَرْبَةَ لَازِبْ

XII

Nathr, p. 66   Ṭawīl

ذَهَبْتُ وَمَا أَدْرِي إِلَى أَيْنَ أَذْهَبُ   وَأَيَّ ٱلْأُمُورِ فِي ٱلْعَزِيمَةِ أَرْكَبُ

فَلَوْ لَمَسَتْ كَفَّايَ عِقْدًا مُنَظَّمًا   مِنَ ٱلدُّرِّ أَضْحَى وَهْوَ وَدْعٌ مُثَقَّبُ
وَلَوْ قَبَضَتْ كَفِّي عَلَى كَفِّ دِرْهَمٍ   لَدَبَّتْ إِلَى رِجْلِي وَفِي ٱلْكَفِّ عَقْرَبُ

XIII

1-4 Ibn ʿAsāk, <u>Tar.</u>, V, 241. 1 <u>Muḥāḍarāt</u>, II, 310 Basīṭ

مَاتَ ٱلثَّلَاثَةُ لَمَّا مَاتَ مُطَّلِبُ   مَاتَ ٱلْحَيَاءُ وَمَاتَ ٱلرَّغْبُ وَٱلرَّهَبُ
لِلّٰهِ أَرْبَعَةٌ قَدْ ضَمَّهَا كَفَنٌ   أَضْحَتْ يُعَزَّى بِهَا ٱلْإِسْلَامُ وَٱلْعَرَبُ
يَا يَوْمَ مُطَّلِبٍ أَصْحَبْتَ أَعْيُنَنَا   دَمْعًا يَدُومُ بِهَا مَا دَامَتِ ٱلْحِقَبُ
هٰذِي خُدُودُ بَنِي قَحْطَانَ قَدْ لَصِقَتْ   بِٱلتُّرْبِ مُنْذُ ٱسْتَوَى مِنْ فَوْقِهِ ٱلتُّرَبُ

XIV

1-7, 9, 12 <u>Aġ.</u>, XVIII, 40: <u>Rifāʿī</u>, III, 260. 5-11 Ibn ʿAsāk, <u>Tar.</u>, V, 236. 5-7, 9-11 Suyūṭī, p. 133; Ḥasan, II, 134. 5-7 <u>Lisān</u>, II, 431. 5-6 <u>Šiʿr</u>, p. 540; <u>ʿUmdah</u>, I, 43; <u>Thimār</u>, p. 314. 9-11 <u>Zuhr</u>, p. 6 Ṭawīl

بَكَى لِشَتَاتِ ٱلدِّينِ مُكْتَئِبٌ صَبُّ   وَفَاضَ بِفَرْطِ ٱلدَّمْعِ مِنْ عَيْنِهِ غَرْبُ
وَقَامَ إِمَامٌ لَمْ يَكُنْ ذَا هِدَايَةٍ   فَلَيْسَ لَهُ دِينٌ وَلَيْسَ لَهُ لُبُّ
وَمَا كَانَتِ ٱلْأَنْبَاءُ تَأْتِي بِمِثْلِهِ   يُمَلَّكُ يَوْمًا أَوْ تَدِينُ لَهُ ٱلْعَرَبُ
وَلٰكِنْ كَمَا قَالَ ٱلَّذِينَ تَتَابَعُوا   مِنَ ٱلسَّلَفِ ٱلْمَاضِينَ إِذْ عَظُمَ ٱلْخَطْبُ
5 مُلُوكُ بَنِي ٱلْعَبَّاسِ فِي ٱلْكُتْبِ سَبْعَةٌ   وَلَمْ تَأْتِنَا عَنْ ثَامِنٍ لَهُمُ كُتْبُ
كَذٰلِكَ أَهْلُ ٱلْكَهْفِ فِي ٱلْكَهْفِ سَبْعَةٌ   خِيَارٌ إِذَا عُدُّوا وَثَامِنُهُمْ كَلْبُ
وَإِنِّي لَأُعْلِي كَلْبَهُمْ عَنْكَ رِفْعَةً   لِأَنَّكَ ذُو ذَنْبٍ وَلَيْسَ لَهُ ذَنْبُ

كَأَنَّكَ إِذَا مُلِّكْتَنَا لِشَقَائِنَا   عَجُوزٌ عَلَيْهَا ٱلتَّاجُ وَٱلْعِقْدُ وَٱلْإِتْبُ

لَقَدْ ضَاعَ مُلْكُ ٱلنَّاسِ إِذْ سَاسَ مُلْكَهُمْ   وَصِيفٌ وَأَشْنَاسٌ وَقَدْ عَظُمَ ٱلْكَرْبُ

وَإِنِّي لَأَرْجُو أَنْ يُرَى مِنْ مَغِيبِهَا   مَطَالِعُ شَمْسٍ قَدْ يَغَصُّ بِهَا ٱلشَّرْبُ

وَهَمُّكَ تُرْكِيٌّ عَلَيْهِ مَهَانَةٌ   فَأَنْتَ لَهُ أُمٌّ وَأَنْتَ لَهُ أَبُ

وَفَضْلُ ٱبْنِ مَرْوَانٍ يُثَلِّمُ ثُلْمَةً   يَظَلُّ لَهَا ٱلْإِسْلَامُ لَيْسَ لَهُ شَعْبُ

6b Šiʻr; ʻUmdah كرام Ibn ʻAsāk. غداة نوو 7a Ibn ʻAsāk.; Ḥasan لازمكز رغبة
9 Zuhr فقد ضاع امر الناس حين يسوسهم وحل بهم عسر وقد عظم الخطب 10a Ḥasan ترى
11a Ibn ʻAsāk. ان تدلى Amīn تدلى

XV

Aġ, XVIII, 45; Rifāʻī, III, 261   Ṭawīl

لَقَدْ عَجِبَتْ سَلْمَى وَذَاكَ عَجِيبُ   رَأَتْ بِيَ شَيْبًا عَجَّلَتْهُ خُطُوبُ

وَمَا شَيَّبَتْنِي كَبْرَةٌ غَيْرَ أَنَّنِي   بِدَهْرٍ بِهِ رَأْسُ ٱلْفَطِيمِ يَشِيبُ

XVI

Aġ, XVIII, 45; Rifāʻī, III, 261; Muwaššaḥ, p. 351; Dīwān al-Maʻānī, II, 277   Ṭawīl

سَرَى طَيْفُ لَيْلَى حِينَ آنَ هُبُوبُ   وَقَضَّيْتُ شَوْقًا حِينَ كَادَ يَذُوبُ

فَلَمْ أَرَ مَطْرُوقًا يَحِلُّ بِرِحْلَةٍ   وَلَا آرِقًا يَقْرِي ٱلْمُنَى وَيُثِيبُ

1a Dīwān حان ;Muwaššaḥ بان 1b Dīwān; Muwaššaḥ شوقى ;
Muwaššaḥ يئوب 2a Dīwān; Muwaššaḥ بطارق 2b Ibid.; Rifāʻī يثيب

XVII

<u>Muntaḫab</u>, p. 121 Ṭawīl

إِذَا مَا ٱغْتَدَوْا فِي رَوْعَةٍ مِنْ خُيُولِهِمْ   وَأَثْوَابِهِمْ قُلْتَ ٱلْبُرُوقُ ٱلْكَوَاذِبُ
وَإِنْ لَبِسُوا دُكْنَ ٱلْخُزُوزِ وَخُضْرَهَا   وَرَاحُوا فَقَدْ رَاحَتْ عَلَيْكَ ٱلْمَشَاجِبُ

XVIII

Ibn ʿAsāk, <u>Tar.</u>, V, 231; <u>Dīwān al-Maʿānī</u>, II, 194; <u>MM</u>, p. 100 Ṭawīl

أَخٌ لَكَ عَادَاهُ ٱلزَّمَانُ فَأَصْبَحَتْ   مُذَمَّمَةً فِيمَا لَدَيْهِ ٱلْعَوَاقِبُ
مَتَى مَا تُخَبِّرْهُ ٱلتَّجَارِبُ صَاحِبًا   مِنَ ٱلنَّاسِ تَرْدُدْهُ إِلَيْكَ ٱلتَّجَارِبُ

1b Ibn ʿAsāk المطالب 2a <u>MM</u>. تعذره ; <u>Dīwān</u> تدوقه 2b <u>Dīwān</u> ردبه

XIX

<u>Muḥāḍarāt</u>, II, 107 Ṭawīl

أُسُودٌ إِذَا مَا كَانَ يَوْمُ كَرِيهَةٍ   وَلَٰكِنَّهُمْ يَوْمَ ٱللِّقَاءِ ثَعَالِبُ

XX

<u>Aġ.</u>, XVIII, 48; Ibn ʿAsāk, <u>Tar.</u>, V, 238 Munsariḥ

أَبَعْدَ مِضَرٍ وَبَعْدَ مُطَّلِبٍ   تَرْجُو ٱلْغِنَى إِنَّ ذَا مِنَ ٱلْعَجَبِ
إِنْ كَثَّرُونَا جِئْنَا بِأُسْرَتِهِ   أَوْ وَاحَدُونَا جِئْنَا بِمُطَّلِبِ

1b Ibn ʿAsāk. نرجو

XXI

__Aġ__, XVIII, 59; __ʿUyūn__, III, 133; __ʿIqd__, I, 89; Rifāʿī, III, 263; Ibn ʿAsāk, __Tar.__, V, 232, __Taʾrīḫ Baghdād__, VIII, 384; __Ḫizānah__, I, 541; __Nujūm__, II, 198 Munsariḥ

جِئْتُ بِلَا حُرْمَةٍ وَلَا سَبَبِ   إِلَيْكَ إِلَّا بِحُرْمَةِ ٱلْأَدَبِ

فَٱقْضِ ذِمَامِي فَإِنَّنِي رَجُلٌ   غَيْرُ مُلِحٍّ عَلَيْكَ فِي ٱلطَّلَبِ

1a ʿ__Uyūn__; ʿ__Iqd__ جئتك ; Ibn ʿAsāk أتيت ; ʿ__Uyūn__; __Nujūm__; Ibn ʿAsāk; مستشفعا ; ʿ__Iqd__ مسترفدا 2a Ibn ʿAsāk. زمامي

XXII

__Wasāṭah__, p. 311 Basīṭ

وَقَدْ عَلِمْتُ وَمَا أَصْبَحْتُ مُرْتَيِبًا   أَنَّ ٱلَّتِي أَدْرَكَتْنِي حِرْفَةُ ٱلْأَدَبِ

XXIII

__Muḥāḍarāt__, I, 209 Basīṭ

لَوْ لَمْ تَكُنْ لَكَ أَجْدَادٌ تَنُوبُهُمُ   أَلَا بِنَفْسِكَ نِلْتَ ٱلنَّجْمَ مِنْ كَثَبِ

XXIV

__Muḥāḍarāt__, I, 231 Basīṭ

لَأَشْكُرَنَّ لِنُوحٍ فَضْلَ نِعْمَتِهِ   شُكْرًا تُصَادِرُ عَنْهُ أَلْسُنُ ٱلْعَرَبِ

XXV

__Tashbīhāt__, p. 61; Ibn Šaj, __Ḥamāsah__, p. 229; __Nihāyah__, I, 92 Ṭawīl

أَرِقْتُ لِبَرْقٍ آخِرَ ٱللَّيْلِ مُنْصِبٍ   خَفِيٍّ كَبَطْنِ ٱلْحَيَّةِ ٱلْمُتَقَلِّبِ

XXVI

<u>Šiʿr</u>, p. 541 Munsariḥ

هُمْ قَعَدُوا فَٱنْتَقَوْا لَهُمْ حَسَبًا   يَجُوزُ بَعْدَ ٱلْعِشَاءِ فِى ٱلْعَرَبِ

حَتَّى إِذَا مَا ٱلصَّبَاحُ لَاحَ لَهُ   بُيِّنَ سَتُّوقُهُ مِنَ ٱلذَّهَبِ

وَٱلنَّاسُ قَدْ أَصْبَحُوا صَيَارِفَةً   أَبْصَرَ شَيْءٍ بِزِيبَقِ ٱلنَّسَبِ

XXVII

Ibn ʿAsāk, <u>Tar.</u>, V, 231 Kāmil

اَلْعِلْمُ يَنْهَضُ بِٱلْخَسِيسِ إِلَى ٱلْعَلَا   وَٱلْجَهْلُ يَقْعُدُ بِٱلْفَتَى ٱلْمَنْسُوبِ

وَإِذَ الْفَتَى نَالَ ٱلْعُلُومَ بِفَهْمِهِ   وَأُعِينَ بِٱلتَّشْذِيبِ وَٱلتَّهْذِيبِ

جَرَتِ ٱلْأُمُورُ لَهُ فَبَرَّزَ سَابِقًا   فِى كُلِّ مَحْضَرِ مَشْهَدٍ وَمَغِيبِ

XXVIII

Ibn al-Muʿtazz, <u>Ṭab.</u>, p. 126 Kāmil

وَيَدُلُّ ضَيْفِى فِى ٱلظَّلَامِ عَلَى ٱلْقِرَى   إِشْرَاقُ نَارِى أَوْ نُبَاحُ كِلَابِى

حَتَّى إِذَا وَاجَهْنَهُ وَلَقِينَهُ   أَحْيَيْنَهُ بِبَصَابِصِ ٱلْأَذْنَابِ

فَتَكَادُ مِنْ عِرْفَانِ مَا قَدْ عَوَّدَتْ   مِنْ ذَاكَ يُفْصِحْنَ بِٱلتَّرْحَابِ

XXIX

Ibn al-Muʿtazz, <u>Ṭab.</u>, p. 126 Rajaz

1 يَا سَلْمُ ذَاتَ ٱلْوُضَّحِ ٱلْعِذَابِ   2 وَرَبَّةَ ٱلْمِعْصَمِ وَٱلْخِضَابِ

3 وَٱلكَفَلِ ٱلرَّجْرَاجِ فِي ٱلعِقَابِ … 4 وَٱلفَاحِمِ ٱلأَسْوَدِ كَٱلغُرَابِ

5 بِحَقِّ تِلْكَ ٱلقُبَلِ ٱلطِّيَابِ … 6 بَعْدَ ٱلتَّجَنِّي مِنْكِ وَٱلعِتَابِ

7 إِلَّا كَشَفْتِ ٱليَوْمَ عَنِّي مَا بِي

XXX

Muwaššā, p. 36 Kāmil

وَأَرَى ٱلنَّوَالَ يَزِينُهُ تَعْجِيلُهُ … وَٱلمَطْلُ آفَةُ نَائِلِ ٱلوَهَّابِ

XXXI

Aǧ, XVIII, 42; 59; Rifāʿī, III, 258 Ḫafīf

إِنَّمَا ٱلعَيْشُ فِي مُنَادَمَةِ ٱلإِخْـ … وَانِ لَا فِي ٱلجُلُوسِ عِنْدَ ٱلكِعَابِ

وَبِصِرْفٍ كَأَنَّهَا أَلْسُنُ ٱلبَرْ … قِ إِذَا ٱسْتَعْرَضَتْ رَقِيقَ ٱلسَّحَابِ

إِنْ تَكُونُوا تَرَكْتُمُ لَذَّةَ ٱلعَيْـ … شِ حِذَارَ ٱلعِقَابِ يَوْمَ ٱلعِقَابِ

فَدَعُونِي وَمَا أَلَذُّ وَأَهْوَى … وَٱدْفَعُوا بِي فِي صَدْرِ يَوْمِ ٱلحِسَابِ

XXXII

1-4 Ibn ʿAsāk, *Tar*, V, 238. 1-3 *Aǧ*, XVIII, 37-38; *Waraqah*, p. 33
Basīṭ

نُهْتُمْ عَلَيْنَا بِأَنَّ ٱلذِّئْبَ كَلَّمَكُمْ … فَقَدْ لَعَمْرِي أَبُوكُمْ كَلَّمَ ٱلذِّئْبَا

فَكَيْفَ لَوْ كَلَّمَ ٱللَّيْثُ ٱلهَصُورُ إِذًا … أَفْنَيْتُمُ ٱلنَّاسَ مَأْكُولًا وَمَشْرُوبَا

هٰذَا ٱلسُّنَيْدِيُّ لَا أَصْلٌ وَلَا طَرَفٌ … يُكَلِّمُ ٱلفِيلَ تَصْعِيدًا وَتَصْوِيبَا

فَٱذْهَبْ إِلَيْهِ فَإِنِّي لَا أَرَى أَحَدًا … بِبَابِ دَارِكَ طَلَّابًا وَمَطْلُوبَا

1b Waraqah نعم 2b Ibid. تركتم Ibn ʿAsāk. جعلت

3a Waraqah ما ساوى اتاونة ; Ibn ʿAsāk. لا يسوى اتاوية 3b Ibn ʿAsāk. الذئب

XXXIII

Muḥāḍarāt, I, 223 Wāfir

لِيَهْنِكَ دَوْلَةٌ حَدِثَتْ   فَأَحْدَثَ عِزُّهَا نَسَبَا

XXXIV

1-11 Amālī, III, 99 (n.e. 97-98). 2-3 Muḥāḍarāt, I, 314; Ṭirāz, p. 175. 2 Aġ, XVIII, 42 Basīṭ

بَانَتْ سُلَيْمَى وَأَمْسَى حَبْلُهَا ٱنْقَضَبَا   وَزَوَّدُوكَ وَلَمْ يَرْثُوا لَكَ ٱلْوَصَبَا
قَالَتْ سَلَامَةُ أَيْنَ ٱلْمَالُ قُلْتُ لَهَا   ٱلْمَالُ وَيْحَكِ لَاقَى ٱلْحَمْدَ فَٱصْطَحَبَا
ٱلْحَمْدُ فَرَّقَ مَالِي فِي ٱلْحُقُوقِ فَمَا   أَبْقَيْنَ ذَمًّا وَلَا أَبْقَيْنَ لِي نَشَبَا
قَالَتْ سَلَامَةُ دَعْ هٰذِي ٱللَّبُونَ لَنَا   لِصِبْيَةٍ مِثْلِ أَفْرَاخِ ٱلْقَطَا زُغُبَا
قُلْتُ ٱحْبِسِيهَا فَفِيهَا مُتْعَةٌ لَهُمُ   إِنْ لَمْ تُنِخْ طَارِقٌ يَبْغِي ٱلْقِرَى سَغِبَا
لَمَّا ٱحْتَبَى ٱلضَّيْفُ وَٱعْتَلَّتْ حَلُوبَتُهَا   بَكَى ٱلْعِيَالُ وَغَنَّتْ قِدْرُنَا طَرَبَا
هٰذِي سَبِيلِي وَهٰذَا فَٱعْلَمِي خُلُقِي   فَٱرْضَيْ بِهِ أَوْ فَكُونِي بَعْضَ مَنْ غَضِبَا
مَا لَا يَفُوتُ وَمَا قَدْ فَاتَ مَطْلَبُهُ   فَلَنْ يَفُوتَنِيَ ٱلرِّزْقُ ٱلَّذِي كُتِبَا
أَسْعَى لِأَطْلُبَهُ وَٱلرِّزْقُ يَطْلُبُنِي   وَٱلرِّزْقُ أَكْثَرُ مِنِّي لَهُ طَلَبَا
هَلْ أَنْتَ وَاجِدُ شَيْءٍ لَوْ عُنِيتَ بِهِ   كَٱلْأَجْرِ وَٱلْحَمْدِ مُرْتَادًا وَمُكْتَسَبَا

قَوْمٌ جَوَادُهُمُ فَرْدٌ وَفَارِسُهُمْ   فَرْدٌ وَشَاعِرُهُمْ فَرْدٌ إِذَا نُسِبَا

3a Muḥāḍarāt الحقوق

XXXV

Muntaḥal, p. 151   Ṭawīl

وَإِنِّي لَأَرْثِي لِلْكَرِيمِ إِذَا غَدَا   عَلَى مَطْمَعٍ عِنْدَ اللَّئِيمِ يُطَالِبُهْ
وَأَرْثِي لَهُ مِنْ مَوْقِفِ السُّوءِ عِنْدَهُ   كَمَا قَدْ رَثَوْا لِلطِّرْفِ وَالْعِلْجُ رَاكِبُهْ

XXXVI

1, 3-5 Muntaḥal, p. 133. 2-5 Ag., XVIII, 35; Rifāʿī, III, 258. 4-5 Ḥāṣṣ, p. 18; Tashbīhāt, p. 382. 1, 6 Wasāṭah, p. 190 (n.e. 242); Nihāyah, III, 92   Basīṭ

تِلْكَ الْمَسَاعِي إِذَا مَا أَخْوَتْ رَجُلًا   أَحَبَّ لِلنَّاسِ عَيْبًا كَالَّذِي عَابَهْ
يَا بُؤْسَ لِلْفَضْلِ لَوْ لَمْ يَأْتِ مَا عَابَهْ   يَسْتَفْرِغُ السَّمَّ مِنْ صَمَّاءِ قِرْضَابَهْ
مَا إِنْ يَزَالُ وَفِيهِ الْعَيْبُ يَجْمَعُهُ   جَهْلًا لِأَعْرَاضِ أَهْلِ الْمَجْدِ عَيَّابَهْ
إِنْ عَابَنِي لَمْ يَعِبْ إِلَّا مُؤَدِّبَهُ   وَنَفْسَهُ عَابَ لَمَّا عَابَ أُدَّابَهْ
فَكَانَ كَالْكَلْبِ ضَرَّاهُ مُكَلِّبُهُ   لِصَيْدِهِ فَعَدَا فَاصْطَادَ كَلَّابَهْ
كَذَلِكَ مَنْ كَانَ هَدْمُ الْمَجْدِ عَادَتَهُ   فَإِنَّهُ لِبِنَاءِ الْمَجْدِ عَيَّابَهْ

4b Tashbīhāt فنفسه ; Muntaḥal آدابه   5a Tashbīhāt وكان

5b *Ḫāṣṣ* بصطار ; Rifāʿī لغيره 6a *Wasāṭah* 190 غياته ; *Wasāṭah* 242 سبابه 6b *Ibid.* لبناة

XXXVII

Aǧ., XVIII, 49 Mutaqārib

فَأَيْرُ عَلِيٍّ لَهُ آلَةٌ   وَنَفْقَحَةُ عَمْرٍو لَهُ رَبَّهْ
مَطَوْرًا تُصَادِفُهُ جَعْبَةٌ   وَطَوْرًا تُصَادِفُهُ حَرْبَةٌ

XXXVIII

Kāmil, p. 525 Basīṭ

مَا يَرْحَلُ ٱلضَّيْفُ عَنِّي بَعْدَ تَكْرِمَةٍ   إِلَّا بِرِفْدٍ وَتَشْيِيعٍ وَمَعْذِرَتِ

XXXIX

1-13, 15-17 *Amālī*, III, 112 (n.e. 111-12). 3, 5-8, 14-15, 17 *Kāmil*, p. 229. 11, 13-15 *Muḥāḍarāt*, I, 353. 14-15, 17 *Muwaššaḥ*, p. 380. 1 *ʿUmdah*, I, 47; Murtaḍā, IV, 182. 14-15 *Muwāzanah*, p. 6. 17 *ʿIqd*, III, 39 Basīṭ

إِذَا غَزَوْنَا فَمَغْزَانَا بِأَنْقِرَةٍ   وَأَهْلُ سَلْمَى بِسِيفِ ٱلْبَحْرِ مِنْ جُرُتِ
هَيْهَاتِ هَيْهَاتِ بَيْنَ ٱلْمَنْزِلَيْنِ لَقَدْ   أَنْضَيْتَ شَوْقِي وَقَدْ طَوَّلْتَ مُلْتَفَتِي
أَحْبَبْتُ أَهْلِي وَلَمْ أَظْلِمْ بِحُبِّهِمِ   قَالُوا تَعَصَّبْتَ جَهْلًا قَوْلَ ذِي بَهَتِ
لَهُمْ لِسَانِي بِتَقْرِيظِي وَمُمْتَدَحِي   نَعَمْ وَقَلْبِي وَمَا تَحْوِيهِ مَقْدُرَتِي
دَعْنِي أَصِلْ رَحِمِي إِنْ كُنْتَ قَاطِعَهَا   لَا بُدَّ لِلرَّحِمِ ٱلدُّنْيَا مِنَ ٱلصِّلَةِ
فَٱحْفَظْ عَشِيرَتَكَ ٱلْأَدْنَيْنَ إِنَّ لَهُمْ   حَقًّا يُفَرِّقُ بَيْنَ ٱلزَّوْجِ وَٱلْمَرَتِ

قَوْمِي بَنُو حِمْيَرٍ وَٱلْأَزْدُ إِخْوَتُهُم ... وَآلُ كِنْدَةَ وَٱلْأَحْيَاءُ مِنْ عَلَتِ
ثُبْتُ ٱلْحُلُومِ فَإِنْ سُلَّتْ حَفَائِظُهُم ... سَلُّوا ٱلسُّيُوفَ فَأَرْدَوْا كُلَّ ذِي عَنَتِ
نَفْسِي تُنَافِسُنِي فِي كُلِّ مَكْرُمَةٍ ... إِلَى ٱلْمَعَالِي وَلَوْ خَالَفْتُهَا أَبَتِ
وَكَمْ زَحَمْتُ طَرِيقَ ٱلْمَوْتِ مُعْتَرِضًا ... بِٱلسَّيْفِ ضَيْقًا فَأَدَّانِي إِلَى ٱلسَّعَتِ
قَالَ ٱلْعَوَاذِلُ أَوْدَى ٱلْمَالُ قُلْتُ لَهُم ... مَا بَيْنَ أَجْرٍ وَفَخْرٍ لِي وَمَحْمَدَتِ
أَفْسَدْتَ مَالَكَ قُلْتُ ٱلْمَالُ يُفْسِدُنِي ... إِذَا بَخِلْتُ بِهِ وَٱلْجُودُ مَصْلَحَتِي
أَرْزَاقُ رَبٍّ لِأَقْوَامٍ يُقَدِّرُهَا ... مِنْ حَيْثُ شَاءَ فَيُجْرِيهِنَّ فِي هِبَةِ
لَا تَعْرِضَنَّ بِمَزْحٍ لِٱمْرِئٍ طَبِنٍ ... مَا رَاضَهُ قَلْبُهُ أَجْرَاهُ فِي ٱلشَّفَتِ
فَرُبَّ قَافِيَةٍ بِٱلْمَزْحِ قَائِلُهَا ... مَشْؤُومَةٍ لَمْ يُرِدْ إِنْمَاؤُهَا نَمَتِ
رَدُّ ٱلسُّلَى مُسْتَتِمًّا بَعْدَ قِطْعَتِهِ ... كَرَدِّ قَافِيَةٍ مِنْ بَعْدِ مَا مَضَتِ
إِنِّي إِذَا قُلْتُ بَيْتًا مَاتَ قَائِلُهُ ... وَمَنْ يُقَالُ لَهُ وَٱلْبَيْتُ لَمْ يَمُتِ

3a *Kāmil* اعدل قومي 3b *Amālī* تعصب 5b *Kāmil* الصلت
7a *Ibid.* مذحج 11a *Muḥāḍarāt* نعم 11b *Ibid.* ألقار
14a Murtaḍā فطن 14b *Ibid.* السنة 15a *Kāmil*; *ʿUmdah*;
Murtaḍā; *Amālī*; *Muwaššaḥ* جارية 15b *ʿUmdah* في محفل

XL

Wulāh, p. 161 Mutaqārib

فَكَيْفَ رَأَيْتَ سُيُوفَ ٱلْحَرِيشِ ... وَوَقْعَةَ مَوْلَى بَنِي ضَبَّةِ

أَحَجَّتَنْدَ أَسْيَافُهُمْ كَاهِرًا   وَمَا لَكَ فِي ٱلْحَجِّ مِنْ رَغْبَةِ

XLI

2-11; 13-47 Irshād, IV, 194-97. 2-4, 6, 29, 32-36 Ḥuṣrī, I, 133. 1-2, 5-9, 11-12, 25-27, 32, 37-40 Ḥasan, II, 133-34. 2, 32-37 Ibn ʿAsāk, Tar, V, 234. 37-38; 42-43 Bad', V, 127. 2, 4, 24, 26 Ağ, XVIII, 39-40. 2, 11, 12 Masʿūdī, VI, 195. 2, 4 Thimār, p. 233. 4, 24 Tarīḫ Baghdād, VIII, 383. 1 Ahlward, 7539. 2 Ibn al-Muʿtazz, Ṭab, p. 126; Lisān, II, 431, Murtaḍā, II, 130. 12 Buldān, I, 459 Ṭawīl

ذَكَرْتُ مَحَلَّ ٱلرَّبْعِ مِنْ عَرَفَاتِ   فَأَجْرَيْتُ دَمْعَ ٱلْعَيْنِ بِٱلْعَبَرَاتِ
مَدَارِسُ آيَاتٍ خَلَتْ مِنْ تِلَاوَةٍ   وَمَنْزِلُ وَحْيٍ مُقْفِرُ ٱلْعَرَصَاتِ
لِآلِ رَسُولِ ٱللّٰهِ بِٱلْخَيْفِ مِنْ مِنًى   وَبِٱلرُّكْنِ وَٱلتَّعْرِيفِ وَٱلْجَمَرَاتِ
دِيَارُ عَلِيٍّ وَٱلْحُسَيْنِ وَجَعْفَرٍ   وَحَمْزَةَ وَٱلسَّجَّادِ ذِي ٱلثَّفِنَاتِ
دِيَارٌ عَفَاهَا كُلُّ جَوْرٍ مُبَادِرٍ   وَلَمْ تَعْفُ لِلْأَيَّامِ وَٱلسَّنَوَاتِ
قِفَا نَسْأَلِ ٱلدَّارَ ٱلَّتِي خَفَّ أَهْلُهَا   مَتَى عَهْدُهَا بِٱلصَّوْمِ وَٱلصَّلَوَاتِ
وَأَيْنَ ٱلْأُولَى شَطَّتْ بِهِمْ غُرْبَةُ ٱلنَّوَى   أَفَانِينَ فِي ٱلْآفَاقِ مُفْتَرِقَاتِ
هُمُ أَهْلُ مِيرَاثِ ٱلنَّبِيِّ إِذَا ٱعْتَزَوْا   وَهُمْ خَيْرُ قَادَاتٍ وَخَيْرُ حُمَاةِ
وَمَا ٱلنَّاسُ إِلَّا حَاسِدٌ وَمُكَذِّبٌ   وَمُضْطَغِنٌ ذُو إِحْنَةٍ وَتِرَاتِ
إِذَا ذَكَرُوا قَتْلَى بِبَدْرٍ وَخَيْبَرٍ   وَيَوْمِ حُنَيْنٍ أَسْبَلُوا ٱلْعَبَرَاتِ
قُبُورٌ بِكُوفَتٍ وَأُخْرَى بِطَيْبَةٍ   وَأُخْرَى بِفَخٍّ نَالَهَا صَلَوَاتِي

وَأُخْرَى بِأَرْضِ ٱلْجُوزَجَانِ مَحَلُّهَا   وَقَبْرٌ بِبَاخَمْرَى لَدَى ٱلْغَرُبَاتِ
وَقَبْرٌ بِبَغْدَادٍ لِنَفْسٍ زَكِيَّةٍ   تَضَمَّنَهَا ٱلرَّحْمٰنُ فِي ٱلْغُرُفَاتِ
فَأَمَّا ٱلْمُصِمَّاتُ ٱلَّتِي لَسْتُ بَالِغًا   مَبَالِغَهَا مِنِّي بِكُنْهِ صِفَاتِ
إِلَى ٱلْحَشْرِ حَتَّى يَبْعَثَ ٱللّٰهُ قَائِمًا   يُفَرِّجُ مِنْهَا ٱلْهَمَّ وَٱلْكُرُبَاتِ
نُفُوسٌ لَدَى ٱلنَّهْرَيْنِ مِنْ أَرْضِ كَرْبَلَا   مُعَرَّسُهُمْ فِيهَا بِشَطِّ فُرَاتِ
تَقَسَّمَهُمْ رَيْبُ ٱلزَّمَانِ كَمَا تَرَى   لَهُمْ عُقْرَةٌ مَغْشِيَّةُ ٱلْحُجُرَاتِ
سِوَى أَنَّ مِنْهُمْ بِٱلْمَدِينَةِ عُصْبَةً   مَدَى ٱلدَّهْرِ أَنْضَاءً مِنَ ٱلْأَزَمَاتِ
قَلِيلَةَ زُوَّارٍ سِوَى بَعْضِ زُوَّرٍ   مِنَ ٱلضَّبْعِ وَٱلْعِقْبَانِ وَٱلرَّخَمَاتِ
لَهُمْ كُلَّ حِينٍ نَوْمَةٌ بِمَضَاجِعٍ   لَهُمْ فِي نَوَاحِي ٱلْأَرْضِ مُخْتَلِفَاتِ
وَقَدْ كَانَ مِنْهُمْ بِٱلْحِجَازِ وَأَهْلِهَا   مَغَاوِيرُ يَخْتَارُونَ فِي ٱلسَّرَوَاتِ
تَنَكَّبُ لَأْوَاءُ ٱلسِّنِينَ جِوَارَهُمْ   فَلَا تَصْطَلِيهِمْ جَمْرَةُ ٱلْجَمَرَاتِ
إِذَا وَرَدُوا خَيْلًا تَشَمَّسُ بِٱلْقَنَا   مَسَاعِرَ جَمْرِ ٱلْمَوْتِ وَٱلْغَمَرَاتِ
وَإِنْ فَخَرُوا يَوْمًا أَتَوْا بِمُحَمَّدٍ   وَجِبْرِيلَ وَٱلْفُرْقَانِ ذِي ٱلسُّوَرَاتِ
مَلَامَكَ فِي أَهْلِ ٱلنَّبِيِّ فَإِنَّهُمْ   أَحِبَّايَ مَا عَاشُوا وَأَهْلُ ثِقَاتِي
تَخَيَّرْتُهُمْ رُشْدًا لِأَمْرِي فَإِنَّهُمْ   عَلَى كُلِّ حَالٍ خِيَرَةُ ٱلْخِيَرَاتِ
فَيَا رَبِّ زِدْنِي مِنْ يَقِينِي بَصِيرَةً   وَزِدْ حُبَّهُمْ يَا رَبِّ فِي حَسَنَاتِي
بِنَفْسِي أَنْتُمْ مِنْ كُهُولٍ وَفِتْيَةٍ   لِفَكِّ عُنَاةٍ أَوْ لِحَمْلِ دِيَاتِ
أُحِبُّ قَصِيَّ ٱلرَّحْمِ مِنْ أَجْلِ حُبِّكُمْ   وَأَهْجُرُ فِيكُمْ أُسْرَتِي وَبَنَاتِي

وَأَكْتُمُ بَثِّيكُمْ مَخَافَةَ كَاشِحٍ	عَنِيدٍ لِأَهْلِ ٱلْحَقِّ غَيْرِ مُوَاتِ
لَقَدْ حَفَّتِ ٱلْأَيَّامُ حَوْلِي بِشَرِّهَا	وَإِنِّي لَأَرْجُو ٱلْأَمْنَ بَعْدَ وَفَاتِي
أَلَمْ تَرَ أَنِّي مِنْ ثَلَاثِينَ حِجَّةً	أَرُوحُ وَأَغْدُو دَائِمَ ٱلْحَسَرَاتِ
أَرَى فَيْئَهُمْ فِي غَيْرِهِمْ مُتَقَسَّمًا	وَأَيْدِيهِمْ مِنْ فَيْئِهِمْ صِفِرَاتِ
فَآلُ رَسُولِ ٱللَّهِ نُحْفٌ جُسُومُهُمْ	وَآلُ زِيَادٍ حُفَّلُ ٱلْقَصَرَاتِ
بَنَاتُ زِيَادٍ فِي ٱلْقُصُورِ مَصُونَةٌ	وَآلُ رَسُولِ ٱللَّهِ فِي ٱلْفَلَوَاتِ
إِذَا وُتِرُوا مَدُّوا إِلَى أَهْلِ وِتْرِهِمْ	أَكُفًّا مِنَ ٱلْأَوْتَارِ مُنْقَبِضَاتِ
فَلَوْلَا ٱلَّذِي أَرْجُوهُ فِي ٱلْيَوْمِ أَوْ غَدٍ	لَقَطَّعَ قَلْبِي إِثْرَهُمْ حَسَرَاتِي
خُرُوجُ إِمَامٍ لَا مَحَالَةَ خَارِجٌ	يَقُومُ عَلَى ٱسْمِ ٱللَّهِ وَٱلْبَرَكَاتِ
يُمَيِّزُ فِينَا كُلَّ حَقٍّ وَبَاطِلٍ	وَيَجْزِي عَلَى ٱلنَّعْمَاءِ وَٱلنَّقِمَاتِ
سَأَقْصُرُ نَفْسِي جَاهِدًا عَنْ جِدَالِهِمْ	كَفَانِي مَا أَلْقَى مِنَ ٱلْعَبَرَاتِ
فَيَا نَفْسُ طِيبِي ثُمَّ يَا نَفْسُ أَبْشِرِي	فَغَيْرُ بَعِيدٍ كُلُّ مَا هُوَ آتِ
فَإِنْ قَرَّبَ ٱلرَّحْمٰنُ مِنْ تِلْكَ مُدَّتِي	وَأَخَّرَ مِنْ عُمْرِي لِطُولِ حَيَاتِي
شَفَيْتُ وَلَمْ أَتْرُكْ لِنَفْسِي رَزِيَّةً	وَرَوَّيْتُ مِنْهُمْ مُنْصُلِي وَقَنَاتِي
أُحَاوِلُ نَقْلَ ٱلشَّمْسِ مِنْ مُسْتَقَرِّهَا	وَأُسْمِعُ أَحْجَارًا مِنَ ٱلصَّلَدَاتِ
فَمِنْ عَارِفٍ لَمْ يَنْتَفِعْ وَمُعَانِدٍ	يَمِيلُ مَعَ ٱلْأَهْوَاءِ وَٱلشُّبُهَاتِ
قُصَارَايَ مِنْهُمْ أَنْ أَمُوتَ بِغُصَّةٍ	تُرَدَّدُ بَيْنَ ٱلصَّدْرِ وَٱللَّهَوَاتِ

كَأَنَّكَ بِٱلْأَضْلَاعِ قَدْ ضَاقَ رَحْبُهَا   لِمَا ضُمِّنَتْ مِنْ شِدَّةِ ٱلزَّفَرَاتِ

1b Ḥasan فاسلبت   2b Ḥuṣrī عفت   3b Ibid. والبيت
4a Aġ. الخيرمنهم ; اناس   4b Ḥuṣrī النفثات ; Aġ. ذو   5a Irshād كل حون مبادر   5b Ḥasan جور كل منابذ   7a Ḥuṣrī الالى
11a Ḥasan; Masʿūdī كفان   11b Ḥasan مالها ; Masʿūdī يالها صلوات
12a Irshād وقبر   12b Ḥasan العبرات   29 Ḥuṣrī احب قصي الدار من اجل حبهم واهجر فيهم اسرتي وثقاتي   32a Ḥuṣrī مذ   34a Ibid. وآل   34b Ibid. غلظ   35b Ibid. وبنت   37a Bad' نرجوه   37b Ibid. نفسي   42b Ibid. ربة ; شغبت   43a Ibid. ووقت وفاتي

XLII

Aġ., XVIII, 44; Rifāʿī, III, 259; Ibn ʿAsāk., Tar., V, 229   Basīṭ

سَقْيًا وَرَعْيًا لِأَيَّامِ ٱلصَّبَابَاتِ   أَيَّامَ أَرْفُلُ فِي أَثْوَابِ لَذَّاتِي

أَيَّامَ غُصْنِي رَطِيبٌ مِنْ لِيَانَتِهِ   أَصْبُو إِلَى غَيْرِ جَارَاتِي وَكَنَّاتِي

دَعْ عَنْكَ ذِكْرَ زَمَانٍ فَاتَ مَطْلَبُهُ   وَٱقْذِفْ بِرِجْلِكَ عَنْ مَتْنِ ٱلْجَهَالَاتِ

وَٱقْصِدْ بِكُلِّ مَدِيحٍ أَنْتَ قَائِلُهُ   نَحْوَ ٱلْهُدَاةِ بَنِي بَيْتِ ٱلْكَرَمَاتِ

1a Ibn ʿAsāk. شكرا   1b Ibid. لذات   2a Ibid. لدونته
2b Ibid. كناتي وجاراتي

XLIII

1-5 Ibn al-Muʿtazz, Ṭab. p. 127. 2-3 Lisān, II, 431   Kāmil

طَرَقَتْكِ طَارِقَةُ ٱلْمُنَى بِبَيَاتِ   لَا تُظْهِرِي جَزَعًا فَأَنْتِ بَدَأْتِ

فِي حُبِّ آلِ ٱلْمُصْطَفَى وَوَصِيِّهِ   شُغُلٌ عَنِ ٱللَّذَّاتِ وَٱلْقَيْنَاتِ

إِنَّ ٱلنَّشِيدَ بِحُبِّ آلِ مُحَمَّدٍ   أَزْكَى وَأَنْفَعُ لِي مِنَ ٱلْقَيْنَاتِ

فَٱحْشُ ٱلْقَصِيدَ بِهِمْ وَفَرِّغْ فِيهِمِ   قَلْبًا حَشَوْتَ هَوَاهُ بِٱللَّذَّاتِ

وَٱقْطَعْ حِبَالَةَ مَنْ يُرِيدُ سِوَاهُمُ   فِي حُبِّهِمْ تَحْلُلْ بِدَارِ نَجَاتِ

3a <u>Lisān</u> اليسير

XLIV

1-3 <u>Aḡ</u>, XVIII, 39; <u>Tā'rīḫ Baghdād</u>, VIII, 383; Ibn ʿAsāk, <u>Tar.</u>, V, 239-40. 2-3 Ibn Šaj, <u>Ḥamāsah</u>, p. 135 Ṭawīl

وَنُبِّئْتُ كَلْبًا مِنْ كِلَابٍ يَسُبُّنِي   وَمَحْضُ كِلَابٍ يَقْطَعُ ٱلصَّلَوَاتِ

فَإِنْ أَنَا لَمْ أَعْلَمْ كِلَابًا بِأَنَّهَا   كِلَابٌ وَإِنِّي بَاسِلُ ٱلنَّقِمَاتِ

فَكَانَ إِذًا مِنْ قَيْسِ عَيْلَانَ وَالِدِي   وَكَانَتْ إِذًا أُمِّي مِنَ ٱلْحَبِطَاتِ

1a Ibn ʿAsāk. تسبني 1b <u>Ibid</u>. مرز تقطع 2a Ibn Šaj. نانهم زلئن 2b <u>Ibid</u>. فان الموت من نقماتى 3a <u>Ibid</u>. اذن 3b <u>Ibid</u>. وامي اذن من نسوة الحبطات

XLV

Ibn ʿAsāk, <u>Tar.</u>, V, 241 Mutaqārib

فَشَهِدْتُ ٱلزُّطَاطِيَّ فِي مَجْلِسٍ   وَقَدْ كَانَ عِنْدِي بَغِيضًا مَقِيتًا

فقال آقترح بعض ما تشتهي   فقلت آقترحت عليك آلسكوتا

XLVI

Ag., XVIII, 42   Kāmil

ما جعفر بن محمد بن الأشعث   عندي بخير أبوة من عثعث

عبثا تمارس بي تمارس حية   سوارة إن هجتها لم تلبث

لو يعلم آلمغرور ماذا حاز من   خزي لوالده إذا لم يعبث

XLVII

Maḥāsin, p. 241   Rajaz

1 نلنا لذيذ آلعيش في بطياثا   2 لما حثثنا أقدحا ثلاثا

3 وآمرأتي طالقة ثلاثا

Text has حَثَثْنا

XLVIII

1-2 ʿUmdah, II, 28 (n.e. 32). 2 Ag., XVIII, 42   Ramal

وإذا عاندنا ذو نخوة   غضب آلروح عليه فعرج

فعلى أيماننا يجري آلندى   وعلى أسيافنا تجري آلمهج

XLIX

ʿIqd, I, 237 (n.e. II, 334)   Ṭawīl

وقد قطع آلواشون ما كان بيننا   ونحن إلى أن نوصل آلحبل أحوج

رأوا عورة فآستقبلوها ببالهم   فلم ينههم حلم ولم يتحرجوا

وكانوا أناسا كنت آمن غيبهم   فراحوا على ما لا يحب فأدلجوا

2a <u>ʿIqd</u>, II, 334 بألبهم 3b <u>Ibid</u>. نعب

L

<u>Ibn ʿAsāk, Tar.</u>, V, 237; <u>Buldān</u>, IV, 186 Kāmil

ظَلَّتْ بِقُمّ مَطِيَّتِي يَعْتَادُهَا ... هَمَّانِ غُرْبَتُهَا وَبُعْدُ ٱلْمُدْلَجِ

مَا بَيْنَ عِلْجٍ قَدْ تَعَرَّبَ فَٱنْتَمَى ... أَوْ بَيْنَ آخَرَ مُعْرِبٍ مُسْتَعْلِجِ

1a <u>Buldān</u> مظيتى

LI

<u>Tashbīhāt</u>, p. 221; <u>Amālī</u>, I, 110, <u>Laṭāʾif</u>, p. 100; <u>Nathr</u>, p. 92 Kāmil

أَهْلًا وَسَهْلًا بِٱلْمَشِيبِ فَإِنَّهُ ... سِمَةُ ٱلْعَفِيفِ وَحِلْيَةُ ٱلْمُتَحَرِّجِ

وَكَأَنَّ شَيْبِي نَظْمُ دُرٍّ زَاهِرٍ ... فِي تَاجِ ذِي مُلْكٍ أَغَرَّ مُتَوَّجِ

1b <u>Laṭāʾif</u> وهيئة

LII

<u>Tashbīhāt</u>, p. 406 Sarīʿ

كَأَنَّهُ كَبْشٌ إِذَا مَا بَدَا ... لٰكِنَّهُ فِي طَبْعِهِ نَعْجَهْ

فَأَنْتَ إِنْ تَقْعُدْ إِلَى جَنْبِهِ ... تَخَالُ فِي خُصْيَتِهِ قُنْبُجَهْ

LIII

<u>Wasāṭah</u>, p. 297 (n.e. 409); <u>Nihāyah</u>, III, 91 Ṭawīl

هِيَ ٱلنَّفْسُ مَا حَسَّنْتَهُ فَمُحَسَّنٌ ... لَدَيْهَا وَمَا قَبَّحْتَهُ فَمُقَبَّحُ

LIV

Wasāṭah, p. 266 (n.e. 363) Ṭawīl

إِذَا أُقْحِمَ ٱلرُّكْبَانُ فِيهَا تَبَتَّلُوا فَمُسْتَغْفِرٌ مِنْ ذَنْبِهِ وَمُسَبِّحُ

LV

1-3 Tashbīhāt, p. 132. 2 Tashbīhāt, p. 138; Muḥāḍarāt, II, 187; Dīwān al-Ma'ānī, I, 207 Sarī'

إِنَّ ٱبْنَ زَيَّاتٍ لَهُ قَيْنَةٌ أَرْبَتْ عَلَى ٱلشَّيْطَانِ فِي ٱلْقُبْحِ

سَوْدَاءُ فَوْهَاءُ لَهَا شَعْرَةٌ كَأَنَّهَا خَمْلٌ عَلَى مِسْحِ

فَلَوْ بَدَتْ حَاسِرَةً فِي ٱلضُّحَى لَٱسْوَدَّ مِنْهُ فَلَقُ ٱلصُّبْحِ

2a Muḥāḍarāt بطراء سوداء ; Dīwān al-Ma'ānī فوهاء سوداء 2b Tashbīhāt نمل

LVI

Muḥāḍarāt, II, 79 Wāfir

هُمُ ٱلْمُتَخَيَّرُونَ عَلَى ٱلْمَنَايَا نُفُوسُ ذَوِي ٱلرِّيَاسَةِ بِٱقْتِرَاحِ

LVII

Muḥāḍarāt, II, 107 Basīṭ

كَأَنَّ نَفْسَهُ مِنْ طُولِ حَيْرَتِهَا مِنْهَا عَلَى نَفْسِهِ يَوْمَ ٱلْوَغَى رَصَدُ

LVIII

Ag., XVIII, 53 Basīṭ

مَا كُنْتُ أَحْسِبُ أَنَّ ٱلدَّهْرَ يُمْهِلُنِي حَتَّى أَرَى أَحَدًا يَهْجُوهُ لَا أَحَدُ

إِنِّي لَأَعْجَبُ مِمَّنْ فِي حَقِيبَتِهِ مِنَ ٱلْمَنِيِّ بُحُورٌ كَيْفَ لَا يَلِدُ

فَإِنْ سَمِعْتَ بِهِ بِعْتَ ٱلْقَنَا عَبَثًا فَقَدْ أَرَادَ قَنًا لَيْسَتْ لَهُ عُقَدُ

LIX

1-3 <u>Bidāyah</u>, X, 309. 1-2 <u>Aġ</u>, XVIII, 41; Rifāʿī, III, 261; <u>Tārīḫ Guzīdah</u>, pp. 323-24 Basīṭ

ٱلْحَمْدُ لِلّٰهِ لَا صَبْرٌ وَلَا جَلَدُ   وَلَا عَزَاءٌ إِذَا أَهْلُ ٱلْبَلَا رَقَدُوا

خَلِيفَةٌ مَاتَ لَمْ يَحْزَنْ لَهُ أَحَدُ   وَآخَرُ قَامَ لَمْ يَفْرَحْ بِهِ أَحَدُ

فَمَرَّ هٰذَا وَمَرَّ ٱلشُّؤْمُ يَتْبَعُهُ   وَقَامَ هٰذَا فَقَامَ ٱلْوَيْلُ وَٱلنَّكَدُ

1b <u>Bidāyah</u> الهوى

LX

<u>Šiʿr</u>, p. 541; <u>ʿUyūn</u>, III, 247 Ḫafīf

إِنَّ مَنْ ضَنَّ بِٱلْكَنِيفِ عَنِ ٱلضَّيْـ   ـفِ بِغَيْرِ ٱلْكَنِيفِ كَيْفَ يَجُودُ

مَا رَأَيْنَا وَلَا سَمِعْنَا بِحُشٍّ   قَبْلَ هٰذَا لِبَابِهِ إِقْلِيدُ

إِنْ يَكُنْ فِي ٱلْكَنِيفِ شَيْءٌ تَخَبَّا   هُ فَعِنْدِي إِنْ شِئْتَ فِيهِ مَزِيدُ

LXI

<u>Aġ</u>, XVIII, 41 Wāfir

وَلَسْتُ بِقَائِلٍ تَذْعًا وَلٰكِنْ   لِأَمْرٍ مَا تَعَبَّدَكَ ٱلْعَبِيدُ

LXII

<u>Muḥāḍarāt</u>, II, 186 Wāfir

لَهَا عَيْنَانِ مِنْ أَقَطٍ وَتَمْرٍ   وَسَائِرُ خَلْقِهَا بَعْدُ ٱلثَّرِيدُ

LXIII

Ibn 'Asāk, <u>Tar.</u>, V, 236   Wāfir

فَيَا عَبْدَ ٱلإِلٰهِ أَصِخْ لِقَوْلِي ... وَبَعْضُ ٱلْقَوْلِ يَصْحَبُهُ ٱلسَّدَادُ
تَرَى طَسْمًا تَعُودُ بِهَا ٱللَّيَالِي ... إِلَى ٱلدُّنْيَا كَمَا رَجَعَتْ إِيَادُ
قَبَائِلُ جُذَّ أَصْلُهُمُ فَبَادُوا ... وَأَوْدَى ذِكْرُهُمْ زَمَنًا فَعَادُوا
وَكَانُوا غَرَّزُوا فِي ٱلرَّمْلِ بَيْضًا ... فَأَمْسَكَهُ كَمَا غَرَزَ ٱلْجَرَادُ
فَلَمَّا إِنْ سُقُوا دَرَجُوا وَدَبُّوا ... وَزَادُوا حِينَ جَادَهُمُ ٱلْعِهَادُ
هُمُ بَيْضُ ٱلرَّمَادِ يُشَقُّ عَنْهُمْ ... وَبَعْضُ ٱلْبَيْضِ يُشْبِهُهُ ٱلرَّمَادُ
غَدًا تَأْتِيكَ إِخْوَتُهُمْ جَدِيسُ ... وَجُرْهُمُ قَصْرًا وَتَعُودُ عَادُ
فَتَعْجِزُ عَنْهُمُ ٱلْأَمْصَارُ ضِيقًا ... وَتَمْتَلِئُ ٱلْمَنَازِلُ وَٱلْبِلَادُ
فَلَمْ أَرَ مِثْلَهُمْ بَادُوا فَعَادُوا ... وَلَمْ أَرَ مِثْلَهُمْ قَلُّوا وَزَادُوا
تَوَغَّلَ فِيهِمِ سَفْكٌ وَجَوْرٌ ... وَأَوْبَاشٌ فَهُمْ لَهُمُ مِدَادُ
وَأَنْبَاطُ ٱلسَّوَادِ قَدِ ٱسْتَحَالُوا ... بِهَا عَرَبًا فَقَدْ خَرِبَ ٱلسَّوَادُ
فَلَوْ شَاءَ ٱلْإِمَامُ أَقَامَ سُوقًا ... فَبَاعَهُمُ كَمَا بِيعَ ٱلسَّمَادُ

4a Text has غرزا   7b Text has يشبهها

LXIV

1-4 <u>Ag.</u>, XVIII, 29. 1 <u>Ag.</u>, XVIII, 41. 4 <u>'Uyūn</u>, I, 130; <u>Tashbīhāt</u>, p. 147; <u>Nihāyah</u>, VI, 221; <u>Thimār</u>, p. 339; <u>Muwāzanah</u>, p. 39   Sarī'

أَيْنَ مَحَلُّ ٱلْحَيِّ يَا وَادِي ... خَبِّرْ سَقَاكَ ٱلرَّائِحُ ٱلْغَادِي

مُسْتَصْحِبٌ لِلْحَرْبِ خَيْفَانَةً　　مِثْلَ عُقَابِ ٱلسَّرْحَةِ ٱلْعَادِي

بَيْنَ خُدُورِ ٱلظَّعْنِ مَحْجُوبَةً　　حَدَا بِقَلْبِي مَعَهَا ٱلْحَادِي

وَأَسْمَرٍ فِي رَأْسِهِ أَزْرَقٌ　　مِثْلُ لِسَانِ ٱلْحَيَّةِ ٱلصَّادِي

1a *Aǧ.* حادي

LXV

1-3, 5, 7 *Šir*, p. 539. 1-2, 4-6 Ibn ʿAsāk, *Tar.*, V, 235. 1-2, 5-6 Ḥuṣrī, *Dhail*, p. 298. 1-3, 7 *K. Baghdād*, p. 296; Ḥasan, II, 134; Ṭabarī, III, 1155. 1, 5-6 *Aǧ*, XVIII, 55; Rifāʿī, III, 259. 5-6 *Ašʿār*, p. 33; Ḥuṣrī, I, 33. *Thimār*, p. 419; *Mustaṭraf*, II, 2; Suyūṭī, p. 128 Kāmil

وَيَسُومُنِي ٱلْمَأْمُونُ خُطَّةَ عَارِفٍ　　أَمَا رَأَى بِٱلْأَمْسِ رَأْسَ مُحَمَّدِ

تُوفِي عَلَى رُوسِ ٱلْخَلَائِقِ مِثْلَ مَا　　تُوفِي ٱلْجِبَالُ عَلَى رُؤُوسِ ٱلْفَرْدَدِ

وَيَحِلُّ فِي أَكْنَافِ كُلِّ مُمَنَّعٍ　　حَتَّى يُذَلِّلَ شَاهِقًا لَمْ يُصْعَدِ

لَا تَحْسِبَنْ جَهْلِي كَحِلْمِ أَبِي فَمَا　　حِلْمُ ٱلْمَشَائِخِ مِثْلُ جَهْلِ ٱلْأَمْرَدِ

إِنِّي مِنَ ٱلْقَوْمِ ٱلَّذِينَ سُيُوفُهُمْ　　قَتَلَتْ أَخَاكَ وَشَرَّفَتْكَ بِمَقْعَدِ

رَفَعُوا مَحَلَّكَ بَعْدَ طُولِ خُمُولِهِ　　وَٱسْتَنْقَذُوكَ مِنَ ٱلْحَضِيضِ ٱلْأَوْهَدِ

إِنَّ ٱلتِّرَاتِ مُسَهَّدٌ طُلَّابُهَا　　فَٱكْفُفْ لُعَابَكَ عَنْ لُعَابِ ٱلْأَسْوَدِ

1a Ibn ʿAsāk; Ḥuṣrī, *Dhail* ظالم Ḥuṣrī, *Dhail* اسومني
2a *K. Baghdād*; Ibn ʿAsāk هام ; Ḥuṣrī, *Dhail* يربي ; Ḥuṣrī, *Dhail*; Ibn ʿAsāk. مثلها ; *K. Baghdād* يوفي ; Ḥuṣrī, *Dhail* راس ; Ibn ʿAsāk. توني
2b Ḥuṣrī, *Dhail* روس زتربى ; Ḥasan يوفي 3a *K. Baghdād*; Ḥasan يحل
5a Ḥuṣrī, *Dhail* هم هم 5b *Šir*; Ḥuṣrī, *Dhail* شرفوك ; Ḥuṣrī, *Dhail*

فتلوا 6a Ibn ʿAsāk. ساروا بذكره ; Thimār; Ašʿār; Mustaṭraf;

Ḥuṣrī, Dhail شادوا بذكره 6b Ibn ʿAsāk. الابعد

7a Ḥasan التراث 7b Šiʿr مذاقه

LXVI

Muwaššā, p. 36 Munsariḥ

إِيَّاكَ وَٱلْمَطْلَ أَنْ تُفَارِقَهُ فَإِنَّهُ آفَةٌ لِكُلِّ يَدِ

إِذَا مَطَلْتَ ٱمْرَءًا بِحَاجَتِهِ فَٱمْضِ عَلَى مَطْلِهِ وَلَا تَجُدِ

فَلَسْتَ تَلْقَاهُ شَاكِرًا لِيَدٍ قَدْ كَدَّهَا ٱلْمَطْلُ آخِرَ ٱلْأَبَدِ

LXVII

Waraqah, p. 36 Ṭawīl

أَمَا فِي صُرُوفِ ٱلدَّهْرِ أَنْ يَرْجِعَ ٱلنَّوَى بِهِمْ وَيُدَالَ ٱلْقُرْبُ يَوْمًا مِنَ ٱلْبُعْدِ

بَلَى فِي صُرُوفِ ٱلدَّهْرِ كُلُّ ٱلَّذِي أَرَى وَلٰكِنَّمَا أَغْفَلْنَ حَظِّي عَلَى عَمْدِ

فَوَٱللّٰهِ مَا أَدْرِي بِأَيِّ سِهَامِهَا رَمَتْنِي وَكُلٌّ عِنْدَنَا لَيْسَ بِٱلْمُكْدِي

أَبِٱلْجِيدِ أَمْ مَجْرَى ٱلْوِشَاحِ وَإِنَّنِي لَأَتَّهِمُ عَيْنَيْهَا مَعَ ٱلْفَاحِمِ ٱلْجَعْدِ

LXVIII

1-3 Tashbīhāt, p. 136; Ḥamāsah, pp. 798-99. 2 Muḥāḍarāt, II, 186

Basīṭ

لَا بَارَكَ ٱللّٰهُ فِي لَيْلٍ يُقَرِّبُنِي إِلَى مُضَاجَعَةٍ كَٱلدَّلْكِ بِٱلْمَسَدِ

لَقَدْ لَمَسْتُ مُعَرَّاهَا فَمَا وَقَعَتْ مِمَّا لَمَسْتُ يَدِي إِلَّا عَلَى وَتَدِ

فِي كُلِّ عُضْوٍ لَهَا قَرْنٌ تَصُكُّ بِهِ جَنْبَ ٱلضَّجِيعِ فَيُضْحِي وَاهِيَ ٱلْجَسَدِ

1a Hamāsah اعوذ بالله 1b Ibid. مضاجعه 3a Ibid. قرون

LXIX

ʿUyūn, III, 240 Ṭawīl

وَإِنِّي لَعَبْدُ ٱلضَّيْفِ مِنْ غَيْرِ ذِلَّةٍ   وَمَا فِيَّ إِلَّا تِلْكَ مِنْ شِيمَةِ ٱلْعَبْدِ

LXX

1-4 Buldān, III, 812. 1 Iklīl, p. 51. 1a Aġ, XVIII, 56 Basīṭ

مَنَازِلُ ٱلْحَيِّ مِنْ غُمْدَانَ فَٱلنَّضَدِ   فَمَأْرِبٍ فَظَفَارِ ٱلْمُلْكِ فَٱلْجَنَدِ
أَرْضُ ٱلتَّبَابِعِ وَٱلْأَقْيَالِ مِنْ يَمَنٍ   أَهْلُ ٱلْجِيَادِ وَأَهْلُ ٱلْبِيضِ وَٱلزَّرَدِ
مَا دَخَلُوا قَرْيَةً إِلَّا وَقَدْ كَتَبُوا   بِهَا كِتَابًا فَلَمْ يَدْرُسْ وَلَمْ يَبِدِ
بِٱلْقَيْرَوَانِ وَبَابِ ٱلصِّينِ قَدْ زَبَرُوا   وَبَابِ مَرْوٍ وَبَابِ ٱلْهِنْدِ وَٱلصُّغْدِ

1a Iklīl العز Ag عمدان مانصد

LXXI

Muḥāḍarāt, II, 77 Kāmil

مِنْ مَعْشَرٍ إِنْ تَدْعُهُمْ لِمُلِمَّةٍ   وَصَلُوا ٱلْحَيَاةَ إِلَى ٱلْعُلَا بِحَدِيدِ

LXXII

Amālī, III, 127 (n.e. 126) Basīṭ

وَصَاحِبٍ مُغْرَمٍ بِٱلْجُودِ قُلْتُ لَهُ   وَٱلْبُخْلُ يَصْرِفُهُ عَنْ شِيمَةِ ٱلْجُودِ.
لَا تَقْضِيَنْ حَاجَةً أَتْعَبْتَ صَاحِبَهَا   بِٱلْمَطْلِ مِنْكَ فَنَزْرًا غَيْرَ مَحْمُودِ
كَأَنَّنِي رُحْتُ مِنْهُ حِينَ نَوَّلَنِي   بِمُدْمَجِ ٱلصَّدْرِ مِنْ مَتْنَيْهِ مَقْدُودِ

كَأَنَّ أَعْضَاءَهُ فِي كُلِّ مَكْرُمَةٍ   يُنْزَعْنَ مُسْتَكْرَهَاتٍ بِٱلسَّفَافِيدِ

LXXIII

1-2 *Aǧ*, XVIII, 37; 46. 1 *Muntaḥal*, p. 152 Sarīʿ

أَحْسَنُ مَا فِي صَالِحٍ وَجْهُهُ   فَقِسْ عَلَى ٱلْغَائِبِ بِٱلشَّاهِدِ
تَأَمَّلَتْ عَيْنِي لَهُ خِلْقَةً   تَدْعُو إِلَى تَزْنِيَةِ ٱلْوَالِدِ

1b *Muntaḥal* شاهد بالغائب

LXXIV

Aǧ, XVIII, 54 Sarīʿ

إِنَّ أَبَا سَعْدٍ فَتًى شَاعِرٌ   يُعْرَفُ بِٱلْكُنْيَةِ لَا ٱلْوَالِدِ
يَنْشُدُ فِي حَيِّ مَعَدٍّ أَبًا   ضَلَّ عَنِ ٱلْمَنْشُودِ وَٱلنَّاشِدِ
فَرَحْمَةُ ٱللّٰهِ عَلَى مُسْلِمٍ   أَرْشَدَ مَفْقُودًا إِلَى فَاقِدِ

LXXV

Muhāḍarāt, II, 44 Kāmil

إِنِّي وَجَدْتُكِ فِي ٱلْهَوَى ذَوَّاقَةً   لَا تَصْبِرِينَ عَلَى طَعَامٍ وَاحِدِ

LXXVI

1-4 *Fihrist*, p. 99. 1-3 Ibn ʿAsāk, *Tar.*, V, 239 Wāfir

سَأَلْتُ أَبِي وَكَانَ أَبِي عَلِيمًا   بِسَاكِنَةِ ٱلْجَزِيرَةِ وَٱلسَّوَادِ
فَقُلْتُ أَهَيْثَمٌ مِنْ حَيِّ قَيْسٍ   فَقَالَ كَأَحْمَدَ بْنِ أَبِي دُؤَادِ
فَإِنْ يَكُ هَيْثَمٌ مِنْ حَيِّ قَيْسٍ   فَأَحْمَدُ غَيْرُ شَكٍّ مِنْ إِيَادِ

مَتَى كَانَتْ إِيَادُ يَرُوسُ قَوْمًا ‏ ‏ لَقَدْ غَضِبَ ٱلْإِلٰهُ عَلَى ٱلْعِبَادِ

1b Fihrist باخبار الحواضر والبوادى   2a Ibid. عدى
2b Ibn ʿAsāk. نعم كاحمد بن دواد   3a Fihrist منهم صيما

LXXVII

Ṣināʿatain, p. 365   Kāmil

قَالَتْ وَقَدْ ذَكَّرْتُهَا عَهْدَ ٱلصِّبَى ‏ ‏ بِٱلْيَأْسِ يَقْطَعُ عَادَةَ ٱلْمُعْتَادِ
إِلَّا ٱلْإِمَامُ فَإِنَّ عَادَةَ جُودِهِ ‏ ‏ مَوْصُولَةٌ بِزِيَادَةِ ٱلْمُزْدَادِ

LXXVIII

1-5 Aǵ, XVIII, 39; Rifāʿī, III, 256. 1-4 Thimār, p. 419. 1-2, 4 Buldān, II, 709. 1, 3-4 ʿUyūn, I, 151. 1, 4 Aǵ, XVIII, 30; Ḥuṣrī Dhail, p. 297. 4 Ṭabarī, III, 1156; K. Baghdād, p. 297
Kāmil

أَوْلَى ٱلْأُمُورِ بِضَيْعَةٍ وَفَسَادِ ‏ ‏ أَمْرٌ يُدَبِّرُهُ أَبُو عَبَّادِ
خَرِقٌ عَلَى جُلَسَائِهِ فَكَأَنَّهُمْ ‏ ‏ حَضَرُوا لِمَلْحَمَةٍ وَيَوْمِ جِلَادِ
يَسْطُو عَلَى كُتَّابِهِ بِدَوَاتِهِ ‏ ‏ فَمُضَمَّخٌ بِدَمٍ وَنَضْحِ مِدَادِ
وَكَأَنَّهُ مِنْ دَيْرِ هِزْقِلَ مُفْلَتٌ ‏ ‏ حَرِدٌ يَجُرُّ سَلَاسِلَ ٱلْأَقْيَادِ
فَٱشْدُدْ أَمِيرَ ٱلْمُؤْمِنِينَ وَثَاقَهُ ‏ ‏ فَأَصَحُّ مِنْهُ بَقِيَّةُ ٱلْحَدَّادِ

3 ʿUyūn حنق على جلساء بدواته فمرمل و مضمخ بمداد
Thimār سمح على اصحابه بدواته فمرمل ومضمخ بمداد
Buldān حرق على جلساء بدواته ومضمخ ومرمل بمداد

4a Aǧ.; 'Uyūn; Thimār; Ḥuṣrī, Dhail هرقل ; Buldān مكانه ; Ḥuṣrī, Dhail خارج 4b نحو ; Thimār مردا ; Ḥuṣrī, Dhail خوبا ; Buldān جرد

LXXIX

Aǧ., XVIII, 40 Mutaqārib

وَكَانَ أَبُو خَالِدٍ مَرَّةً إِذَا بَاتَ مُتَّخِمًا قَاعِدًا
يَضِيقُ بِأَوْلَادِهِ بَطْنُهُ فَيَخْرَأُهُم وَاحِدًا وَاحِدًا
فَقَدْ مَلَأَ ٱلْأَرْضَ مِنْ سَلْحِهِ خَنَافِسَ لَا تُشْبِهُ ٱلْوَالِدَا

LXXX

'Iqd, I, 106; 222; 392 (n.e. I, 281) Basīṭ

مَا أَكْثَرَ ٱلنَّاسَ لَا بَلْ مَا أَقَلَّهُمْ وَٱللّٰهُ يَعْلَمُ أَنِّي لَمْ أَقُلْ فَنَدَا
إِنِّي لَأُغْلِقُ عَيْنِي ثُمَّ أَفْتَحُهَا عَلَى كَثِيرٍ وَلٰكِنْ مَا أَرَى أَحَدَا

2a 'Iqd, I, 202; 392 حين لافتح

LXXXI

Aǧ., XVIII, 36 Rajaz

1 تَخْضِبُ كَفًّا قُطِعَتْ مِنْ زَنْدِهَا 2 مُتَخْضَبُ ٱلْحِنَّاءُ مِنْ مُسْوَدِّهَا
3 كَأَنَّهَا وَٱلْكُحْلُ فِي مِرْوَدِهَا 4 تَكْحَلُ عَيْنَيْهَا بِبَعْضِ جِلْدِهَا
5 أَشْبَهُ شَيْءٍ آسْتُهَا بِخَدِّهَا

LXXXII

Aġ., XVIII, 46 Rajaz

1 وَذِي يَمِينَيْنِ وَعَيْنٍ وَاحِدَهْ 2 نُقْصَانِ عَيْنٍ وَيَمِينٍ زَائِدَهْ

3 نَزْرُ ٱلْعَطِيَّاتِ قَلِيلُ ٱلْفَائِدَهْ 4 أَعْطَاهُ ٱللّٰهُ بِبَظْرِ ٱلْوَالِدَهْ

Text has ۃ

LXXXIII

Muḥāḍarāt, II, 358 Ramal

وَفَضَاءٍ يَرْجِعُ ٱلطَّرْفُ بِهِ قَبْلَ أَنْ يَرْجِعَ مَأْوَاهُ ٱلْبَصَرْ

LXXXIV

Ibn ʿAsāk., Tār., V, 238 Basīṭ

يَا هَيْثَمَ يَا ٱبْنَ عُثْمَانِ ٱلَّذِي ٱفْتَخَرَتْ بِهِ ٱلْمَكَارِمُ وَٱلْأَيَّامُ تَفْتَخِرُ

أَضْحَتْ رَبِيعَةُ وَٱلْأَحْيَاءُ مِنْ يَمَنٍ تِيهًا بِنَجْدَتِهِ لَا وَحْدَهَا مُضَرُ

LXXXV

Ṭirāz, p. 206 Ṭawīl

وَإِنْ طُوَّةٌ رَابَتْكَ فَٱنْظُرْ فَرُبَّمَا أُمِرَّ مَذَاقُ ٱلْعُودِ وَٱلْعُودُ أَخْضَرُ

LXXXVI

Aʿyān, XXX, 353 Basīṭ

لَا أَضْحَكَ ٱللّٰهُ سِنَّ ٱلدَّهْرِ إِنْ ضَحِكَتْ وَآلُ أَحْمَدَ مَظْلُومُونَ قَدْ قُهِرُوا

مُشَرَّدُونَ نُفُوا عَنْ عُقْرِ دَارِهِمِ كَأَنَّهُمْ قَدْ جَنَوْا مَا لَيْسَ يُغْتَفَرُ

LXXXVII

<u>Aǧ</u>, XVIII, 35 Wāfir

خَرَجْتُ مُبَكِّرًا مِنْ سُرَّ مَنْ رَى   أُبَادِرُ حَاجَةً فَإِذَا عُمَيْرُ
فَلَمْ أَثْنِ ٱلْعِنَانَ وَقُلْتُ أَمْضِي   فَوَجْهُكَ يَا عُمَيْرُ خَرًا وَخَيْرُ

LXXXVIII

<u>Šiʿr</u>, p. 541 Sarīʿ

اُنْظُرْ إِلَيْهِ وَإِلَى ظَرْفِهِ   كَيْفَ تَطَايَا وَهُوَ مَنْشُورُ
وَيْلَكَ مَنْ دَلَّاكَ فِي نِسْبَةٍ   قَلْبُكَ مِنْهَا ٱلدَّهْرَ مَذْعُورُ
لَوْ ذُكِرَتْ طَيٌّ عَلَى فَرْسَخٍ   أَظْلَمَ فِي نَاظِرِكَ ٱلنُّورُ

LXXXIX

Ibn ʿAsāk, <u>Tar</u>, V, 232 Wāfir

أَرَى مَنَّا قَرِيبًا بَيْتَ زُورٍ   وَزُورٌ لَا يَزُورُ وَلَا يُزَارُ
وَلَا يَهْدِي وَلَا يُهْدَى إِلَيْهِ   وَلَيْسَ كَذَاكَ فِي ٱلْعُرْبِ ٱلْجِوَارُ

XC

<u>Muḥāḍarāt</u>, I, 359 Basīṭ

اَلْجُودُ يَعْلَمُ أَنِّي مُنْذُ عَاهَدَنِي   مَا خُنْتُهُ وَقْتَ مَيْسُورِي وَمَعْسُورِي

XCI

Muntaḥal, pp. 73-74 Basīṭ

لَا تُحْزِنَنَّكَ حَاجَتِي أَبَا عُمَرٍ　　فَإِنَّهَا مِنْكَ بَيْنَ ٱلْفِكْرِ وَٱلْعِذَرِ

مَا رَاحَ مِنْهَا فَإِنَّ ٱللَّهَ يَسَّرَهُ　　وَمَا تَأَخَّرَ مَحْمُولٌ عَلَى ٱلْقَدَرِ

XCII

Muntaḫab, pp. 47-48 Basīṭ

إِذَا رَأَيْتَ بَنِي فَضْلٍ بِمَنْزِلَةٍ　　لَمْ تَدْرِ أَيُّهُمُ ٱلْأُنْثَى مِنَ ٱلذَّكَرِ

قَمِيصُ أُنْثَاهُمُ يُنْقَدُّ مِنْ قُبُلٍ　　وَقُمْصُ ذُكْرَانِهِمْ تُنْقَدُّ مِنْ دُبُرِ

مُحَنَّكُونَ عَنِ ٱلْفَحْشَاءِ فِي صِغَرٍ　　مُحَنَّكُونَ عَنِ ٱلْفَحْشَاءِ فِي ٱلْكِبَرِ

مُحَنَّكُونَ وَلَمْ تُقْطَعْ تَمَائِمُهُمْ　　مَعَ ٱلْفَوَاطِمِ وَٱلدَّايَاتِ بِٱلْكِبَرِ

XCIII

Aġ, XVIII, 35 Ṭawīl

لَقَدْ خَلَّفَ ٱلْأَهْوَازَ مِنْ خَلْفِ ظَهْرِهِ　　يَزِيدُ وَرَاءَ ٱلزَّابِ مِنْ أَرْضِ كَسْكَرِ

يُهَوِّدُ إِسْمَعِيلُ بِٱلْبِيضِ وَٱلْقَنَا　　وَقَدْ فَرَّ مِنْ زَيْدِ بْنِ مُوسَى بْنِ جَعْفَرِ

وَعَايَنْتُهُ فِي يَوْمِ خَلَّى حَرِيمَهُ　　فَيَا قُبْحَهَا مِنْهُ وَيَا حُسْنَ مَنْظَرِ

XCIV

Aġ, XVIII, 50 Hazaj

أَتَانَا طَالِبًا وَغْرًا　　فَأَعْقَبْنَاهُ بِٱلْوَغْرِ

وَتَرْنَاهُ فَلَمْ يَرْضَ　　فَأَعْقَبْنَاهُ بِٱلْوِتْرِ

XCV

1-10 Ibn ʿAsāk, <u>Tar</u>, V, 233. 1-4, 7-10 <u>Aǧ</u>, XVIII, 57; Rifāʿī, III, 262. 4, 6-10 <u>T. Qumm</u>, p. 200. 1-3 <u>Buldān</u>, II, 436. 7-10 Ḥuṣrī, I, 133; <u>Buldān</u>, II, 562 Basīṭ

وَلَيْسَ حَيٌّ مِنَ ٱلْأَحْيَاءِ نَعْلَمُهُ   مِنْ ذِي يَمَانٍ وَمِنْ بَكْرٍ وَمِنْ مُضَرِ
إِلَّا وَهُمْ شُرَكَاءُ فِي دِمَائِهِمِ   كَمَا تَشَارَكَ أَيْسَارٌ عَلَى جُزُرِ
قَتْلٌ وَأَسْرٌ وَتَحْرِيقٌ وَمَنْهَبَةٌ   فِعْلَ ٱلْغُزَاةِ بِأَهْلِ ٱلرُّومِ وَٱلْخَزَرِ
أَرَى أُمَيَّةَ مَعْذُورِينَ إِنْ قَتَلُوا   وَلَا أَرَى لِبَنِي ٱلْعَبَّاسِ مِنْ عُذُرِ
أَبْنَاءُ حَرْبٍ وَمَرْوَانٍ وَأُسْرَتُهُمْ   بَنُو مُعَيْطٍ وُلَاةُ ٱلْحِقْدِ وَٱلذُّعْرِ
قَوْمٌ قَتَلْتُمْ عَلَى ٱلْإِسْلَامِ أَوَّلَهُمْ   حَتَّى إِذَا ٱسْتَمْكَنُوا جَازُوا عَلَى ٱلْكُفْرِ
اِرْبَعْ بِطُوسَ عَلَى ٱلْقَبْرِ ٱلزَّكِيِّ بِهِ   إِنْ كُنْتَ تَرْبَعُ مِنْ دِينٍ عَلَى وَطَرِ
قَبْرَانِ فِي طُوسَ خَيْرُ ٱلنَّاسِ كُلِّهِمِ   وَقَبْرُ شَرِّهِمِ هٰذَا مِنَ ٱلْعِبَرِ
مَا يَنْفَعُ ٱلرِّجْسَ مِنْ قَبْرِ ٱلزَّكِيِّ وَلَا   عَلَى ٱلزَّكِيِّ بِقُرْبِ ٱلرِّجْسِ مِنْ ضَرَرِ
هَيْهَاتَ كُلُّ ٱمْرِئٍ رَهْنٌ بِمَا كَسَبَتْ   يَدَاهُ حَقًّا فَخُذْ مَا شِئْتَ أَوْ فَذَرِ

1a Ibn ʿAsak. يعرفه ; <u>Buldān</u> نعرفه 1b <u>Buldān</u> ولا بكر ولا مضر
2b <u>Ibid</u>. حزر 7a <u>Aǧ</u>.; Rifāʿī اذا ; Ḥuṣrī بها
7a-b Ibn ʿAsāk. الذكى 7b <u>Aǧ</u>; Rifāʿī ماكنت ; <u>T. Qumm</u> من طين على
<u>Aǧ</u>. ديرالى ; <u>Buldān</u> وطرى 8b Ibn ʿAsāk. القبر ; <u>T. Qumm</u> على
9a-b Ibn ʿAsāk. النحس 9b <u>Ibid</u>. بقرن 10b <u>Aǧ</u>; Rifāʿī له يداه ;
<u>T. Qumm</u> له يدا ; <u>Buldān</u> نذر ; Ḥuṣrī من ذاك
Order in Ḥuṣrī is verses 7, 9, 10, 8.

XCVI

1, 3-5 Ibn Šaj., Ḥamāsah, p. 117. 2-5 Dīwān al-Maʿānī, I, 127; Nujūm, II, 198. 2-4 Ibn ʿAsāk, Tar., V, 228. 2, 5 Tārīḫ Baghdād, IX, 488. Ṭawīl

تَعلَّمْ أَبا عِيسَى بِأَنْ لَيْسَ عَنْ قِلًى   وَلا مَلَلٍ كَانَ ٱبْتِدَاءُكَ بِٱلْهَجْرِ
هَجَرْتُكَ لَمْ أَهْجُرْكَ مِنْ كُفْرِ نِعْمَةٍ   وَهَلْ يُرْتَجَى نَيْلُ ٱلزِّيَادَةِ بِٱلْكُفْرِ
وَلٰكِنَّنِي لَمَّا أَتَيْتُكَ زَائِرًا   فَأَفْرَطْتَ فِي بِرِّي عَجَزْتُ عَنِ ٱلشُّكْرِ
فَإِنْ زِدْتَ فِي بِرِّي تَزَيَّدْتُ جَفْوَةً   فَلَمْ تَلْقَنِي حَتَّى ٱلْقِيَامَةِ وَٱلْحَشْرِ
فَمِلْآنَ لَا آتِيكَ إِلَّا مُعَذِّرًا   أَزُورُكَ فِي ٱلشَّهْرَيْنِ يَوْمًا أَوِ ٱلشَّهْرِ

1b Ibn Šaj. ابتدائك 2 Dīwān al-Maʿānī هجرتك لا عن جفوة وملالة ترتجى نيلك 2a Nujūm كفرا النعمة 2b Ibn ʿAsāk. ولا لقلى ابطات عنك ابا بكر 3a Dīwān al-Maʿānī راغبا, 4a Ibn Šaj. زدتني برا 4b Ibid.; Dīwān al-Maʿānī تزايدت; Ibn ʿAsāk. ولم نلتقي ; Dīwān al-Maʿānī فلا نلتقي 5a Ibn Šaj. مسلما 5b Ibid. وفي شهر

In Dīwān al-Maʿānī, verse 5 precedes verse 4.

XCVII

ʿUyūn, I, 334 Ṭawīl

لَئِنْ كُنْتَ لا تُولِي يَدًا دُونَ إِمْرَةٍ   فَلَسْتَ بِمُولٍ نَائِلًا آخِرَ ٱلدَّهْرِ
فَأَيُّ إِنَاءٍ لَمْ يَفِضْ عِنْدَ مَلْئِهِ   وَأَيُّ بَخِيلٍ لَمْ يُنِلْ سَاعَةَ ٱلْوَفْرِ
وَلَيْسَ ٱلْفَتَى ٱلْمُعْطِي عَلَى ٱلْيُسْرِ وَحْدَهُ   وَلٰكِنَّهُ ٱلْمُعْطِي عَلَى ٱلْعُسْرِ وَٱلْيُسْرِ

XCVIII

Ibn 'Asāk, Tar., V, 239 Ṭawīl

مَهَدْتُ لَهُ وُدِّي صَغِيرًا وَنُصْرَتِي   وَقَاسَمْتُهُ مَالِي وَبَوَّأْتُهُ حِجْرِي

وَقَدْ كَانَ يَكْفِيهِ مِنَ ٱلْعَيْشِ كُلِّهِ   رَجَاءٌ وَيَأْسٌ يَرْجَحَانِ إِلَى ٱلْفَقْرِ

وَفِيهِ عُيُوبٌ لَيْسَ يُحْصَى عِدَادُهَا   فَأَصْغَرُهَا عَيْبًا يَجِلُّ عَنِ ٱلْفِكْرِ

وَلَوْ أَنَّنِي أَبْدَيْتُ لِلنَّاسِ بَعْضَهَا   لَأَصْبَحَ مِنْ بَصْقِ ٱلْأَحِبَّةِ فِي بَحْرِ

وَدُونَكَ عِرْضِي فَٱهْجُ حَيًّا وَإِنْ أَمُتْ   فَأُقْسِمُ إِلَّا مَا خَرِيتَ عَلَى قَبْرِي

XCIX

Muḥāḍarāt, I, 406 Wāfir

وَبَاتَتْ قِدْرُنَا طَرِبًا تُغَنِّي   عَلَانِيَةً بِأَعْضَاءِ ٱلْجَزُورِ

C

Nihāyah, II, 92; Mustaṭraf, II, 19 Wāfir

أَتَاحَ لَكَ ٱلْهَوَى بِيضٌ حِسَانٌ   سَلَبْنَكَ بِٱلْعُيُونِ وَبِٱلنُّحُورِ

نَظَرْتَ إِلَى ٱلنُّحُورِ وَكِدْتَ تَقْضِي   فَكَيْفَ إِذَا نَظَرْتَ إِلَى ٱلْخُصُورِ

1a Mustatraf بيضا حسنا 1b Ibid. تبلى بالعيوب 2b Nihāyah فاولى لو

CI

1-3 Aġ, XVIII, 38. 1-2 Tashbīhāt, p. 346; Kināyāt, p. 9 Basīṭ

يَا مَنْ يُقَلِّبُ طُومَارًا وَيَنْشُرُهُ   مَاذَا بِقَلْبِكَ مِنْ حُبِّ ٱلطَّوَامِيرِ

فِيهِ مُشَابَهُ مِنْ شَيْءٍ تُسَرُّ بِهِ طُولًا بِطُولٍ وَتَدْوِيرًا بِتَدْوِيرِ

لَوْ كُنْتَ تَجْمَعُ أَمْوَالًا كَجَمْعِكَهَا إِذَنْ جَمَعْتَ بُيُوتًا مِنْ دَنَانِيرِ

1a Aǵ. بِلِينَتِه

CII

Muhādarāt, II, 186 Rajaz

1 وَذَاتُ جِسْمٍ مُشْبِهِ ٱلسَّاجُورِ

2 وَجُؤْجُؤٍ كَجُؤْجُؤِ ٱلطُّنْبُورِ

CIII

1-5 Ibn ʿAsāk, Tar., V, 239. 1-4 MM, p. 215. 3-5 Tashbīhāt, p. 137; Aḥsan Mā Samiʿtu, p. 100 Kāmil

يَا رُكْبَتَيْ جَزَرٍ وَسَاقَ نَعَامَةٍ وَزَبِيلَ كَنَّاسٍ وَرَأْسَ بَعِيرِ

يَا مَنْ أُشَبِّهُهَا بِحُمَّى نَافِضٍ قَطَّاعَةٍ لِلظَّهْرِ ذَاتِ زَفِيرِ

صُدْغَاكِ قَدْ شَمِطَا وَنَحْرُكِ يَابِسٌ وَالصَّدْرُ مِنْكِ كَجُؤْجُؤِ ٱلطُّنْبُورِ

يَا مَنْ مُعَانِقُهَا يَبِيتُ كَأَنَّهُ فِي مَحْبِسٍ قَمِلٍ وَفِي سَاجُورِ

5 قَبَّلْتُهَا فَوَجَدْتُ طَعْمَ لِثَاتِهَا فَوْقَ ٱللِّسَانِ كَلَدْغَةِ ٱلزُّنْبُورِ

1a MM. حرز نعامه 1b Ibid. شدق ; Ibn ʿAsāk. زنبيل

2b MM. للقلب ذات زفير 3a Aḥsan بارز 4a Ibid. مجلس صعب

5a Tashbīhāt; Aḥsan لدغة ريقها 5b Ibn ʿAsāk. كسلعة اللثام

CIV

Muntaḫab, p. 48 Ḫafīf

وَمِنَ ٱلنَّاسِ مَنْ يُحِبُّكَ حُبًّا ... ظَاهِرُ ٱلْوُدِّ لَيْسَ بِٱلتَّقْصِيرِ

وَإِذَا مَا خَبَرْتَهُ شَهِدَ ٱلطَّرْ ... فُ عَلَى حُبِّهِ بِمَا فِي ٱلضَّمِيرِ

وَإِذَا مَا بَحَثْتَ قُلْتَ لِهٰذَا ... ثِقَةٌ لِي وَرَأْسُ مَالٍ كَبِيرِ

فَإِذَا مَا سَأَلْتَهُ رُبْعَ فَلْسٍ ... أَلْحَقَ ٱلْوُدَّ بِٱللَّطِيفِ ٱلْخَبِيرِ

CV

Dīwān al-Ma'ānī, II, 180 Kāmil

حَنَّطْتَهُ يَا نَصْرُ بِٱلْكَافُورِ ... وَرَفَعْتَهُ لِلْمَنْزِلِ ٱلْمَهْجُورِ

هَلَّا بِبَعْضِ خِلَالِهِ حَنَّطْتَهُ ... فَيَضُوعَ أُفْقُ مَنَازِلٍ وَقُبُورِ

CVI

Tashbīhāt, p. 248 Ṭawīl

وَقَدْ كَانَ هٰذَا ٱلْبَحْرُ لَيْسَ يَجُوزُهُ ... سِوَى خَائِفٍ مِنْ ذَنْبِهِ أَوْ مُخَاطِرِ

وَأَضْحَى لِمَنْ يَنْتَابُ جُودَكَ عَامِرًا ... كَأَنَّ عَلَيْهِ مُحْكَمَاتِ ٱلْقَنَاطِرِ

CVII

Muhāḍarāt, II, 84 Ṭawīl

هُوَ ٱلْجَاعِلُ ٱلْبِيضَ ٱلْقَوَاطِعَ وَٱلْقَنَا ... طَعَامًا لِأَفْوَاهِ ٱلثُّغُورِ ٱلْفَوَاغِرِ

CVIII

Muhāḍarāt, II, 186 Ṭawīl

وَوَجْهٌ كَوَجْهِ ٱلْغُولِ فِيهِ سَمَاجَةٌ ... مُفَوَّهَةٌ شَوْهَاءُ ذَاتُ مَشَافِرِ

CIX

Ibn ʿAsāk, <u>Tar.</u>, V, 240 Basīṭ

قَوْمٌ إِذَا أَكَلُوا أَخْفَوْا كَلَامَهُمْ   وَٱسْتَوْثَقُوا مِنْ لُزُومِ ٱلْبَابِ وَٱلدَّارِ
لَا يَقْبِسُ ٱلْجَارُ مِنْهُمْ فَضْلَ نَارِهِمِ   وَلَا يَكُفُّ يَدٌ عَنْ حُرْمَةِ ٱلْجَارِ

CX

1-5 <u>Hamāsah</u>, p. 818. 1, 3 <u>Tashbīhāt</u>, p. 135 Ḫafīf

إِصْرِمِينِي يَا خِلْقَةَ ٱلْمِقْدَارِ   وَصِلِينِي بِطُولِ بُعْدِ ٱلْمَزَارِ
فَلَقَدْ سُمْتِنِي بِوَجْهِكِ وَٱلْوَصْلِ   قُرُوحًا أَعْيَتْ عَلَى ٱلْمِسْبَارِ
ذَقَنٌ نَاقِصٌ وَأَنْفٌ غَلِيظٌ   وَجَبِينٌ كَسَاحَةِ ٱلْقِسْطَارِ
طَالَ لَيْلِي بِهَا فَبِتُّ أُنَادِي   يَا لَثَارَاتِ مُسْتَضَاءِ ٱلنَّهَارِ
5 قَامَةُ ٱلْفَصْعَلِ ٱلضَّئِيلِ وَكَفٌّ   خِنْصِرَاهَا كَذِينَقَا قَصَّارِ

1a <u>Tashbīhāt</u> المسمار 3a <u>Ibid.</u> طويل

CXI

1-2 <u>Aǧ.</u>, XVIII, 46; <u>Kināyāt</u>, p. 18; <u>Buldān</u>, II, 519 Basīṭ

مَا زَالَ عِصْيَانُنَا لِلّٰهِ يُرْذِلُنَا   حَتَّى دُفِعْنَا إِلَى يَحْيَى وَدِينَارِ
وَغْدَيْنِ عِلْجَيْنِ لَمْ تُقْطَعْ ثِمَارُهُمَا   قَدْ طَالَمَا سَجَدَا لِلشَّمْسِ وَٱلنَّارِ

1a <u>Kināyāt</u> يربتنا 1b <u>Ibid.</u> فتح 2a <u>Ibid.</u>; <u>Buldān</u> الى عليجين

CXII

Muwāzanah, p. 46 Ṭawīl

تَنَافَسَ فِيهِ ٱلْحَزْمُ وَٱلْبَأْسُ وَٱلتُّقَى … وَبَذْلُ ٱللُّهَى حَتَّى ٱصْطَبَحْنَ ضَرَائِرَا

CXIII

Aḡ, XVIII, 53 Ṭawīl

هُمُ كَتَبُوا ٱلصَّكَّ ٱلَّذِي قَدْ عَلِمْتَهُ … عَلَيْكَ وَشَنُّوا فَوْقَ هَامَتِكَ ٱلْقَفْرَا

CXIV

1-7 Ibn al-Muᶜtazz, Ṭab, p. 140. 1-3 Aḡ, XVIII, 51; 55 Ḫafīf

يَا أَبَا سَعْدٍ قَوْصَرَهْ … زَانِيَ ٱلْأُخْتِ وَٱلْمَرَهْ

لَوْ تَرَاهُ مُحَبَّبًا … خِلْتَهُ عَقْدَ قَنْطَرَهْ

أَوْ تَرَى ٱلْأَيْرَ فِي ٱسْتِهِ … قُلْتَ سَاقٌ بِمِقْطَرَهْ

أَوْ تَرَاهُ يَلُوكُهُ … قُلْتَ زُبْدٌ بِسُكَّرَهْ

أَوْ تَرَاهُ يَشُمُّهُ … قُلْتَ مِسْكٌ بِعَنْبَرَهْ

أَرْسَلَ ٱلْعَبْدُ بَارَهُ … وَهْوَ لِلْعَبْدِ كُنْدُرَهْ

أَبَعَ ٱلدَّهْرِ خَلْفَهُ … فَارِسٌ فِي مُؤَخَّرَهْ

1b Ibn al-Muᶜtazz has المرة corrected in Notes p. 36 to المره
2a Ibn al-Muᶜtazz مدجنا ; Aḡ. مجيبا 2b Ibn al-Muᶜtazz text has حلته corrected in Notes to خلته 5a Text has يسمه. corrected in Notes to يشمه 5b Text has ميسك corrected in Notes to مسك 6a Reading above is that of M edition. Text has أجج العبد ناره 6b Text has للنار

CXV

1-4 Aġ, XVIII, 59. 3-4 Muntaḥal, p. 139 Sarīʿ

إِنَّ ٱبنَ طَوقٍ وَبَنِي تَغلِبٍ   لَو قُتِلُوا أَو جُرِحُوا قَصْرَهْ
لَم يَأخُذُوا مِن دِيَةٍ دِرهَمًا   يَومًا وَلا مِن أَرشِهِم بَعْرَهْ
دِمَاؤُهُمْ لَيسَ لَهَا طَالِبٌ   مَطلُولَةٌ مِثلُ دَمِ ٱلعُذرَهْ
وُجُوهُهُم بِيضٌ وَأَحسَابُهُم   سُودٌ وَفِي آذَانِهِم صُفرَهْ

4b Muntaḥal أعراضهم

CXVI

1-3 Muḥāḍarāt, I, 221. 1-2 Gefährte, p. 278 Sarīʿ

إِنَّ بَنِي عَمرٍو لَأُعجُوبَةٌ   تَعجِزُ عَن وَصفِهِمِ ٱلفِكرَهْ
أَبُوهُمُ أَسمَرُ فِي لَونِهِ   وَهَؤُلَاءِ لَونُهُم شُقرَهْ
أَظُنُّهُ حِينَ أَتَى أُمَّهُم   صَيَّرَ فِي نُطفَتِهِ مَغرَهْ

1a Gefährte لا عجوبة   2b Ibid. ألوانهم

CXVII

Tashbīhāt, p. 306 Wāfir

يُلَوِّثُ لِحيَةً عَرُضَت وَطَالَت   وَيَمرُثُهَا كَتَمرِيثِ ٱلخَمِيرَهْ
فَيَا لَكَ لِحيَةً وَضَرًى وَشَيبًا   كَأَنَّكَ قَد أَكَلتَ بِهَا مَضِيرَهْ

CXVIII

Muḥāḍarāt, I, 223   Ramal

كُلَّ يَوْمٍ لِأَبِي سَعْدٍ   وعَلَى ٱلْأَنْسَابِ غَارَهْ

فَهْوَ يَوْمًا فِي تَمِيمٍ   وَهْوَ يَوْمًا فِي فَزَارَهْ

CXIX

Kāmil, p. 523; Ibn ʿAsāk, Tar, V, 241   Ṭawīl

رَأَيْتَ أَبَا عِمْرَانَ يَبْذُلُ عِرْضَهُ   وَخُبْزُ أَبِي عِمْرَانَ فِي أَحْرَزِ ٱلْحِرْزِ

يَحِنُّ إِلَى جَارَاتِهِ بَعْدَ شِبْعِهِ   وَجَارَاتُهُ غَرْثَى تَحِنُّ إِلَى ٱلْخُبْزِ

2a Ibn ʿAsāk. سبعه

CXX

K. Baghdād, p. 226   Kāmil

لَوْلَا تَكُونُ كَكَاتِبٍ لَكَ رَبْعَةٍ   يَقْضِي ٱلْحَوَائِجَ مُسْتَطِيلِ ٱلرَّأْسِ

لَمْ تَغْدَ بِٱلْمَلْبُونِ عِنْدَ فِطَامِهِ   يَوْمًا وَلَا بِمُطَجَّنِ ٱلْقُلْقَاسِ

أَوْ كَانَ مَسْعَدَةَ ٱلْكَرِيمِ نِجَارُهُ   بَيْتُ ٱلْكِتَابَةِ فِي بَنِي ٱلْعَبَّاسِ

يَغْدُو عَلَى أَضْيَافِهِ مُسْتَطْعِمًا   كَٱلْكَلْبِ يَأْكُلُ فِي بُيُوتِ ٱلنَّاسِ

CXXI

1-9 Ḥamāsah, pp. 822-23. 1, 3, 8 ʿUyūn, IV, 38. 3, 8 ʿUyūn, II, 188. 7 Muḥāḍarāt, II, 186   Mutaqārib

مُنِيتُ بِزَنْمَرْدَةٍ كَالْعَصَا ... أَلَصَّ وَأَخْبَثَ مِنْ كُنْدُشِ
تُحِبُّ النِّسَاءَ وَتَأْبَى الرِّجَالَ ... وَتَمْشِي مَعَ الْأَخْبَثِ الْأَطْيَشِ
لَهَا وَجْهُ قِرْدٍ إِذَا ازَّيَّنَتْ ... وَلَوْنٌ كَبَيْضِ الْقَطَا الْأَبْرَشِ
وَثَدْيٌ يَجُولُ عَلَى نَحْرِهَا ... كَقِرْبَةِ ذِي الثَّلَّةِ الْمُعْطِشِ
لَهَا رَكَبٌ مِثْلُ ظِلْفِ الْغَزَالِ ... أَشَدُّ اصْفِرَارًا مِنَ الْمِشْمِشِ
وَفَخْذَانِ بَيْنَهُمَا نَفْنَفٌ ... يُجِيزُ الْمَحَامِلَ لَمْ تُخْدَشِ
وَسَاقٌ مُخَلْخَلُهَا حَمْشَةٌ ... كَسَاقِ الْجَرَادَةِ أَوْ أَحْمَشِ
كَأَنَّ الثَّآلِيلَ فِي وَجْهِهَا ... إِذَا سَفَرَتْ بَدَدُ الْكِشْمِشِ
لَهَا جُمَّةٌ فَوْقَهَا جَثْلَةٌ ... كَمِثْلِ الْخَوَافِي مِنَ الْمُرْعَشِ

1a ʿUyūn بليث بزمردة 1b Ibid. أسرق 3a ʿUyūn, IV, 38; II, 88
شعر 3b ʿUyūn ووجه 7a Ḥamāsah التاابيل 8a Ibid. أحمش

CXXII

ʿUyūn, IV, 39 Kāmil

تَمَّتْ مَقَابِحُ وَجْهِهِ فَكَأَنَّهُ ... طَلَلٌ تَحَمَّلَ سَاكِنُوهُ فَأَوْحَشَا
لَوْ كَانَ لِاسْتِكَ ضِيقُ صَدْرِكَ أَوْ بِصَدْ ... رِكَ رَحْبُ دُبْرِكَ كُنْتَ أَكْمَلَ مَنْ مَشَى

CXXIII

Aġ., XVIII, 33-34 Basīṭ

أَبَا نُضَيْرٍ تَحَلْحَلْ عَنْ مَجَالِسِنَا ... فَإِنَّ فِيكَ لِمَنْ جَارَكَ مُنْتَقَصَا

أَنْتَ ٱلْحِمَارُ حُرُونًا إِنْ وَقَفْتَ بِهِ ... وَإِنْ قَصَدْتَ إِلَى مَعْرُوفِهِ قَمَصَا

إِنِّي هَزَزْتُكَ لَا آلُوكَ مُجْتَهِدًا ... لَوْ كُنْتَ سَيْفًا وَلَكِنِّي هَزَزْتُ عَصَا

CXXIV

ʿIqd, III, 426; Muslim, pp. 242-43; Ibn ʿAsāk, Tar., V, 230; Azdī, p. 25 Munsariḥ

دُمُوعُ عَيْنِي بِهَا ٱنْبِسَاطُ ... وَنَوْمُ عَيْنِي بِهِ ٱنْقِبَاضُ

وَذَا قَلِيلٌ لِمَنْ دَهَتْهُ ... بِلَحْظِهَا ٱلْأَعْيُنُ ٱلْمِرَاضُ

فَهَلْ لِمَوْلَايَ عَطْفُ قَلْبٍ ... أَوْ لِلَّذِي بِي ٱلْحَشَا ٱنْقِرَاضُ

3a Ibn ʿAsāk. فهل لمولاتي 3b Ibid. أم 3b Azdī بسحرها.

CXXV

Ibn ʿAsāk, Tar., V, 232 Basīṭ

أَحْمَلْتُهُ حِينَ لَمْ أَمْلِكْ مَقَادَتَهُ ... ثُمَّ ٱنْقَبَضْتُ بِوُدِّي عَنْهُ وَٱنْقَبَضَا

وَقُلْتُ لِلنَّفْسِ تَنْدُبُهُ مَتَى نَزَحَتْ ... بِهِ ٱلنَّوَى أَوْ مِنَ ٱلْقَرْنِ ٱلَّذِي ٱنْقَرَضَا

فَمَا بَكَيْتُ عَلَيْهِ حِينَ فَارَقَنِي ... وَلَا وَجَدْتُ لَهُ بَيْنَ ٱلْحَشَا مَضَضَا

CXXVI

1-6 Aġ., XVIII, 30; Rifāʿī, III, 255. 1-4 Waraqah, p. 21; Ibn ʿAsāk, Tar., II, 272; Tāʾrīḫ Baghdād, VI, 144; Bidāyah, X, 290 Sarīʿ

يا معشر الأجناد لا تقنطوا — وارضوا بما كان ولا تسخطوا

فسوف تعطون حنينية — يلتذها الأمرد والأشمط

والمعبديات لقوادكم — لا تدخل الكيس ولا تربط

وهكذا يرزق قواده — خليفة مصحفه البربط

قد ختم الصك بأرزاقكم — وصحح العزم فلا تسخطوا

بيعة إبراهيم مشؤومة — يقتل فيها الخلق أو يقحطوا

1a Ibn ʿAsāk تغلطوا ,الاعراب ; Ta'rīẖ Baghdād لا تغلطوا ; Bidāyah Waraqah الاعراب 1b Bidāyah; Waraqah; Ta'rīẖ Baghdād لا تغلطوا ; Ibn ʿAsāk. عطاياكم 2 Bidāyah; Ibn ʿAsāk; Ta'rīẖ Baghdād خذوا عطاياكم ; بعطيكم 2a Waraqah فسوف يعطيكم حنينية لاتدخل الكيس ولا توبط In Waraqah 2a and 3a are added by editor. 3 Bidāyah; Ibn ʿAsāk; Ta'rīẖ Baghdād والمعبديات لقوادكم ومابهااحد يغبط 4a Bidāyah هكذا ,اجناده ; Ibn ʿAsāk فهكذا ,اصحابه ; Ta'rīẖ Baghdād ; اصحابه

CXXVII

1-6 Kāmil, p. 457; Tashbīhāt, p. 25 Rajaz

1 لم أر صفا مثل صف الزط — 2 تسعين منهم صلبوا في خط

3 كأنما غمستهم في نفط — 4 كأنه في جذعه المشتط

5 أخو نعاس جد في التمطي — 6 كأنه خامر النوم ولم يغط

1 Tashbīhāt لم ار عيني 2 Tashbīhāt خمسين 3 Kāmil من كل عال بجدعه بالشط is missing in Tashbīhāt. After verses 1, 2 have كانما غمستهم في نفط واُفرد واحد فقال then follow verses 4, 5, 6.

CXXVIII

Ibn ʿAsāk, Tar., V, 237   Ṭawīl

أَلَا أَبْلِغَا عَنِّي ٱلْإِمَامَ رِسَالَةً   رِسَالَةَ نَاءٍ عَنْ جَنَابَيْهِ شَاحِطِ
بِأَنَّ ٱبْنَ وَهْبٍ حِينَ يَشْمَخُ شَامِخٌ   يَمُرُّ عَلَى ٱلْقِرْطَاسِ أَقْلَامُ غَالِطِ

CXXIX

Ag, XVIII, 33; Rifāʿī, III, 257   Kāmil

أَسَرَ ٱلْمُؤَذِّنَ صَالِحٌ وَضُيُوفَهُ   أَسْرَ ٱلْكَمِيِّ هَفَا خِلَالَ ٱلْمَأْقِطِ
بَعَثُوا عَلَيْهِ بَنِيهِمُ وَبَنَاتِهِمْ   مِنْ بَيْنِ نَاتِفَةٍ وَآخَرَ سَامِطِ
يَتَنَازَعُونَ كَأَنَّهُمْ قَدْ أَوْثَقُوا   خَاقَانَ أَوْ هَزَمُوا كَتَائِبَ نَاعِطِ
نَهَشُوا فَٱنْتَزَعَتْ لَهُ أَسْنَانُهُمْ   وَتَهَشَّمَتْ أَقْفَاؤُهُمْ بِٱلْحَائِطِ

3b Rifāʿī قبائل

CXXX

Ibn ʿAsāk, Tar., V, 238   Ḫafīf

رُفِعَ ٱلْكَلْبُ فَٱتَّضَعْ   لَيْسَ فِي ٱلْكَلْبِ مُصْطَنَعْ
بَلَغَ ٱلْغَايَةَ ٱلَّتِي   دُونَهَا كُلُّ مُرْتَفَعْ
إِنَّمَا قَصْرُ كُلِّ شَيْ   ءٍ إِذَا طَارَ أَنْ يَقَعْ

قُلْ لِيَحْيَى ٱبْنِ أَكْثَمْ إِنَّ مَا خِفْتَ قَدْ وَقَعْ
لَعَنَ ٱللهُ نَحْوَهُ كَانَ مِنْ بَعْدِهَا ضَرَعْ

CXXXI

__Irshād__, IV, 197 Kāmil

رَأْسُ ٱبْنِ بِنْتِ مُحَمَّدٍ وَوَصِيِّهِ يَا لَلرِّجَالِ عَلَى قَنَاةٍ تُرْفَعُ
وَٱلْمُسْلِمُونَ بِمَنْظَرٍ وَبِمَسْمَعٍ لَا جَازِعٌ مِنْ ذَا وَلَا مُتَخَشِّعُ
أَيْقَظْتَ أَجْفَانًا وَكُنْتَ لَهَا كَرًى وَأَنَمْتَ عَيْنًا لَمْ تَكُنْ بِهَا تَهْجَعُ
كُحِلَتْ بِمَنْظَرِكَ ٱلْعُيُونُ عَمَايَةً وَأَصَمَّ نَعْيُكَ كُلَّ أُذْنٍ تَسْمَعُ
مَا رَوْضَةٌ إِلَّا تَمَنَّتْ أَنَّهَا لَكَ مَضْجَعٌ وَلِخَطِّ قَبْرِكَ مَوْضِعُ

CXXXII

1-5 Ibn ʿAsāk, __Tar__, V, 229. 2-5 __Aġ__, XVIII, 44-45; Rifāʿī, III, 261
Ṭawīl

وَقَائِلَةٍ لَمَّا ٱسْتَمَرَّتْ بِهَا ٱلنَّوَى وَمَحْجِرُهَا فِيهِ دَمٌ وَدُمُوعُ
أَلَمْ يَأْنِ لِلسَّفْرِ ٱلَّذِينَ تَحَمَّلُوا إِلَى وَطَنٍ قَبْلَ ٱلْمَمَاتِ رُجُوعُ
فَقُلْتُ وَلَمْ أَمْلِكْ سَوَابِقَ عَبْرَةٍ نَطَقْنَ بِمَا ضُمَّتْ عَلَيْهِ ضُلُوعُ
تَبَيَّنْ فَكَمْ دَارٍ تَفَرَّقَ شَمْلُهَا وَشَمْلٍ شَتِيتٍ عَادَ وَهْوَ جَمِيعُ
كَذَاكَ ٱللَّيَالِي صَرْفُهُنَّ كَمَا تَرَى لِكُلِّ أُنَاسٍ جَدْبَةٌ وَرَبِيعُ

2a Ibn ʿAsāk. ترى نقض للسفر 2b __Ibid__. الى بلد فيه السفر رجيع
3b __Ibid__. بطفن 4a __Ibid__. تأن 5a __Aġ__. كذلك

CXXXIII

Aǧ., XXI, 2-3   Ṭawīl

يَقُولُ زِيَادٌ قِفْ بِصَحْبِكَ مَرَّةً   عَلَى ٱلرَّبْعِ مَا لِي وَلِلْوُقُوفِ عَلَى ٱلرَّبْعِ
أَدِرْهَا عَلَى فَقْدِ ٱلْحَبِيبِ فَرُبَّمَا   شَرِبْتُ عَلَى نَأْيِ ٱلْأَحِبَّةِ وَٱلْفَجْعِ
فَمَا بَلَغَتْنِي ٱلْكَأْسُ إِلَّا شَرِبْتُهَا   وَإِلَّا سَقَيْتُ ٱلْأَرْضَ كَأْسًا مِنَ ٱلدَّمْعِ

CXXXIV

1-2 Kāmil, p. 525; Dalā'il, p. 427. 2 Ṭirāz, p. 206   Basīṭ

أَضْيَافُ سَالِمٍ فِي خَفْضٍ وَفِي دَعَةٍ   وَفِي شَرَابٍ وَلَحْمٍ غَيْرِ مَمْنُوعِ
وَضَيْفُ عَمْرٍو وَعَمْرٌو يَسْهَرَانِ   عَمْرٌو لِبَطْنَتِهِ وَٱلضَّيْفُ لِلْجُوعِ

CXXXV

Nihāyah, III, 91   Sarī'

جِئْنَا بِهِ يَشْفَعُ فِي حَاجَةٍ   فَٱحْتَاجَ فِي ٱلْإِذْنِ إِلَى شَافِعِ

CXXXVI

Aǧ., XVIII, 38   Wāfir

إِذَا نَزَلَ ٱلْغَرِيبُ بِأَرْضِ حِمْصٍ   رَأَيْتَ عَلَيْهِ عِزَّ ٱلِامْتِنَاعِ
سُمُوا لِلْمَكْرُمَاتِ بِآلِ عِيسَى   أَحَلَّهُمُ عَلَى شَرَفِ ٱلتِّلَاعِ
هُنَاكَ ٱلْخَزُّ يَلْبَسُهُ ٱلْمُغَالِي   وَعِيسَى مِنْهُمُ سَقَطُ ٱلْمَتَاعِ
فَسَدِّدْ لِٱسْطِ أَشْعَثَ أَيْرَ بَغْلٍ   وَآخَرَ فِي حِرَامِ أَبِي ٱلصَّنَاعِ
فَلَيْسَ بِصَانِعٍ مَجْدًا وَلٰكِنْ   أَضَاعَ ٱلْمَجْدَ فَهْوَ أَبُو ٱلضَّيَاعِ

CXXXVII

<u>Muḥāḍarāt</u>, I, 233 Kāmil

لَا يَقْبَلُونَ ٱلشُّكْرَ مَا لَمْ يُنْعِمُوا   نِعَمًا يَكُونُ لَهَا ٱلثَّنَاءُ تَبِيعَا

CXXXVIII

1-7 <u>Aġ</u>, XVIII, 47; Rifāʿī, III, 262, <u>Muslim</u>, pp. 245-46. 1, 2, 6-7 <u>ʿUyūn</u>, III, 82. 4-7 Ibn Ḫallikān, I, 224; 4, 7 <u>Lisān</u>, II, 430

Ṭawīl

أَبَا مَخْلَدٍ كُنَّا عَقِيدَيْ مَوَدَّةٍ   هَوَانَا وَقَلْبَانَا جَمِيعًا مَعًا مَعَا
أَحُوطُكَ بِٱلْوُدِّ ٱلَّذِي لَا تَحُوطُنِي   وَأَجْزَعُ إِشْفَاقًا مِنْ أَنْ تَتَوَجَّعَا
فَصَيَّرْتَنِي بَعْدَ ٱنْتِكَاثِكَ مُتْهِمًا   لِنَفْسِي عَلَيْهَا أَرْهَبُ ٱلْخَلْقِ أَجْمَعَا
غَشَشْتَ ٱلْهَوَى حَتَّى تَدَاعَتْ أُصُولُهُ   بِنَا وَٱبْتَذَلْتَ ٱلْوَصْلَ حَتَّى تَقَطَّعَا
5 وَأَنْزَلْتَ بِي بَيْنَ ٱلْجَوَانِحِ وَٱلْحَشَا   ذَخِيرَةَ وُدٍّ طَالَمَا قَدْ تَمَنَّعَا
فَلَا تَلْحِيَنِّي لَيْسَ لِي فِيكَ مَطْمَعٌ   تَخَرَّقْتَ حَتَّى لَمْ أَجِدْ لَكَ مَرْقَعَا
فَهَبْكَ يَمِينِي ٱسْتَأْكَلَتْ فَقَطَعْتُهَا   وَجَشَّمْتُ قَلْبِي صَبْرَهُ فَتَشَجَّعَا

1a <u>ʿUyūn</u> خليلي ؛ ابا مسلم 2a <u>Aġ</u>; Rifāʿī; <u>Muslim</u> انت حايطي ؛ بالغيب
2b <u>ʿUyūn</u> وأراب منك الشعب ان يتصدعا ; <u>Aġ</u>. لان ؛ انجع
3a <u>Aġ</u> انتحائك 4a <u>Lisān</u> عسيت 5a Ibn Ḫallikān ما بين
6a <u>Aġ</u>; Ibn Ḫallikān تعذلني ; <u>ʿUyūn</u> لم اجد ؛ حيلة 7a <u>ʿUyūn</u> فاحتسبتها
7b <u>Ibid</u>. قطعتها <u>Lisān</u>; Ibn Ḫallikān وصبرت قلبي بعدها فتشجعا

CXXXIX

<u>Tashbīhāt</u>, p. 62; <u>Nihāyah</u>, I, 92; <u>MM</u>, p. 186; <u>Zahrah</u>, p. 230

Basīṭ

مَا زِلْتَ أَكْلَأُ بَرْقًا فِي جَوَانِبِهِ — كَطَرْفَةِ ٱلْعَيْنِ يَخْبُو ثُمَّ يَخْتَطِفُ
بَرْقٌ تَجَاسَرَ مِنْ خَفَّانِ لَامِعُهُ — يَقْضِي ٱللُّبَانَةَ فِي قَلْبِي وَيَنْصَرِفُ

1b Nihāyah; MM تخبو ثم تختطف   2a MM لامحة

CXL

Ag., IX, 24; K. Baghdād, p. 303; Azdī, p. 118   Hazaj

فَإِذْ فَاتَ ٱلَّذِي فَاتَ — فَكُونُوا مِنْ ذَوِي ٱلظَّرْفِ
وَمُرُّوا نَقْصِفِ ٱلْيَوْمَ — فَإِنِّي بَائِعٌ خُفِّي

1b Azdī اولى

CXLI

1, 3-5 Muntahab, p. 22. 1-3 Ibn Hallikān, I, 424   Basīṭ

اللهُ أَجْرَى مِنَ ٱلْأَرْزَاقِ أَكْثَرَهَا — عَلَى يَدَيْكَ بِخَيْرٍ يَا أَبَا دُلَفِ
مَا خَطَّ لَا كَاتِبَاهُ فِي صَحِيفَتِهِ — كَمَا تَخَطَّطَ فِي سَائِرِ ٱلصُّحُفِ
أَعْطَى أَبُو دُلَفٍ وَٱلرِّيحُ عَاصِفَةٌ — حَتَّى إِذَا وَقَفَتْ أَعْطَى وَلَمْ يَقِفِ
مَا يَصْنَعُ ٱلشَّيْخُ بِٱلْعَذْرَاءِ يَمْلِكُهَا — كَجَوْزَةٍ بَيْنَ فَكَّيْ أَدْرَدٍ خَرِفِ
5 إِنْ رَامَ يَكْسِرُهَا بِٱلسِّنِّ تَثْلِمُهُ — وَكَسْرُهَا رَاحَةٌ لِلْهَائِمِ ٱلدَّنِفِ

1b Ibn Hallikān على يديك تعلم   3a Ibid. بارى الريح فاعطى وهى جارية
4b Muntahab has كجودة

CXLII

'Iqd, III, 427; Muslim, p. 244   Hafif

مَنْ لَهُ فِي خُرَامِهِ قَرْنٌ   قَدْ أَنَافَتْ عَلَى عُلُوٍّ مُنَافِ

CXLIII

Ibn ʿAsāk, Tar., V, 241; Dīwān al-Maʿānī, II, 252   Wāfir

وَعَدْتَ ٱلنَّعْلَ ثُمَّ صَدَفْتَ عَنْهَا   كَأَنَّكَ تَبْتَغِي شَتْمًا وَقَذْفَا

فَإِنْ لَمْ تُهْدِنِي نَعْلًا فَكُنْهَا   إِذَا أَعْجَمْتَ بَعْدَ ٱلنُّونِ حَرْفَا

1b Dīwān al-Maʿānī تشتهى   2a Ibid. تهدلى

CXLIV

Ṣūlī, Abū Tammām, p. 50   Wāfir

وَأَكْثَرْتُ ٱلْهِجَاءَ عَلَى لَئِيمٍ   فَلَمَّا ذَاقَهُ لِلُّؤْمِ عَافَهْ

CXLV

ʿIqd, I, 120 (n.e. I, 315); Ibn Ḫallikān, I, 236   Mutaqārib

عَجِبْتُ لِحَرَّاقَةِ ٱبْنِ ٱلْحُسَيْـ   ـنِ كَيْفَ تَسِيرُ وَلَا تَغْرَقُ

وَبَحْرَانِ مِنْ تَحْتِهَا وَاحِدٌ   وَآخَرُ مِنْ فَوْقِهَا مُطْبِقُ

وَأَعْجَبُ مِنْ ذَاكَ عِيدَانُهَا   إِذَا مَسَّهَا كَيْفَ لَا تُورِقُ

3a Ibn Ḫallikān اعوادها   3b Ibid. وقد

CXLVI

1-2 Ṣūlī, Abū Tammām, p. 63; Aġ, XV, 101; Ṣinā'atain, p. 160; Muwāzanah, p. 28. 2 Ibn al-Athīr, Mathal, I, 306 Ṭawīl

وَإِنَّ ٱمْرَأً أَسْدَى إِلَيَّ بِشَافِعٍ   إِلَيْهِ وَيَرْجُو ٱلشُّكْرَ مِنِّي لَأَحْمَقُ

شَفِيعُكَ فَٱشْكُرْ فِي ٱلْحَوَائِجِ إِنَّهُ   يَصُونُكَ عَنْ مَكْرُوهِهَا وَهُوَ يَخْلُقُ

1a Ṣūlī, Abū Tammām ان 1b Muwāzanah لدى يرجو

CXLVII

Muhāḍarāt, II, 107 Kāmil

عَيْرٌ رَأَى أَسَدَ ٱلْعَرِينِ فَرَاعَهُ   حَتَّى إِذَا وَلَّى تَوَلَّى يَنْهَقُ

CXLVIII

1-12; 14 Aġ, XVIII, 58; Rifā'ī, III, 263. 4-5, 9, 11, 13-14 'Iqd, III, 130; 4-5, 9, 11, 14 'Iqd, I, 94 (n.e. I, 251-52). 14 Ṭirāz, p. 109 Kāmil

دَلَّيْتَنِي بِغُرُورِ وَعْدِكَ فِي   مُتَلَاطِمٍ مِنْ حَوْمَةِ ٱلْغَرَقِ

حَتَّى إِذَا شَمِتَ ٱلْعَدُوُّ وَقَدْ   شُهِرَ ٱنْتِقَاصُكَ شُهْرَةَ ٱلْبَلَقِ

أَنْشَأْتَ تَحْلِفُ أَنَّ وُدَّكَ لِي   صَافٍ وَحَبْلَكَ غَيْرُ مُنْحَذِقِ

وَظَنَنْتَ أَرْضَ ٱللّٰهِ ضَيِّقَةً   عَنِّي فَأَرْضُ ٱللّٰهِ لَمْ تَضِقِ

5 وَحَسِبْتَنِي فَقْعًا بِقَرْقَرَةٍ   فَوَطِئْتَنِي وَطْأً عَلَى حَنَقِ

وَنَصَبْتَنِي عَلَمًا عَلَى غَرَضٍ   تَرْمِينَنِي ٱلْأَعْدَاءُ بِٱلْحَدَقِ

مِنْ غَيْرِ مَا جُرْمٍ سِوَى ثِقَةٍ   مِنِّي بِوَعْدِكَ حِينَ قُلْتَ ثِقِ

وَمَوَدَّةٍ تَحْنُو عَلَيْكَ بِهَا   نَفْسِي بِلَا مَنٍّ وَلَا مَلَقِ
فَمَتَى سَأَلْتُكَ حَاجَةً أَبَدًا   فَاشْدُدْ بِهَا قُفْلًا عَلَى غَلَقِ
وَتَقَى ٱلإِخَاءُ عَلَى شَفَا جُرُفٍ   هَارٍ مُبِيعُهُ بَيْعَةَ ٱلخَلَقِ
وَأَعِدَّ لِي قُفْلًا وَجَامِعَةً   فَاشْدُدْ يَدَيَّ بِهَا إِلَى عُنُقِي
أُعْفِيكَ مِمَّا لَا تُحِبُّ بِهَا   وَٱشْدُدْ عَلَيَّ مَذَاهِبَ ٱلأُفُقِ
ثُمَّ ٱرْمِ بِي فِي قَعْرِ مُظْلِمَةٍ   إِنْ عُدْتُ بَعْدَ ٱليَوْمِ فِي ٱلحُمُقِ
مَا أَطْوَلَ ٱلدُّنْيَا وَأَعْرَضَهَا   وَأَدَلَّنِي بِمَسَالِكِ ٱلطُّرُقِ

4a ʿ*Iqd*, I, 94; III, 130 احسبن 5a ʿ*Iqd*, I, 94; I, 251 وجعلتني
5b ʿ*Iqd*, III, 130 فقعها 9a ʿ*Iqd*, I, 94; III, 130; I, 251 فاذا
9b *Ibid*. فاضرب لها 11a *Ibid*. غلا 11b ʿ*Iqd*, I, 94; III, 130
14a ʿ*Iqd*, I, 94; III, 130; I, 252; *Tirāz* فاجمع ز عنق
14b *Aġ*. وادلني اوسعها

CXLIX

1-3 Ibn ʿAsāk., *Tar*., V, 240; *Thimār*, p. 212; *Aġ*., XVIII, 54. 1-2 *Muntahab*, p. 12 Wāfir

عَدُوٌّ رَاحَ فِي ثَوْبِ ٱلصَّدِيقِ   شَرِيكٌ فِي ٱلصَّبُوحِ وَفِي ٱلغَبُوقِ
لَهُ وَجْهَانِ ظَاهِرُهُ ٱبْنُ عَمٍّ   وَبَاطِنُهُ ٱبْنُ زَانِيَةٍ عَتِيقِ
يَسُرُّكَ ظَاهِرًا وَيَسُوءُ سِرًّا   كَذَاكَ يَكُونُ أَبْنَاءُ ٱلطَّرِيقِ

2a Ibn ʿAsāk. ابن عمرو 2b *Ibid.* وباطن وجهه ابن ضيق
3a *Ibid.* مقبلا ويسوك هيبا ; *Aǧ.* يسوك معلنا

CL

1-4, 5-7 Ibn ʿAsāk, *Tar.*, V, 234. 1, 2, 5, 7 *Aǧ.*, XVIII, 58. 4-7 *Ašʿār*, p. 33; Ibn Ḫallikān, I, 8. 5-7 *Šiʿr*, p. 540; Ṭabarī, III, 1156; *K. Baghdād*, p. 296, 194; Ḥasan, II, 134. 4-5 Ibn Šaj., *Amālī*, I, 59; *Tārīḫ Baghdād*, VI, 144. 5-6 *Waraqah*, p. 21; *Muḥāḍarāt*, I, 441-42. 4 Ibn Ḫallikān, I, 179. 5 *Fiqh*, p. 323 Kāmil

عِلْمٌ وَتَحْكِيمٌ وَشَيْبُ مَفَارِقِ   طَلَّسْنَ رَيْعَانَ ٱلشَّبَابِ ٱلرَّائِقِ
وَإِمَارَةٌ مِنْ دَوْلَةٍ مَيْمُونَةٍ   كَانَتْ عَلَى ٱللَّذَّاتِ أَشْغَبَ عَائِقِ
فَٱلْآنَ لَا أَغْدُو وَلَسْتُ بِرَائِحٍ   فِي كِبْرِ مَعْشُوقٍ وَذِلَّةِ عَاشِقِ
نَفَرَ ٱبْنُ شِكْلَةَ بِٱلْعِرَاقِ وَأَهْلِهِ   فَهَفَا إِلَيْهِ كُلُّ أَطْلَسَ مَائِقِ
إِنْ كَانَ إِبْرَاهِيمُ مُضْطَلِعًا بِهَا   فَلَتَصْلُحَنْ مِنْ بَعْدِهِ لِمُخَارِقِ
وَلَتَصْلُحَنْ مِنْ بَعْدِ ذَاكَ لِزُلْزُلٍ   فَلَتَصْلُحَنْ مِنْ بَعْدِهِ لِلْمَارِقِ
أَنَّى يَكُونُ وَلَا يَكُونُ وَلَمْ يَكُنْ   لِيَنَالَ ذَٰلِكَ فَاسِقٌ عَنْ فَاسِقِ

1b *Aǧ.* تطميس 2a *Ibid.* في 4a Ibn ʿAsāk; Ibn Ḫallikān نعر
4b *Ašʿār* الجيش 6a *K. Baghdād* من بعده في عشعش 6b *Ašʿār* ولتصلحن وراثة
7a Ibn ʿAsāk; *Aǧ.*; *Ašʿār*; Ibn Ḫallikān ليس ذاك بكائن
7b Ibn ʿAsāk; *Aǧ.*; *Ašʿār*; Ibn Ḫallikān يرث الخلافة
Order in Ibn ʿAsāk. is 1, 2, 3, 7, 4, 5. In *Aǧ* 1, 2, 7, 5. In *K. Baghdād* 7, 5, 6.

CLI

Muslim, p. 243; ʿIqd, III, 426 Kāmil

أترى الزمان يسرنا بتلاقِ   ويضمّ مشتاقا إلى مشتاقِ

CLII

1-8 Ibn ʿAsāk, Tar., V, 134. 1-6, 8 Tashbīhāt, p. 134. 3, 6, 7 Muḥāḍarāt, II, 186 Mutaqārib

رأيت غزالا وقد أطلعت   فأبدت لعيني عن منطقه
قصيرة الخلق دحداحة   تدحرج في المشي كالبندقه
كأنّ ذراعا على كفّها   إذا حسرت ذنب الملعقه
تخطّط حاجبها بالمداد   وتربط في عجزها مرفقه
5 وأنف على وجهها ملصق   قصير المناخر كالفستقه
وثديان ثدي كبلّوطة   وآخر كالقربة المدهقه
وصدر نحيف كثير العظام   تقعقع من فوقه المخنقه
وثغر إذا كشرت خلته   تخاتخ قائمة مغلقه

1a Ibn ʿAsāk. غربالا اقبلت 1b Ibid. مبصقه 2b Ibid. كالبندقة
6b Ibid. المنهفه 7a Muḥāḍarāt فسيح 7b Ibid. يسبح
8b Ibn ʿAsāk. تخاليج قامية

CLIII

Aġ., XVIII, 36 Basīṭ

غصبت عجلا على فرجين في سنة   أفسدتهم ثمّ ما أصلحت من نسبك

وَلَوْ خَطَبْتَ إِلَى طَوْقٍ وَأُسْرَتِهِ   فَزَوَّجُوكَ لَمَا زَانُوكَ فِي حَسَبِكَ

بِنْتَ مَنْ هَوَيْتَ وَبِنْتَ مَا شِئْتَ مِنْ نَسَبٍ   أَنْتَ ٱبْنُ زِرْيَابَ مَنْسُوبًا إِلَى نَسَبِكَ

إِنْ كَانَ قَوْمٌ أَرَادَ ٱللّٰهُ خِزْيَهُمُ   فَزَوَّجُوكَ ٱرْتِغَابًا مِنْكَ فِي ذَهَبِكَ

فَذَاكَ يُوجِبُ أَنَّ ٱلْفِقْهَ يَجْمَعُهُ   إِلَى خِلَافِكَ فِي ٱلْعِيدَانِ أَوْ غَرَبِكَ

وَلَوْ سَكَتَّ وَلَمْ تَخْطُبْ إِلَى عَرَبٍ   لَمَا نَشَبْتَ ٱلَّذِي تَطْوِيهِ مِنْ سَبَبِكَ

عَدَّ ٱلْبُيُوتَ ٱلَّتِي تَرْضَى بِخِطْبَتِهَا   تَجِدْ فَزَارَةَ ٱلْعُكْلِيَّ مِنْ عَرَبِكَ

CLIV

Muhādarāt, I, 260   Basīṭ

هٰذِي هَدِيَّةُ عَبْدٍ أَنْتَ مُلْبِسُهُ   ثَوْبَ ٱلْغِنَى فَاقْبَلِ ٱلْمَيْسُورَ مِنْ خَدَمِهْ

CLV

1-2, 4-7 Ibn 'Asāk, Tar, V, 229-230. 1-4, 6-7 Hizānah, II, 487; Murtaḍā, II, 92-93. 1-2, 6-7 'Iqd, III, 163 (n.e. V, 375); Aǧ, XVIII, 32; Rifā'ī, III, 259; Irshād, IV, 197. 2, 6-7 Ibn Hallikān I, 179; Nujūm, II, 323. 1-2 Hāṣṣ, p. 95. 1-2, 7 Tārīh Baghdād, VIII, 384. 2, 4 Šir, p. 540. 2, 7 Ibn al-Mu'tazz, Tab, p. 24; I'jāz, p. 56. 2 Ṣinā'atain, p. 239; Aǧ, XVIII, 45; Muhāḍarāt, II, 189; Dīwān al-Ma'ānī, II, 159; Lisān, II, 430; Ma'ālim, p. 74; Wasāṭah, pp. 44, 74; Naqd, p. 86; Qānūn, p. 436. Ḥamawī, p. 87. 4 Muhāḍarāt, II, 139. 7 Yatīmah, I, 103; Waḥidī, p. 265   Kāmil

أَيْنَ ٱلشَّبَابُ وَأَيَّةً سَلَكَا   لَا أَيْنَ يُطْلَبُ ضَلَّ بَلْ هَلَكَا

لا تَعْجَبِي يا سَلْمَ مِنْ رَجُلٍ ... ضَحِكَ ٱلْمَشِيبُ بِرَأْسِهِ فَبَكَى
يا سَلْمَ ما بِٱلشَّيْبِ مَنْقَصَةٌ ... لا سُوقَةٌ يُبْقِي وَلا مَلِكَا
قَصَرَ ٱلْغَوايَةَ عَنْ هَوَى قَمَرٍ ... وَجَدَ ٱلسَّبِيلَ إِلَيْهِ مُشْتَرِكا
وَعَدا بِأُخْرَى عَنْ مُطَلِّبِها ... صَبًّا يَطَأْ مِنْ دُونِها ٱلْحَسَكا
يا لَيْتَ شِعْرِي كَيْفَ يَوْمُكُما ... يا صاحِبَيَّ إِذا دَمِي سُفِكا
لا تَأْخُذا بِظُلامَتِي أَحَدًا ... قَلْبِي وَطَرْفِي فِي دَمِي ٱشْتَرَكا

1b ʿ__Iqd__, III, 163; V, 375 ام ابن يطلب ضل ام ; Murtaḍa حلا ; __Ḫāṣṣ__ لم يطلبن
2a __Muḥāḍarāt__, Maᶜālim هنر 3a Murtaḍā اسلم 3b __Ibid__. تبتغي
4b __Ibid__. البيداء 6a Ibn ʿAsāk; Ibn Ḫallikān; __Nujūm__; __Irshād__
نومكما ; ʿ__Iqd__, III, 163; V, 375 صبركما 7a ʿ__Iqd__, III, 163; V,
375; __Yatīmah__ تطلبا ; __Ījāz__ تأخذي 7b Ibn ʿAsāk. عيني وقلبي ; __Ījāz__;
__Tārīḫ Baghdād__ طرفي وقلبي Order in __Tārīḫ Baghdād__ is 2, 1, 7.

CLVI

__Buldān__, III, 856 Munsariḥ

أَصْبَحَ وَجْهُ ٱلزَّمانِ ضَحِكًا ... بِرَدِّ مَأْمُونِ هاشِمٍ فَدَكَا

CLVII

__Thimār__, p. 132 Sarīᶜ

مَنْ مُبْلِغٌ عَنِّي إِمامَ ٱلْهُدَى ... قافِيَةً لِلسِّتْرِ هَتّاكَهْ
هٰذا جَناحُ ٱلْمُسْلِمِينَ ٱلَّذِي ... قَدْ قَصَّهُ تَوْلِيَةُ ٱلْحاكَهْ

أَضْمَنْ بِعَازِ ٱلْبُرْدِ مَنْظُومَةً   إِلَى ٱبْنِ وَهْبٍ نَعْلُ ٱلنَّاكِهْ

CLVIII

1-4 ʿIqd, I, 102 (n.e. I, 272). 1-2, 4 Ibn ʿAsāk, Tar., V, 232
Kāmil

مَا ذَا أَقُولُ إِذَا أَتَيْتُ مَعَاشِرِى   صِفْرًا يَدَاىَ مِنَ ٱلْجَوَادِ ٱلْمُجْزِلْ

إِنْ قُلْتُ أَعْطَانِى كَذَبْتُ وَإِنْ أَقُلْ   ضَنَّ ٱلْأَمِيرُ بِمَالِهِ لَمْ يَجْمُلْ

وَلَأَنْتَ أَعْلَمُ بِٱلْمَكَارِمِ وَٱلْعُلَى   مِنْ أَنْ أَقُولَ فَعَلْتَ مَا لَمْ تَفْعَلْ

فَٱخْتَرْ لِنَفْسِكَ مَا أَقُولُ فَإِنَّنِى   لَا بُدَّ مُخْبِرُهُمْ وَإِنْ لَمْ أُسْأَلْ

1a Ibn ʿAsāk. انصرفت وقيل لي   1b Ibid. ماذا اخذت من الجواد المفضل
ʿIqd, I, 102 صفرا يدى من عند أروع مجزل   2b Ibn ʿAsāk. يجعل
4a Ibid. خير شئت   4b ʿIqd, I, 102 مخبرهم ز اسئل

CLIX

Muwāzanah, p. 52   Mutaqārib

فَبَاطِنُهَا لِلنَّدَى   وَظَاهِرُهَا لِلْقُبَلْ

CLX

Ibn ʿAsāk, Tar., V, 237; Buldān, IV, 176   Wāfir

تَلَاشَى أَهْلُ قُمَّ فَاضْمَحَلُّوا   تُحِلُّ ٱلْمُخْزِيَاتُ بِحَيْثُ حَلُّوا

وَكَانُوا شَيَّدُوا فِى ٱلْفَقْرِ مَجْدًا   فَلَمَّا جَاءَتِ ٱلْأَمْوَالُ مَلُّوا

1b <u>Buldān</u> المعزيات

CLXI

1-2 Masʿūdī, VI, 405. 2 <u>Muntaḥal</u>, p. 106 Ṭawīl

أَلَمْ تَرَ صَرْفَ ٱلدَّهْرِ فِي آلِ بَرْمَكٍ … فِي ٱبْنِ نُهَيْكٍ وَٱلْقُرُونِ ٱلَّتِي تَخْلُو

لَقَدْ غُرِسُوا غَرْسَ ٱلنَّخِيلِ تَمَكُّنًا … فَمَا حُصِدُوا إِلَّا كَمَا حُصِدَ ٱلْبَقْلُ

2a <u>Muntaḥal</u> الكريم 2b <u>Ibid</u>. وما يحصد

CLXII

<u>Dīwān al-Maʿānī</u>, I, 184 Wāfir

أَتُقْفِلُ مَطْبَخًا لَا شَيْءَ فِيهِ … مِنَ ٱلدُّنْيَا تَخَافُ عَلَيْهِ أَكْلُ

فَهٰذَا ٱلْمَطْبَخُ ٱسْتَوْثَقْتَ مِنْهُ … فَمَا بَالُ ٱلْكَنِيفِ عَلَيْهِ قُفْلُ

وَلٰكِنْ قَدْ بَخِلْتَ بِكُلِّ شَيْءٍ … فَحَتَّى ٱلسَّلْحُ مِنْكَ عَلَيْكَ بُخْلُ

CLXIII

1-14, 16 <u>Aǧ</u>, XVIII, 49. 5, 8, 12, 16 <u>Aǧ</u>, XVIII, 48. 12-13, 15-16 Ibn ʿAsāk, <u>Tar</u>, V, 238. 1-2 Azdī, p. 96; <u>Aǧ</u>, IX, 23. 1 <u>Aǧ</u>, XVIII, 59 Mutaqārib

أَمُطَّلِبُ أَنْتَ مُسْتَعْذِبٌ … حُمَيَّا ٱلْأَفَاعِي وَمُسْتَقْتِلُ

فَإِنْ أَشْفِ مِنْكَ تَكُنْ سُبَّةً … وَإِنْ أَعْفُ عَنْكَ فَمَا تَفْعَلُ

سَتَأْتِيكَ إِمَّا وَرَدْتَ ٱلْعِرَاقَ … صَحَائِفُ يَأْثُرُهَا دِعْبِلُ

صُنَيْعَةُ بَيْنَ أَثْنائِها … مَخازٍ تَحُطُّ فَلا تَرْحَلُ
وَضَعْتَ رِجالًا فَما ضَرَّهُمْ … وَشَرَّفْتَ قَوْمًا فَما يَنْبُلُوا
فَأَيُّهُمُ الزَّيْنُ وَسْطَ المَلا … عُطَيَّةُ أَمْ صالِحُ الأَحْوَلُ
أَمِ البَاذْجانِيُّ أَمْ عامِرٌ … أَمِينُ الحَمامِ الَّتِي يَزْجُلُ
تُنَوِّطُ مِصْرُ بِكَ المُخْزِياتِ … وَتَبْصُقُ فِي وَجْهِكَ المَوْصِلُ
وَيَوْمَ السَّراةِ تَحَسَّيْتَها … يَطِيبُ لَدَى مِثْلِها الحَنْظَلُ
تَوَلَّيْتَ رَكْضًا وَفِتْيانُنا … صُدُورُ القَنا فِيهِمُو تَعْسِلُ
إِذا الحَرْبُ كُنْتَ أَمِيرًا لَها … فَحَظُّهُمُ مِنْكَ أَنْ يُقْتَلُوا
فَمِنْكَ الرُّؤُوسُ غَداةَ اللِّقا … وَمِمَّنْ يُحارِبُكَ المُنْصُلُ
شِعارُكَ فِي الحَرْبِ يَوْمَ الوَغا … إِذا انْهَزَمُوا عَجِّلُوا عَجِّلُوا
هَزائِمُكَ الغُرُّ مَشْهُورَةٌ … يُقَرْطِسُ فِيهِنَّ مَنْ يَنْضُلُ
فَذَلِكَ ذاتُكُما إِذْ عَوَتْ … مِنَ القَوْمِ بَيْنَكُما الأَعْجَلُ
فَأَنْتَ إِذا ما التَقَوْا آخِرٌ … وَأَنْتَ إِذا انْهَزَمُوا أَوَّلُ

1b Aḡ, XVIII, 59 سمام ; Aḡ, IX, 23 لسم ; Azdī لسم المنايا ; Aḡ, XVIII, 49 مستقبل 2a Azdī اسف 2b Aḡ, XVIII, 49 تعقل 5a Aḡ, XVIII, 48 وعاديت قوما 8a Aḡ, XVIII, 48 تعلق 12b Ibn ʿAsāk. شعارك عند الحروب النجا وصاحبك الاخور الافشل 13 Aḡ, XVIII, 48 المفصل 13b Ibn ʿAsāk. لفرسانك الاول فالاول 16 Aḡ, XVIII, 49 فانت لاولهم آخر فانت اذا اقبلوا آخر فانت اذا دبروا اول ; Ibn ʿAsāk. وانت لآخرهم اول

Order in Ibn ʿAsāk. is 13, 16, 12, 15.

CLXIV

ʿ<u>Iqd</u>, I, 102 (n.e. I, 271)   Mutaqārib

أَيَا ذَا ٱلْيَمِينَيْنِ وَٱلدَّعْوَتَيْنِ ‏ ‏ ‏ وَمَنْ عِنْدَهُ ٱلْعُرْفُ وَٱلنَّائِلُ
أَتَرْضَى بِمِثْلِي فَتًى أَنْ يُقِيمَ ‏ ‏ ‏ بِبَابِكَ مُطَّرَحٌ خَامِلُ
رَضِيتَ مِنَ ٱلْوُدِّ وَٱلْعَائِدَاتِ ‏ ‏ ‏ وَمِنْ كُلِّ مَا أَمَلَ ٱلْآمِلُ
بِتَسْلِيمَةٍ بَيْنَ خَمْسٍ وَسِتٍّ ‏ ‏ ‏ إِذَا ضَمَّهُ ٱلْمَجْلِسُ ٱلْحَافِلُ
وَمَا كُنْتُ أَرْضَى بِذَا مِنْ سِوَاكَ ‏ ‏ ‏ أَيَرْضَى بِذَا رَجُلٌ عَاقِلُ
وَإِنْ نَابَ شُغْلٌ فَفِي دُونِ مَا ‏ ‏ ‏ تُدَبِّرُهُ شُغُلٌ شَاغِلُ
عَلَيْكَ ٱلسَّلَامُ فَإِنِّي ٱمْرُؤٌ ‏ ‏ ‏ إِذَا ضَاقَ بِي بَلَدٌ رَاحِلُ

CLXV

1-2 Ibn ʿAsāk, <u>Tar</u>, V, 232. 1 <u>Muḥāḍarāt</u>, I, 403   Wāfir

كَيْفَ ٱحْتِيَالِي لِبَسْطِ ٱلضَّيْفِ إِنْ حَصَرَ ‏ ‏ ‏ عِنْدَ ٱلطَّعَامِ فَقَدْ ضَاقَتْ بِهِ حِيَلِي
أَخَافُ يَزْدَادُ قَوْلِي كُلْ فَأَحْشِمُهُ ‏ ‏ ‏ وَٱلْكَفُّ يَحْمِلُهُ مِنِّي عَلَى ٱلْبُخْلِ

1a Ibn ʿAsāk. حصرا

CLXVI

Ibn ʿAsāk, <u>Tar</u>, V, 230   Kāmil

لَمَّا رَأَتْ شَيْبًا يَلُوحُ بِمَفْرِقِي   صَدَّتْ صُدُودَ مُفَارِقٍ مُتَجَمِّلِ

فَظَلِلْتُ أَطْلُبُ وَصْلَهَا بِتَذَلُّلٍ   وَالشَّيْبُ يَغْمِزُهَا بِأَنْ لَا تَفْعَلِي

CLXVII

Ag, XVIII, 38 Ṭawīl

نَصَحْتُ فَأَخْلَصْتُ النَّصِيحَةَ لِلْفَضْلِ   وَقُلْتُ فَسَيَّرْتُ الْمَقَالَةَ فِي الْفَضْلِ

أَلَا إِنَّ فِي الْفَضْلِ بْنِ سَهْلٍ لَعِبْرَةً   إِنِ اعْتَبَرَ الْفَضْلُ بْنُ مَرْوَانَ بِالْفَضْلِ

وَلِلْفَضْلِ فِي الْفَضْلِ بْنِ يَحْيَى مَوَاعِظٌ   إِذَا فَكَّرَ الْفَضْلُ ابْنُ مَرْوَانَ فِي الْفَضْلِ

فَأَبْقِ جَمِيلًا مِنْ حَدِيثٍ تُعَزُّ بِهِ   وَلَا تَدَعِ الْإِحْسَانَ وَالْأَخْذَ بِالْفَضْلِ

فَإِنَّكَ قَدْ أَصْبَحْتَ لِلْمُلْكِ قَيِّمًا   وَصِرْتَ مَكَانَ الْفَضْلِ وَالْفَضْلِ وَالْفَضْلِ

وَلَمْ أَرَ أَبْيَاتًا مِنَ الشِّعْرِ قَبْلَهَا   جَمِيعُ قَوَافِيهَا عَلَى الْفَضْلِ وَالْفَضْلِ

وَلَيْسَ لَهَا عَيْبٌ إِذَا هِيَ أُنْشِدَتْ   سِوَى أَنَّ نُصْحِي الْفَضْلَ كَانَ فِي الْفَضْلِ

CLXVIII

‘Iqd, I, 120 (n.e. I, 315) Kāmil

طَلَعَتْ قَنَاتُكَ بِالسَّعَادَةِ فَوْقَهَا   مَعْقُودَةً بِلِوَاءِ مُلْكٍ مُقْبِلِ

تَهْتَزُّ فَوْقَ طَرِيدَتَيْنِ كَأَنَّمَا   تَهْفُو يُقَصُّ لَهَا جَنَاحَا أَجْدَلِ

رِبْحَ الْبَخِيلِ عَلَى احْتِيَالِ عِرْضِهِ   بِنَدَى يَدَيْكَ وَوَجْهِكَ الْمُتَهَلِّلِ

لو كان يعلم أن نيلك عاجل ‏ ‏ ما فاض منه جدول في جدول

2b ʿIqd, I, 20 يفضلها

CLXIX

Muḥāḍarāt, I, 401 Kāmil

الله يعلم أنني ما سرني ‏ ‏ شيء كطارقة الضيوف النزل

ما زلت بالترحيب حتى خلتني ‏ ‏ ضيفا له والضيف رب المنزل

CLXX

1-3 Muslim, p. 242; Ṣūlī, Abū Tammām, p. 41. 2-3 Kāmil, p. 476; Muwāzanah, p. 25 Kāmil

ميّاس قل لي أين أنت من الورى ‏ ‏ لا أنت معلوم ولا مجهول

أما الهجاء فدقّ عرضك دونه ‏ ‏ والمدح فيك كما علمت جليل

فاذهب فأنت طليق عرضك إنه ‏ ‏ عرض عززت به وأنت ذليل

1a Ṣūlī, Abū Tammām أمويس 2b Ibid. عنك 3a Kāmil عتيق

CLXXI

Tashbīhāt, p. 136; Muḥāḍarāt, II, 186 Basīṭ

قوهاء شوهاء يبدي الكبد مضحكها ‏ ‏ قنواء بالعرض والعيناء بالطول

لها فم ملتقى شدقيه نقرتها ‏ ‏ كأن مشفرها قد طرّ من فيل

1a Muḥāḍarāt رقطاء كبداء الكبد 1b Ibid. تنوء العينان

CLXXII

Muwāzanah, p. 39   Sarī'

1 إنْ جاءه مُرتغِبًا سائلٌ   2 آلت عليه رغبةُ السائلِ

2 Text has جاره

CLXXIII

Ag, XVIII, 40   Basīṭ

حَواجبٌ كالجبالِ سُودٌ   إلى عَثانينَ كالمَخالي
وأوجهٌ جَهمةٌ غِلاظٌ   عُطلٌ منَ الحُسنِ والجمالِ

CLXXIV

Muḥāḍarāt, I, 212   Mujtathth

سألتُه عن أبيهِ   فقالَ دينارُ خالي
فقلتُ دينارُ مَن هو   فقالَ والي الجبالِ

CLXXV

Muslim, p. 242; Nihāyah, III, 276   Kāmil

لا تَعجبَنْ بابنِ الوليدِ فإنّهُ   يَرميكَ بعدَ ثلاثةٍ بِملالِ
إنّ الملولَ وإنْ تقادمَ عهدُهُ   كانتْ مودّتُهُ كفيءِ ظِلالِ

CLXXVI

'Iqd, I, 238   Munsariḥ

أسقِهِمُ السمَّ إنْ ظفرتَ بهم   وامزجْ لهم من لسانكَ العسلا

CLXXVII

ʿUyūn, III, 43   Mutaqārib

بَعَثْتَ إِلَيَّ بِأُضْحِيَّةٍ   وَكُنْتَ حَرِيًّا بِأَنْ تَفْعَلَا

وَلَكِنَّهَا خَرَجَتْ غَثَّةً   كَأَنَّكَ أَرْعَيْتَهَا حَرْمَلَا

فَإِنْ قَبِلَ ٱللَّهُ قُرْبَانَهَا   فَسُبْحَانَ رَبِّكَ مَا أَعْدَلَا

CLXXVIII

Ibn ʿAsāk., Tar., V, 232   Wāfir

هَدَايَا ٱلنَّاسِ بَعْضُهُمْ لِبَعْضٍ   تُوَلِّدُ فِي قُلُوبِهِمُ ٱلْوِصَالَا

وَتَزْرَعُ فِي ٱلضَّمِيرِ هَوًى وَوُدًّا   وَتَكْسُوهُمْ إِذَا حَضَرُوا جَمَالَا

CLXXIX

1-4 Kāmil, p. 229; Murtaḍā, IV, 181; Amālī, III, 112 (n.e. III, 111). 2-4 Muwaššaḥ, p. 381. 3-4 Tashbīhāt, p. 229; Dīwān al-Maʿānī, II, 238; Ḫāṣṣ, p. 60; 95; Ījāz, p. 57; ʿUmdah, I, 73 (n.e. I, 95). 4 ʿIqd, III, 139; Šiʿr, p. 541   Ṭawīl

نَعَوْنِي وَلَمَّا يَنْعَنِي غَيْرُ شَامِتٍ   وَغَيْرُ عَدُوٍّ قَدْ أُصِيبَتْ مَقَاتِلُهْ

يَقُولُونَ إِنْ ذَاقَ ٱلرَّدَى مَاتَ شِعْرُهُ   وَهَيْهَاتَ عُمْرُ ٱلشِّعْرِ طَالَتْ طَوَائِلُهْ

سَأَقْضِي بِبَيْتٍ يَحْمَدُ ٱلنَّاسُ أَمْرَهُ   وَيَكْثُرُ مِنْ أَهْلِ ٱلرِّوَايَةِ حَامِلُهْ

يَمُوتُ رَدِيُّ ٱلشِّعْرِ مِنْ قَبْلِ أَهْلِهِ   وَجَيِّدُهُ يَبْقَى وَإِنْ مَاتَ قَائِلُهْ

2a Kāmil; Murtaḍā الرَّدَى 3a Tashbīhāt يعلم الناس فضله

4a Dīwān al-Maʿānī; Murtaḍā ربه ; ʿIqd غير اهله ; Ījāz; Dīwān al-

Maʿānī; Muwaššaḥ; ʿIqd; Amālī ردى 4b Šiʿr يحيا

CLXXX

1-3 K. Baghdād, p. 226. 1-2 Suyūṭī, p. 129 Mutaqārib

شَكَرْنَا ٱلْخَلِيفَةَ إِجْرَاءَهُ ... عَلَى ٱبْنِ أَبِي خَالِدٍ نُزْلَهُ
وَكَفَّ أَذَاهُ عَنِ ٱلْمُسْلِمِينَ ... وَصَيَّرَ فِي بَيْتِهِ أَكْلَهُ
وَقَدْ كَانَ يَقْسِمُ أَشْغَالَهُ ... فَصَيَّرَ فِي نَفْسِهِ شُغْلَهُ

CLXXXI

Bard al-Akbād, p. 134 Ṭawīl

بَدَأْتَ بِإِحْسَانٍ وَثَنَّيْتَ بِٱلْعُلَى ... وَثَلَّثْتَ بِٱلْحُسْنَى وَرَبَّعْتَ بِٱلْكَرَمْ
وَيَسَّرْتَ أَمْرِي وَٱعْتَنَيْتَ بِحَاجَتِي ... وَأَخَّرْتَ لَا عَنِّي وَقَدَّمْتَ لِي نَعَمْ
فَإِنْ نَحْنُ كَافَأْنَا فَأَهْلٌ لِوُدِّنَا ... وَإِنْ نَحْنُ قَصَّرْنَا فَمَا ٱلْوُدُّ مُتَّهَمْ

CLXXXII

Ibn ʿAsāk, Tar., V, 230 Mutaqārib

وَدَاعُكَ مِثْلُ وَدَاعِ ٱلْحَيَاةِ ... وَفَقْدُكَ مِثْلُ ٱفْتِقَادِ ٱلدِّيَمْ
عَلَيْكَ ٱلسَّلَامُ فَكَمْ مِنْ وَفَا ... أُفَارِقُ مِنْكَ وَكَمْ مِنْ كَرَمْ

CLXXXIII

1-6 Ibn ʿAsāk, Tar., V, 235. 1-2, 4-6 Aġ., XVIII, 46 Wāfir

وَأَبقى طاهِرٌ فينا ثَلاثًا   عَجائِبَ تَستَخِفُّ لَها الحُلومُ

ثَلاثَةُ إِخوَةٍ لِأَبٍ وَأُمٍّ   تَمايَزَ عَن ثَلاثَتِهِم أُرومُ

فَبَعضُهُمُ يَقولُ قُرَيشُ قَومي   وَيَدفَعُهُ المَوالي وَالصَميمُ

وَبَعضٌ في خُزاعَةَ مُنتَماهُ   وِلادُ غَيرُ مَجهولٍ قَديمُ

وَبَعضُهُمُ يَهِشُّ لِآلِ كِسرى   وَيَزعَمُ أَنَّهُ عِلجٌ لَئيمُ

فَقَد كَثُرَت مَناسِبُهُم عَلَينا   فَكُلُّهُمُ عَلى حالٍ زَنيمُ

1a Ibn ʿAsāk. خلالا 1b <u>Ibid</u>. تسحق 2a <u>Aǧ</u>. اعبد

2b <u>Ibid</u>. تمير 4a <u>Ibid</u>. قريش 4b <u>Ibid</u>. ولا غيرو 6a <u>Ibid</u>. كسرت

CLXXXIV

<u>Aǧ</u>, XVIII, 34; Ibn ʿAsāk, <u>Tar</u>, V, 240; Ṣūlī, <u>Abū Tammām</u>, p. 268

Sarīʿ

يا عَجَبًا مِن شاعِرٍ مُفلِقٍ   آباؤُهُ في طَيِّئٍ تَنتَمي

أَتَيتُهُ يَشتِمُ مِن جَهلِهِ   أُمّي وَما أُصبِحُ مِن هَمّي

فَقُلتُ لَكِن حَبَّذا أُمُّهُ   طاهِرَةٌ زاكِيَةٌ عِلمي

كَذَبتَ وَاللَهِ عَلى أُمِّهِ   كَكِذبِهِ أَيضًا عَلى أُمّي

1 <u>Aǧ</u>. وشاعر عرض لي نفسه   لحارك آباؤه تنمى

2 <u>Aǧ</u>. يشتم عرضي عند ذكري وما   امسي ولا اصبح من همي

1b Ṣūlī, <u>Abū Tammām</u> تنمى 2a <u>Ibid</u>. انبئته 3a Ibn ʿAsāk. جيرا

<u>Aǧ</u>. لا بل 3b Ag. خيرة طاهرة 4a Ṣūlī; <u>Aǧ</u>. الكذب

CLXXXV

<u>Aǧ</u>, XVIII, 46; Ibn ʿAsāk, <u>Tar</u>, V, 238; <u>Buldān</u>, IV, 442; II, 519   I

ألا فاشتروا منّي ملوك المخرّم   أبع حسنا وابني رجاء بدرهم

وأعط رجاء فوق ذاك زيادة   وأسمح بدينار بغير تندّم

فإن ردّ من عيب عليّ جميعهم   فليس يردّ العيب يحيى بن أكثم

1a Ag. المحزم ; Ibn ʿAsāk. المحرم ; Buldān, IV, 442 دروب 1b Ibn ʿAsāk.; Buldān, IV, 442 ابى هشام 2a Buldān, IV, 442 راعطى ; Ibn ʿAsāk. بعد. 2b Ibn ʿAsāk. واعط ; Buldān, IV, 442 وادفع; دينارا 3a Buldān text has رُدَّ

CLXXXVI

Tashbīhāt, p. 135; Ibn Šaj, Ḥamāsah, p. 272; Muḥāḍarāt, II, 181

Munsariḥ

كأنّها كفّها إذا اختضبت   مخالب البازِ ضُرّجت بدمِ

CLXXXVII

1-3 ʿUyūn, II, 197; Dīwān al-Maʿānī, I, 181; Muntaḥab, p. 16; Ḥarīrī, p. 110   Basīṭ

الناس كلّهم يسعى لحاجته   ما بين ذي فرح منهم ومهموم

ومالك ظلّ مشغولا بنسبته   يرمّ منها خرابا غير مرموم

يبني بيوتا خرابا لا أنيس بها   ما بين طوق إلى عمرو بن كلثوم

1a Ḥarīrī يغدوا 1b Dīwān al-Maʿānī منها 2b Ḥarīrī يروم; بناء مهدوم.

3a Muntaḥab تبنى

CLXXXVIII

Ag, XVIII, 46; Rifa'i, III, 262 Kamil

قل للإمام إمام آل محمد   قول امرئ حدب عليك محام

أنكرت أن تفتر عندك صنيعة   في صالح بن عطية الحجام

ليس الصنائع عنده بصنائع   لكنهن طوائل الإسلام

اضرب به جيش العدو فوجهه   جيش من الطاعون والبرسام

4a Rifa'i فانه

CLXXXIX

Ibn al-Wardi, I, 228 Basit

لكنها خطرات من وساوسه   يعطي ويمنع لا بخلا ولا كرما

CXC

'Iqd, III, 268 Ramal

ومغن إن تغنى   أورث الندمان هما

أحسن الأقوام حالا   فيه من كان أصما

CXCI

Muhadarat, I, 364 Sari'

يعدها أنفق من ماله   غنما وما وفره غرما

CXCII

Ag, XVIII, 44, 48; Rifa'i, III, 259; Ibn 'Asak, Tar, V, 241 Basit

اِضْرِبْ نَدَى طَلْحَةِ الطَّلَحَاتِ مُتَّئِدًا ... بِلُؤْمِ مُطَّلِبٍ فِينَا وَكُنْ حَكَمَا

تَخْرُجْ خُزَاعَةُ مِنْ لُؤْمٍ وَمِنْ كَرَمٍ ... فَلَا تُحِسُّ لَهَا لُؤْمًا وَلَا كَرَمَا

1a Ibn ʿAsāk. بذى زمبتدأ 1b *Ibid.* ببخل مطلبها 2b *Ibid*; *Aǧ*. تعد
Ibn ʿAsākir states that there is also the variant تسلم

CXCIII

1-2 *Ṣināʿatain*, p.41; 129; Ibn Ḫallikān, II, 34. 2 *Aǧ*, XVIII, 36; Rifāʿī, III, 260 Ṭawīl

وَإِنَّ امْرَأً أَمْسَتْ مَسَاقِطُ رَحْلِهِ ... بِأَسْوَانَ لَمْ يَتْرُكْ لَهُ الْحَزْمُ مُعْلَمَا

حَلَلْتُ مَحَلًّا يَقْصُرُ الطَّرْفُ دُونَهُ ... وَيَعْجِزُ عَنْهُ الطَّيْفُ أَنْ يَتَجَشَّمَا

1a Ibn Ḫallikān اضحت مطارح سهمه 1b *Ṣināʿatain*, p. 129 الحرص
2a *Aǧ*; *Ṣināʿatain*, p. 129 البرق

CXCIV

ʿUyūn, II, 36 Basīṭ

صَدَقَ أَلِيَّتَهُ إِذْ قَالَ مُجْتَهِدًا ... لَا وَالرَّغِيفِ فَذَاكَ الْبِرُّ مِنْ قَسَمِهْ

قَدْ كَانَ يُعْجِبُنِي لَوْ أَنَّ غَيْرَتَهُ ... عَلَى جَرَادِقِهِ كَانَتْ عَلَى حُرَمِهْ

فَإِنْ هَمَمْتَ بِهِ فَافْتِكْ بِخُبْزَتِهِ ... فَإِنَّ مَوْقِعَهَا مِنْ لَحْمِهِ وَدَمِهْ

CXCV

1-4 *ʿUyūn*, III, 246. 1-3 *Nihāyah*, III, 309 Kāmil

اِسْتَبِقْ وُدَّ أَبِي ٱلْمُقَا   تِلِ حِينَ تَأْكُلُ مِنْ طَعَامِهْ
بِسِيَّانِ كَسْرُ رَغِيفِهِ   أَوْ كَسْرُ عَظْمٍ مِنْ عِظَامِهْ
فَتَرَاهُ مِنْ خَوْفِ ٱلنَّزِيـ   لِ بِهِ يُرَوَّعُ فِي مَنَامِهْ
فَإِذَا مَرَرْتَ بِبَابِهِ   فَٱحْفَظْ رَغِيفَكَ مِنْ غُلَامِهْ

CXCVI

Muhāḍarāt, II, 142   Munsariḥ

إِنَّ الرَّقَاشِيَّ مِنْ تَكَرُّمِهِ   يَكُدُّهُ مِنْهُ مُنْتَهَى هِمَمِهْ
يَبْلُغُ مِنْ بِرِّهِ وَرَأْفَتِهِ   خِلَّانَ إِخْوَانِهِ عَلَى حُرَمِهْ

CXCVII

Muwāzanah, p. 44   Sarīʿ

تَخَالُ أَحْيَانًا بِهِ غَفْلَةً   مِنْ كَرَمِ ٱلنَّفْسِ وَمَا أَغْفَلَهْ

CXCVIII

1-5 Ṣināʿatain, p. 365. 2 Muhāḍarāt, II, 335. 5 Muhāḍarāt, I, 364   Mutaqārib

وَمَيْشَاءَ خَضْرَاءَ مَوْشِيَّةٍ   بِهَا ٱلنَّوْرُ يَزْهَرُ مِنْ كُلِّ فَنْ
ضَحُوكٍ إِذَا لَاعَبَتْهُ ٱلرِّيَاحُ   تَأَوَّدَ كَٱلشَّارِبِ ٱلْمُرْجَحِنْ
فَشَبَّهَ صَحْبِي نُوَّارَهُ   بِدِيبَاجِ كِسْرَى وَعَصْبِ ٱلْيَمَنْ
فَقُلْتُ بَعُدْتُمْ وَلَكِنَّنِي   أُشَبِّهُهُ بِجَنَابِ ٱلْحَسَنْ
مَتَى لَا يَرَى ٱلْمَالَ إِلَّا ٱلْعَطَاءَ   وَلَا ٱلْكَنْزَ إِلَّا ٱعْتِقَادَ ٱلْمِنَنْ

5a Ṣināʿatain, p. 365   الصنا

CXCIX

Ag., XVIII, 41; Rifāʿī, III, 261   Munsariḥ

قَد قُلتُ إِذ غَيَّبوهُ وَاِنصَرَفوا   في شَرِّ قَبرٍ لِشَرِّ مَدفونِ

اِذهَب إِلى النارِ وَالعَذابِ فَما   خُلِقتَ إِلّا مِنَ الشَياطينِ

ما زِلتَ حَتّى عَقَدتَ بَيعَةَ مَن   أَضَرَّ بِالمُسلِمينَ وَالدينِ

CC

ʿUmdah, II, 32 (n.e. II, 38)   Ṭawīl

خَليلَيَّ مِن كَعبٍ أَعينا أَخاكُما   عَلى دَهرِهِ إِنَّ الكَريمَ مُعينُ

وَلا تَبخَلا بُخلَ اِبنِ قَزعَةَ إِنَّهُ   مَخافَةَ أَن يُرجى نَداهُ حَزينُ

إِذا جِئتَهُ في الفَقطِ أَغلَقَ بابَهُ   فَلَم تَلقَهُ إِلّا وَأَنتَ كَمينُ

CCI

Maqātil, pp. 570-71   Ṭawīl

عَلى الكَرهِ ما فارَقتُ أَحمَدَ وَاِنطَوى   عَلَيهِ بِناءُ جَندَلٍ وَرَزينُ

وَأَسكَنتُهُ بَيتًا حَسيسًا مَتاعُهُ   وَإِنّي عَلى رَغمي بِهِ لَضَنينُ

وَلَولا التَأَسّي بِالنَبِيِّ وَأَهلِهِ   لَأَسبَلَ مِن عَيني عَلَيهِ شُؤونُ

فَوَالنَفسِ إِلّا أَنَّ آلَ مُحَمَّدٍ   لَهُم دونَ نَفسي في الفُؤادِ كَمينُ

أضرّ بهم إرث النبيّ فأصبحوا … يساهم فيه ميتة ومنون
دعتهم ذئاب من أميّة وانتحت … عليهم دراكا أزمة وسنون
وعاثت بنو العبّاس في الدين عيثة … تحكّم فيه ظالم وظنين
وسمّوا رشيدا ليس فيهم لرشده … وها ذاك مأمون وذاك أمين
فما قبلت بالرشد منهم رعاية … ولا لوليّ بالأمانة دين
رشيدهم غاو وطفلاه بعده … لهذا رزايا دون ذاك مجون
ألا أيّها القبر الغريب محلّه … بطوس عليك الساريات هتون
شككت فما أدري أمسقى بشربة … فأبكيك أم ريب الردى فيهون
وأيّهما ما قلت إن قلت شربة … وإن قلت موت إنّه لقمين
أيا عجبا منهم يسمّونك الرضا … ويلقاك منهم كلحة وغضون
أتعجب للأجلاف أن يتخيّفوا … معالم دين الله وهو مبين
لقد سبقت فيهم بفضلك آية … لديّ ولكن ما هناك يقين

CCII

Majmūʿat, p. 61; Aǧ, XVIII, 30 Tawīl

خليليّ ماذا أرتجي من غد امرئ … طوى الكشح عنّي اليوم وهو مكين
وإنّ امرأ قد ضنّ عنّي بمنطق … يسدّ به من خلّتي لضنين

2a Aǧ. منه بمنطق 2b Ibid. مفقر امرئ

CCIII

Aǧ, XVIII, 37 Sarīʿ

لولا حوى لبيت لهياني ما قام أير الغزبه الفاني

له دواة في سراويله يليقها النازح والداني

CCIV

1-3 Dīwān al-Maʿānī, II, 252. 1-2 Tārīḫ Baghdād, VIII, 385; Aǧ, XVIII, 35 Mutaqārib

وأهديته زمنا فانيا فلا للركوب ولا للثمن

حملت على زمن شاعرا فسوف يكافى بشعر زمن

أبا الفضل ذما وغرما معا فما كنت ترجو بهذا الغبن

1a Aǧ. حملت على قارح غامر 2b Ibid.; Tārīḫ Baghdād تكافا ; Aǧ بشكر

CCV

ʿUyūn, III, 20; Šiʿr, p. 541 Basīṭ

وإن أولى البرايا أن تواسيه عند السرور لمن واساك في الحزن

إن الكرام إذا ما أسهلوا ذكروا من كان يألفهم في المنزل الخشن

1a Šiʿr الموالي 1b ʿUyūn آساك

CCVI

Tashbīhāt, p. 353 Basīṭ

سَمْتَ ٱلْمَدِيحِ رِجَالًا دُونَ مَالِهِمِ　　ضِدٌّ قَبِيحٌ وَلَفْظٌ لَيْسَ بِٱلْحَسَنِ
فَلَمْ أَمُرَّ مِنْهُمْ إِلَّا كَمَا حَمَلَتْ　　رِجْلُ ٱلْبَعُوضَةِ مِنْ فَخَّارَةِ ٱللَّبَنِ

CCVII

<u>Aǧ</u>, XVIII, 50; Azdī, p. 48 Basīṭ

عِصَابَةٌ مِنْ بَنِي مَخْزُومَ بِتُّ بِهِمْ　　بِحَيْثُ لَا يَطْمَعُ ٱلْمِسْحَاةُ فِي ٱلطِّينِ

CCVIII

Ibn ʿAsāk, <u>Tar</u>, V, 236-37 Wāfir

أَيَا لِلنَّاسِ مِنْ خَبَرٍ طَرِيفٍ　　يُغَرِّدُ ذِكْرُهُ فِي ٱلْخَافِقَيْنِ
أَعِجْلٌ تَلْحَقُ ٱبْنَ أَبِي دُؤَادٍ　　وَلَمْ يَتَأَمَّلُوا فِيهِ ٱثْنَتَيْنِ
أَرَادُوا بَعْدَ عَاجِلَةٍ فَبَاعُوا　　رَخِيصًا عَاجِلًا نَقْدًا بِدَيْنِ
بِضَاعَةَ خَاسِرٍ بَارَتْ عَلَيْهِ　　فَبَاعَكَ بِٱلنَّوَاةِ ٱلتَّمْرَتَيْنِ
وَلَوْ غَلَطُوا بِوَاحِدَةٍ لَقُلْنَا　　يَكُونُ ٱلْوَهْمُ بَيْنَ ٱلْغَافِلَيْنِ
وَلٰكِنْ تَشْفَعُ وَاحِدَةٌ بِأُخْرَى　　تَدُلُّ عَلَى فَسَادِ ٱلْمَنْصِبَيْنِ
لَحَى ٱللّٰهُ ٱلْمَحَاشَ بِفَرْجِ أُنْثَى　　وَلَوْ زَوَّجْتَهَا مِنْ ذِي رُعَيْنِ
وَلَمَّا إِنْ أَفَادَ طَرِيقَ مَالٍ　　وَأَصْبَحَ رَافِلًا فِي ٱلْحُلَّتَيْنِ
تَكَنَّى وَٱنْتَمَى لِأَبِي دُؤَادٍ　　وَقَدْ كَانَ ٱسْمُهُ ٱبْنَ ٱلْفَاعِلَيْنِ
فَرُدُّوهُ إِلَى فَرَجٍ أَبِيهِ　　وَزِرْيَابٍ فَأَلَامَ وَٱلدَّيْنِ

5b Text has العافلين   10b Text has وذرباب فاكم

CCIX

1-5 Bidāyah, X, 300. 1-4 Tashbīhāt, p. 283   Wāfir

رَأَيْتُ مِنَ ٱلْكَبَائِرِ قَاضِيَيْنِ   هُمَا أُحْدُوثَةٌ فِي ٱلْخَافِقَيْنِ
هُمَا ٱقْتَسَمَا ٱلْعَمَى نِصْفَيْنِ قَدْرًا   كَمَا ٱقْتَسَمَا قَضَاءَ ٱلْجَانِبَيْنِ
وَتَحْسِبُ مِنْهُمَا مَنْ هَزَّ رَأْسًا   لِيَنْظُرَ فِي مَوَارِيثٍ وَدَيْنِ
كَأَنَّكَ قَدْ جَعَلْتَ عَلَيْهِ دَنًّا   فَتَحْتَ بِزَالَهُ مِنْ فَرْدِ عَيْنِ
هُمَا فَأْلُ ٱلزَّمَانِ بِهُلْكِ يَحْيَى   إِذِ ٱفْتَتَحَ ٱلْقَضَاءَ بِأَعْوَرَيْنِ

2a Bidāyah قدرا   4a Ibid. وضعت

CCX

'Iqd, I, 93 (n.e. I, 250-51)   Ḫafīf

يَا جَوَادَ ٱللِّسَانِ مِنْ غَيْرِ فِعْلٍ   لَيْتَ فِي رَاحَتَيْكَ جُودَ ٱللِّسَانِ
عَيْنَ مِهْرَانَ قَدْ لَطَمْتَ مِرَارًا   فَٱتَّقِي ذَا ٱلْجَلَالِ فِي مِهْرَانِ
عَوَرَتْ عَيْنَنَا فَدَعْ لِمِهْرَانَ عَيْنًا   لَا تَدَعْهُ يَطُوفُ فِي ٱلْعُمْيَانِ

CCXI

Kāmil, p. 476   Wāfir

فَلَوْ أَنِّي بُلِيتُ بِهَاشِمِيٍّ   خُؤُولَتُهُ بَنُو عَبْدِ ٱلْمَدَانِ

صَبَرْتُ عَلَى عَدَاوَتِهِ وَلٰكِنْ ... تَعَالَيْ فَانْظُرِي بِمَنِ ٱبْتَلَانِ .

CCXII

Kāmil, p. 525 Ḫafīf

لَمْ يُطِيقُوا أَنْ يَسْمَعُوا وَسَمِعْنَا ... وَصَبَرْنَا عَلَى رَحَى ٱلْأَسْنَانِ

صَوْتُ مَضْغِ ٱلضُّيُوفِ أَحْسَنُ عِنْدِي ... مِنْ غِنَاءِ ٱلْقِيَانِ بِٱلْعِيدَانِ

CCXIII

1-8 Masʿūdī, VI, 44-45. 1 Aǧ, XVIII, 51; Ibn ʿAsāk, Tar, V, 240; Ṣūlī, Abū Tammām, p. 267; Nišwār, p. 177. Iršād, V, 336. 9, 10 Ibn Badrūn, p. 80; Masʿūdī, I, 352; Buldān, I, 818; III, 134. 9, 11 Iklīl, p. 209 Wāfir

أَفِيقِي مِنْ مَلَامِكِ يَا ظَعِينَا ... كَفَاكِ ٱللَّوْمَ مَرُّ ٱلْأَرْبَعِينَا

أَلَمْ تُحْزِنْكِ أَحْدَاثُ ٱللَّيَالِي ... يُشَيِّبْنَ ٱلذَّوَائِبَ وَٱلْقُرُونَا

أُحَيِّي ٱلْغُرَّ مِنْ سَرَوَاتِ قَوْمِي ... لَقَدْ حُيِّيتِ عَنَّا يَا مَدِينَا

فَإِنْ يَكُ آلُ إِسْرَائِيلَ مِنْكُمْ ... وَكُنْتُمْ بِٱلْأَعَاجِمِ فَاخِرِينَا

فَلَا تَنْسَ ٱلْخَنَازِيرَ ٱللَّوَاتِي ... مُسِخْنَ مَعَ ٱلْقُرُودِ ٱلْخَاسِئِينَا

بِأَيْلَةَ وَٱلْخَلِيجِ لَهُمْ رُسُومٌ ... وَآثَارٌ قَدِمْنَ وَمَا مُحِينَا

وَمَا طَلَبَ ٱلْكُمَيْتُ طِلَابَ وِتْرٍ ... وَلٰكِنَّا لِنُصْرَتِنَا هُجِينَا

لَقَدْ عَلِمَتْ نِزَارُ أَنَّ قَوْمِي ... إِلَى نَصْرِ ٱلنُّبُوَّةِ فَاخِرِينَا

ثم كتبوا الكتاب بباب مرو وباب الصين كانوا الكاتبينا

1 وهم سمّوا بشمر سمرقندا وهم غرسوا هناك التبتينا

وفي صنم المغارب فوق رمل يشير بلونه سيل السفينا

1b Sūlī, Abū Tammām كفانى ; Ibn ʿAsāk. شيب 9b Ibn Badrūn الشاش
10a Buldān, I, 818 فديما سمرقندا ; Buldān, III, 134 وهم خربوا سمرقندا ;
Masʿūdī سمرقندا بشمر 10b Ibn Badrūn الثابتينا In Iklīl have
the following arrangement هم كتبوا الكتاب بباب مرو وهم غرسوا هناك التبتينا

CCXIV

Ibn al-Muʿtazz, Ṭab, p. 94 Wāfir

ويخزهم وينصركم عليهم ويشف صدور قوم مؤمنينا

CCXV

Muwaššā, p. 104 Wāfir

أحبّ ذخيرة وأحبّ علق إلى الغانيات وإن غنينا

وكلّ بكاء ربع أو مشيب نبكّيه فهنّ به عنينا

CCXVI

Kāmil, p. 736 Wāfir

قتلنا بالفتى القسري منهم وليدهم أمير المؤمنينا

وَمَرْوانًا قَتَلْنا عَنْ يَزِيدٍ   كَذاكَ قَضاؤُنا فِي ٱلْمُعْتَدِينا
وَبِٱبْنِ ٱلسِّبْطِ مِنّا قَدْ قَتَلْنا   مُحَمَّدًا ٱبْنَ هارُونَ ٱلْأَمِينا
فَمَنْ يَكُ قَتْلُهُ سَرَفًا فَإِنّا   جَعَلْنا قَتْلَ ٱلْخُلَفاءِ دِينا

CCXVII

Laṭā'if, p. 100; Ḥarīrī, p. 285   Wāfir

أُحِبُّ ٱلشَّيْبَ لَمّا قِيلَ ضَيْفٌ   كَحُبِّي لِلضُّيُوفِ ٱلنّازِلِينا

1b Ḥarīrī لحبى

CCXVIII

1-3 Aǧ., XVIII, 49-50; Ibn Ḫallikān, I, 179; Aḫbār, p. 59; Yāfiʿī, II, 146. 2-3 Lisān, II, 431   Kāmil

زَمَنِي بِمُطَّلِبٍ سُقِيتَ زَمانا   ما كُنْتَ إِلّا رَوْضَةً وَجِنانا
كُلُّ ٱلنَّدَى إِلّا نَداكَ تَكَلُّفٌ   لَمْ أَرْضَ غَيْرَكَ كائِنًا مَنْ كانا
أَصْلَحْتَنِي بِٱلْبِرِّ بَلْ أَفْسَدْتَنِي   وَتَرَكْتَنِي أَتَسَخَّطُ ٱلْإِحْسانا

1a Aḫbār بماطاب   1b Yāfʿī صرت   2a Lisān مكلف
2b Aǧ. بعدك   3a Yāfʿī يد   3b Aǧ. فتركتنى
2 Aḫbār من جاد قبلك كان جودك فوقه   لم ارض قبلك كائنا من كانا
In Aḫbār have verses 2 and 3 in reverse order.

CCXIX

Ibn al-Muʿtazz, Ṭab., p. 126   Rajaz

1 إنّ أبا سعدٍ على مجونهِ — 2 ورقّةٍ في عقلهِ ودينهِ

3 يبترك الدهرُ على جبينهِ — 4 لحيةٍ تنسابُ في تشعّبنهِ

5 يزرعُ قتًّا جارهُ في تينهِ

CCXX

1-3 Ibn ʿAsāk, Tar., V, 237. 1, 3 Waraqah, pp. 31-32 Kāmil

أخزاعَ إنْ ذُكِرَ الفخارُ فأمسكوا — وضعوا أكفّكمُ على الأفواهِ

الرّاتقين ولاتَ حينَ مراتقٍ — والفاتقين شرائعَ الأستاهِ

لا تفخروا بسوى اللواطِ فإنّما — عند المفاخرِ فخرُكم بستاهِ

1 Ibn ʿAsāk. اخزاعة غير الكرام فاقصروا — وصنعوا القلم على الافواه

3 Ibid. فدعوا الفخار فلستم من اهله — يوم الفخار فخركم بستاه

CCXXI

1-4 Ibn ʿAsāk, Tar., V, 235. 1, 3 Durrah, p. 180 Munsariḥ

بغدادُ دارُ الملوكِ كانت — حتّى دهاها الذي دهاها

ما غابَ عنها سرورُ ملكٍ — أعادهُ إلى بلدةٍ سواها

ما سُرَّ من را بسُرَّ من را — بل هي بؤسى لمن رآها

عجّلَ ربّي لها خزايا — برغمِ أنفِ الذي ابتناها

1a Durrah بغداذ 3 Ibn ʿAsāk. ليس سامرا تسر من راى — بل هي بوس لمن يراها

CCXXII

<u>Aġ</u>, XVIII, 34; <u>Lubāb</u>, p. 409 Basīṭ

كَانَتْ خُزَاعَةُ مِلْءَ ٱلْأَرْضِ مَا ٱتَّسَعَتْ   فَقَصَّ مَرُّ ٱللَّيَالِي مِنْ حَوَاشِيهَا
هٰذَا أَبُو ٱلْقَاسِمِ ٱلثَّاوِي بِبَلْقَعَةٍ   تَسْفِي ٱلرِّيَاحُ عَلَيْهِ مِنْ سَوَافِيهَا
هَبَّتْ وَقَدْ عَلِمَتْ أَنْ لَا هُبُوبَ بِهِ   وَقَدْ تَكُونُ حَسِيرًا إِذْ يُبَارِيهَا
أَضْحَى قِرًى لِلْمَنَايَا إِذْ نَزَلْنَ بِهِ   وَكَانَ فِي سَالِفِ ٱلْأَيَّامِ يَقْرِيهَا

CCXXIII

1-3 <u>Baṣāʾir</u>, p. 126. 1 <u>Muḥāḍarāt</u>, II, 92 Ṭawīl

فَأَصْبَحَتْ تَشْتَهِي ٱلْقَنَا أَنْ تَوَدَّهَا   وَقَدْ وَرَدَتْ حَوْضَ ٱلْمَنَايَا صَوَادِيَا
إِذَا ٱلنَّاسُ حَلُّوا بِٱللُّجَيْنِ سُيُوفَهُمْ   رَدَدْتَ ٱلسُّيُوفَ بِٱلْقُلُوبِ حَوَالِيَا
مَسَاعِيَ لَا يَفْنَى ٱلْمَقَالُ بِذِكْرِهَا   وَيَنْفَدُ ذِكْرُ ٱلنَّاسِ وَهِيَ كَمَا هِيَا

CCXXIV

ʿ<u>Iqd</u>, III, 32; Ibn Ḫallikān, I, 110 Ṭawīl

وَلَمَّا رَأَيْتُ ٱلسَّيْفَ جَلَّلَ جَعْفَرًا   وَنَادَى مُنَادٍ لِلْخَلِيفَةِ فِي يَحْيَى
بَكَيْتُ عَلَى ٱلدُّنْيَا وَأَيْقَنْتُ أَنَّمَا   قُصَارَى ٱلْفَتَى يَوْمًا مُفَارَقَةُ ٱلدُّنْيَا

1a Ibn Ḫallikān صبح

CCXXV

<u>Aġ</u>, XVIII, 53 Ramal

غيرَ أنَّ الصَّيدَ منهم … مَنفورٌ بخزايهْ
كتبوا الصكَّ عليهِ … فهو بينَ النّاسِ آيهْ
فإذا أقبلَ يوماً … قيلَ قد جاءَ النُّفايهْ

CCXXVI

Aḡ, XVIII, 60 Kāmil

لا حدَّ أخشاهُ على … مَنْ قالَ أمُّكَ زانيهْ
يا زانيَ ابنَ الزاني ابـ … ـنِ الزاني ابنِ الزانيهْ
أنتَ المردَّدُ في الزنا … ءِ على السنينِ الخاليهْ
ومردَّدٌ فيهِ على … كرِّ السنينِ الباقيهْ

CCXXVII

Aḡ, XVIII, 60 Sarī'

سألتُ عنكم يا بني مالكٍ … في منازحِ الأرضينَ والدانيهْ
طرّاً فلم تُعرَفْ لكم نسبةٌ … حتّى إذا قلتُ بني الزانيهْ
قالوا فدعْ داراً على يمينهِ … وتلكَ ها دارُهُمُ ثانيهْ

CCXXVIII

Tauḥīdī, p. 98 Ramal

فَإِذَا جَانَبْتَهُ صَدَّرْتَهُ   وَتَنَحَّيْتَ لَهُ فِى ٱلْجَانِبَهْ

وَإِذَا سَايَرْتَهُ قَدَّمْتَهُ   وَتَأَخَّرْتَ مَعَ ٱلْمُسْتَأْنِيَهْ

وَإِذَا بَاسَرْتَهُ صَادَفْتَهُ   سَلِسَ ٱلْخُلْقِ سَلِيمَ ٱلنَّاحِيَهْ

وَإِذَا عَاشَرْتَهُ أَلْفَيْتَهُ   شَرِسَ ٱلرَّأْىِ أَبِيًّا دَاهِيَهْ

فَٱحْمَدِ ٱللّٰهَ عَلَى صُحْبَتِهِ   وَٱسْأَلِ ٱلرَّحْمٰنَ مِنْهُ ٱلْعَافِيَهْ

CCXXIX

ʿ<u>Umdah</u>, I, 228 (n.e. I, 200)   Kāmil

أَبِنْتَ ذِى حُبًّا لَوْ تَضَمَّنَهُ سَلْمَى   سَمِيُّكِ ذَاكَ ٱلشَّاهِقُ الرَّاسِ ....

3

THE POETRY (ENGLISH TEXT)

I

How GOOD IS LIFE! Yet if I miss seeing your face [but] for a day, then life is without [its charm].
Could one day or an hour with you be bought with the world, [the price] would not be excessive.

II

He [formerly] denied [others], but was himself denied when he neared his end and the disappearance of youth became obvious.
He threw off the garment of frivolity and out of prudence let hang his shirt and wrapper.
How can one hope for the fair one's [pleasure] when what strikes her first is his whiteness?
He who was collyrium for the corner of her eyes became dust for them in his old age.

III

O encampment, where has Salmā gone? If she has died, it has caused his death.
I do not wish for her the rain of the cloud, for in [the tears] of my eye is a substitute for showers.

IV

[O my two friends] divert me with song, wine, and a night-traveling guest seeking hospitality.
The melodious voice of the guest is sweeter to us than the cry of the sheep.
We lodge the alighting guest in the core of our hearts and in the coils of our intestines.
Many a trading guest have I caused to suffer loss in our dealings, [for] I sold him food while I bought praise.
I hate money when I have gathered it; verily, the hatred of money derives from the love of nobility.
[The good] life consists of [certain] virtues —bravo, bravo for these virtues!—
The serving of the guest, a pleasant cup, a boon companion, a young maiden, and song.
And were you to miss one of these, life would be [found] wanting.

V

He whose father is Du'ād—and Iyād had many sons—
His parents have committed unnatural acts. Would that I knew from whence he came!
He comes from two, hard, barren stones who give birth to dust;
[He comes] not from prostitution, nor from marriage, nor from whatever requires mothers and fathers.

VI

Do not marry your daughter to a member of the [Banū] Nahshal and mix your choicest water with scum.

VII

Ibn 'Imrān covets an Arab [and] scorns the daughters of his peers.
If he needs anything he remembers his guest, but he forgets him at breakfast time.

VIII

I asked Generosity—may I never lack it!—which had, for a time, been absent from us:
"It has been a long time since our meeting. By God, have you or have you not been hiding?"
[And] Generosity replied: "Yes, I continued in hiding, but I have [now] arrived with Muttalib."

IX

Crossing sands, scaling mountains, swimming (*lit.* drinking) roaring oceans.
Removing the veil of the Jinn, ascending heaven to Him who rises above all,
Counting the vices of Sa'īd against us, and the bereavement at the death of a favorite child,
Is easier for a human being [to bear] than his being forced to await the fulfillment of his need.
His chamberlain also has a chamberlain, and the chamberlain's chamberlain is [likewise] barred from access.

X

Remember, O Abū Ja'far, a just claim by which I seek access to you; [remember] that you and I have a love for literature;
That we both have sucked the milk from its cup; that [sharing] its milk is a sharing of kinship.

XI

Do not mar the fifty thousand [dirhams] you have bestowed, the friendly times, the duty of relationship,
Nor the thanks which men, coming and going, bring to every region.
[Our relationship] was faultless, but if it were not, you must forgive.

XII

I depart not knowing where to go; nor do I know upon which affair I shall embark with resolution.
Should my two hands touch a strung pearl necklace, it would become a string of pierced seashells;
Should my hand grasp a hand with a dirham, the dirham would fall at my foot and in my hand would be a scorpion.

XIII

With Muttalib's death died three things: modesty, fear, and awe.
What four [wonderful] things has the shroud enveloped! Therewith were consoled Islām and the Arabs.
O day of Muttalib, our eyes are filled with tears which will flow for time everlasting.
These cheeks of the Banū Qahtān have cleaved to the dust from the moment the earth was leveled over you.

. . . .

I. See *Syntax*, p. 371, for construction: *ammā 'alā*. Verse 1 is cited by Ibn ash-Shajarī as an example of *hadhf* (Ibn Saj., *Amālī*, I, 234), and was imitated by al-Mutanabbī (Ibn Hallikān, II, 34).

II. Translation is in K. *Baghdād*, p. 127.

V. Satire against Ahmad b. abī Du'ād, Mu'tazilite judge, d. 240/854. See poems LXIII, CLIII, and CCIII.

VIII. Praises al-Muttalib b. 'Abd Allāh b. Mālik al-Khuzā'ī, governor of Egypt in 198/813-14. See poems XIII, XX, XXXVII, XL, CXLVIII, CLXIII, CXCII, CCXVIII, and CCXXII.

IX. See Wright, II, 536, for change of *fathah* and *kasrah* before fettered rhyme. Poem satirizes Ghassān b. 'Abbād.

XI. Poem is addressed to 'Alī b. 'Īsā al-Ash'arī.

XIV

A broken-hearted lover weeps for the disintegration of religion; a large bucket would overflow with the excess tears streaming from his eyes.
There has arisen an Imām without guidance, intelligence, and religion.
Reports that one like him would rule one day or that the Arabs would submit to him did not come [to us].
But as the followers of our ancestors said, when affairs became grievous,
"In the books, seven are the kings of the Banū 'Abbās; of an eighth, however, it is not written."
Similarly, seven were the noble men in the Cave when counted; the eighth in their company was a dog.
And I regard that dog above you, for you are a sinner whereas he was not.
When, to our distress, you ruled over us, you were as a decrepit old woman wearing a crown, necklace, and coat of mail.
Verily is the people's realm lost, since it is managed by Wasīf and Ashnās; their anxiety has become grievous.
I hope that from the setting sun there be sunrises wherein the night drinkers choke on [their drink].
You are [only] concerned with an abject Turk to whom you are mother and father.
And al-Fadl ibn Marwān has made a breach for which Islām has no repair.

XV

Salmā is amazed, and that is [itself] amazing. She saw a hoariness hastened by misfortune.
Old age has not made me thus. Rather, I live in an age in which the head of the weaned child is hoary.

XVI

When the wind was calm, Lailā's specter traveled through the night, and I fulfilled [my] yearning at a time when it almost consumed [me].
I did not see a well-traveled road halt its traveler, nor a traveler, following his desire, turn back.

XVII

When they set out in the morning with their horses and clothes of surpassing beauty, you say, "[They are as] lightning which gives false promise of rain."
And when they depart at night wearing black and green silk garments, "Clothes-hangers depart."

XVIII

You have a brother whom Time has treated as an enemy, so that his affairs have ended badly.
Whenever trials inform him of a companion, they [always] return him back to you.

XIX

They are lions on the day of disaster, foxes on the day of battle.

. . . .

XIV. Satirizes the caliph al-Mu'tasim. Verses 6-11 are translated in Jarrett, p. 349; verses 1-7, 9, 12 in Hammer, IV, 542. *'Umdah*, I, 43, mentions that al-Mu'tasim was known as the Eighth: *Kāna'l-Mu'tasim yu'raf bi'th-thāmin wa'th-thamnī aidan*. See poem CXCIX. Al-Fadl b. Marwān, d. 250/864, was al-Mu'tasim's vizier. Ashnās and Wasīf were Turkish generals who played important roles in the reigns of al-Mu'tasim and al-Wāthiq.

XVI. Verse 1, according to as-Sūlī, was unsuccessfully imitated by Ahmad b. abī Tāhir (*Muwassah*, p. 351).

XVII. See Lane, p. 2598, for expression *al-Burūq al-Kawādhib*.

XIX. Said of one who shows bravery before the battle but is a coward in the actual fighting.

XX

Do you hope for satisfaction after Egypt and Muttalib? That is a wonder!
If they vie with us [in clans], we offer his family; if they vie in individual [heroes], we offer Muttalib.

XXI

I came to you but for the sake of good manners.
Therefore, give what is due me, for I am a man who does not importune you.

XXII

I knew and had no doubt that the lesson of misfortune had overtaken me.

XXIII

If you had no ancestors to follow, you would, by yourself, have attained the Pleiades.

XXIV

I shall so thank Nūh for his excellent favors that the tongues of the Arabs will take their cue thereof.

XXV

Through the night, I was kept awake by lightning, rising and vanishing like the belly of the turning viper.

XXVI

They sat and selected a pedigree which passed amongst the Arabs after dusk.
But when morning came, the gold showed as counterfeit.
People have become moneychangers who see something [false] in this quicksilvery lineage.

XXVII

Knowledge raises the vulgar to high rank, while ignorance curbs the pedigreed youth.
When a youth comprehends knowledge and is helped by the pruning and polishing [of his character],
His affairs go forward, and he becomes outstanding in every encounter, manifest or hidden.

XXVIII

In darkness, the light of my fire or the barking of my dogs guides my guest to hospitality,
Until, when they meet him, they greet him with wagging tails.
And, being so accustomed to this, they are almost eloquent in their greeting.

XXIX

O Salmā, possessor of pleasant teeth and mistress of a wrist dyed with henna;
Whose buttocks shake in their girdle, and whose hair is as black as the raven;
By the sincerity of these sweet kisses—after your [pretended] remonstration and false accusations—
I beseech thee to reveal [the feeling] hidden in me.

XXX

I hold that speed enhances a gift, that delay damages the gift of the giver.

XX. Verse 2 translated in *Abriss*, II, 23.

XXI. The verses are addressed to 'Abd Allāh b. Tāhir, governor of Khurāsān, d. 230/844. Verses are translated in Hammer, IV, 543. See poems XCVI, CXLV, CLVIII, CLXVIII, and CCX.

XXIX. Addressed to the caliph al-Ma'mūn. See poems LXV and CLVI.

XXXI

The good life [consists] in the camaraderie of one's brothers, not in the society of full-breasted girls,
And in pure wine which [in its redness] is as tongues of lightning directed toward a thin cloud.
If you give up the pleasures of life, fearing punishment on the Day of Requital,
Then leave me with what is dearest and most agreeable to me, and stand aloof from me at the beginning of the Day of Reckoning.

XXXII

You act haughtily toward us because the wolf spoke to you. By my life, your father spoke to the wolf.
How indeed? If he had spoken to the lion, you would have ordered food and drink for the people.
This little Indian, without origin and nobility, talks to the elephant when he makes him descend and rise.
Go away. For I see no one at your door who is [either] seeking or sought.

XXXIII

May a new government give you joy, for its power has created a lineage [for you].

XXXIV

Sulaimā has become remote, and the tie with her has been cut. They provisioned you and they did not lament your emaciation.
Salmā said, "Where is the money?" And I said, "Woe to thee! the money has met Praise and they have kept company."
"Praise has divided my money amongst the wine cups which did not leave me blame nor property."
Salmā said, "Leave this milch ewe for boys who are as downy as the cheek of the Qatā."
And I replied, "Keep her. And let it benefit them [as long as] a starving traveler does not stop seeking food."
When our guest draws up his legs to sit, and the family's milch camels are ill, the family weeps, while our kettle sings with joy.
This is my way. This, know, is my character. You may, therefore, be pleased or angry.
Whether or not the opportune time for attaining one's desire has passed, I will not fail to attain the sustenance decreed for me.
I endeavor to seek a sustenance which seeks me more than I seek it.
Do you obtain anything desired and earned, such as pay and praise, if you are anxious about it?
When pedigrees are traced, they are a people whose generous one, horseman and poet, is without peer.

XXXV

I pity the nobleman who seeks the fulfillment of his desire from a vile person.
I pity him in his wretched state, just as one pities a Thoroughbred ridden by an ass.

XXXVI

Whenever these efforts depose a man, he loves others to have vices like the ones that have shamed him.
What a misfortune for Fadl! If he did not

XXXI. Addressed to Abū Nahshal b. Humaid at-Tūsī. See Ibn Hallikān, Slane, I, 353, where he builds a canopy over the grave of Abū Tammām.

XXXII. Satirizes the Banū Ahbān, who claim that their ancestor spoke to the wolf in the time of Muhammad.

find fault, he would vomit the poison resulting from the distress of his eating.
He does not cease, and his defects include foolishness, to slander the reputation of noble people.
If he slanders me, he slanders his teacher. And therein he only slanders himself.
He is like the dog trained for the chase who afterward chases his trainer.
Indeed, he whose habit is the destruction of nobility slanders the building of nobility.

XXXVII

'Alī's penis is his tool, and 'Amr's anus his mistress.
At times he encounters a dart, and at other times a quiver.

XXXVIII

After I have shown respect to my guest, he does not depart without a gift, escort, and apologies.

XXXIX

When we raided, our aim was Anqarah, while the family of Salmā is at the sea coast of Jurat.
How far! how far! is the distance between the two stations. I have become emaciated from yearning, and have long delayed [seeing] the object of my desire.
I love my family and do not misuse their love. They say, "Out of ignorance, you have supported the statement of a liar."
For them is my tongue, my praising, and my eulogizing. Yes, my heart and my wealth.
Let me join my kindred. [And] though you prevent, the closest kin must join in this world.
Remember your kin, [for] they have rights which separate man and wife.
My people are the Banū Himyar; the Azd are their brothers. [They include] the family of Kindah and the tribe of 'Ulat.
I have gathered the forbearing ones. But if one draws their anger, they draw their swords and destroy every culprit.
My soul inspires me to nobility and virtue. Even were I to disregard her, she would persist.
How often did I, sorely opposed by a sword, enter the path of death, yet it led me to a spacious place!
My reprovers say, "The property is gone." To which I reply, "Yes, both my pay and my fame!"
They say, "You have corrupted your wealth." And I say, "Wealth would corrupt me, if I were stingy therewith; however, generosity furthers my self-interest."
God allots his benefits [as a gift] to whomever he desires.
Do not present a joke to an experienced man, from whose lips pass [only] what his mind has disciplined.
Indeed, many a deadly and ominous verse, whose publishing is not desired, is traced back to a jest.
The restoring of the afterbirth after its severance is as the restoring of a verse after it has become broadcast.
When I recite a verse, its author and the person addressed may die, but the verse does not.

XL

How have you regarded the swords of the [Banū] Jarīsh and the battle of the client of the Banū Dabbah?
Their swords have sent you on a forced pilgrimage. Now what interest have you in pilgrimages?

. . . .

XXXVI. Satirizes al-Fadl b. al-'Abbās b. Ja'far b. Muhammad al-Ash'ath. His father al-'Abbās was governor of Khurāsān in 173/789.

XL. Maulā Banī Dabbah is as-Sarī b. al-Hakam, who forced al-Muttalib to leave Egypt.

XLI

I recall the camp site at 'Arafah and shed tears at 'Abarah.
The schools where the Qur'ān is taught, [there] its recital is no longer; the abodes of Revelation are as vacant courts.
[Oh, how I wish] for the Family of the Prophet of God at al-Khaif at Minā, at the corner of the Ka'bah, at the sacrifice at 'Arafah, and the heaps [at 'Arafah];
[For] the abodes of 'Alī, Husain, Ja'far, Hamzah, and the Worshipper whose knees are calloused—
Abodes effaced by the damage of injustices, not by days and years.
Stop. Let us ask the house, whose people are few, when is the time for fasting and prayer?
Where are they whom distant journeys have estranged from their abode and who have become disordered and dispersed in the lands?
When they trace their lineage, they are the heirs of the Prophet. They are the best leaders and protectors,
Whereas [other] people are envious, liars, hate one another, and are possessed of rancour and revenge.
When they remember those slain at Badr, Khaibar, and Hunain, they shed tears.
The graves at Kufāh, Taibah, and Fakhkh, may my prayers reach them!
Others are [buried] in Juzājān, and there is a tomb at Bākhamrā near al-Ghurbah.
In Baghdād is a tomb for a Pure Soul. May God include him in Paradise!
As for these deaf ones, their intrinsic qualities defy my powers of description;
They await the Resurrection, when God will send a Restorer who will scatter their grief and cares.
Souls at the two rivers of Karbalā, whose [final] abode is by the bank of the Euphrates,
The vicissitudes of Time have dispersed them [and], as you see, they have a dust color and are covered with stones.
There is a band of them in Madīnah, who are forever emaciated from need;
Who have few visitors except the male hyena, the eagle, and the vulture;
They are forever asleep in their various beds in the regions of the earth.
They who formerly were the raiders and chosen leaders of the Hijāz and its people,
The distress of years has overtaken their neighborhood, so that a party of horsemen no longer warm themselves at their fires.
When they joined battle, their spears flashed in the sun—pokers of the coals of death and woe.
If one day they boasted, they brought forth Muhammad, Gabriel, and the Furqān, the possessor of the Sūras.
[Beware of] cursing the Family of the Prophet, for, as long as I live, they are my beloved and the people of my trust.
I choose them as the guides for my affairs, for they are the best in all situations.
O God, add clear vision to my firm belief; add the love of them to my other good qualities.
I swear that you, young and old, are [ever ready] to free slaves and to pay bloodwit.
I love my remotest relation out of love for you, and I avoid for your sake my kin and daughters.
Fearing an enemy, who opposes those alive of the Family of Truth, I hid my love of you.
Time has surrounded me with evil, and I hope for security after death.
Do you not see me go forth for thirty years, eve and morn, continuously sad?
I see booty divided amongst others; their hands are empty thereof.
The bodies of the Family of the Prophet are lean; the necks of the family of Ziyād are distended [with food].
The daughters of Ziyād live in palaces; the Family of the Messenger of God lives in the desert.
When they suffer injury, they stretch out

to their oppressors hands afflicted with past injuries.
Were it not for him, who I hope will come today or tomorrow, my sighing for them would cut my heart.
No doubt an Imām is coming—an Imām who will govern according to the name of God and the Blessings.
He will distinguish those false and true among us; he will requite with favors and revenge.
I will restrain my heart from opposing [your] enemies, for what I have met of tears suffices me.
O my soul, delight! O my soul, rejoice! for what cometh is not remote.
If God will delay the time of my death and will bring this event within my lifespan,
I will recover without damage to my heart, and I will let my lance and sword water in my enemies.
I wish to transfer the sun from her fixed abode and to cause the hard, bare stones to listen.
[However,] many are those who know and do not benefit; many are those who are obstinate and incline to their passions and doubts.
My end is that I will die with grief for them —[a grief] which reverberates in my throat.
[And] it is as though you saw my ribs become narrow with the intensity of [my] sighing.

XLII

May God water and protect the days of yearning—days in which I strutted in garments of pleasure;
Days when my branch was pliant because of its freshness; [days] when I longed for others than my female neighbors and daughters-in-law.
Forgo remembering a time whose attainment is beyond reach; cast forth thy foot from the path of ignorance,
And aim with every eulogy, whose author you are, toward the leaders, the sons of the House of Excellences.

XLIII

Do not grieve that misfortune knocked, at night, at thy house, for you are a novice [thereof].
In the love of the Family of the Chosen, of God's Trustee, is a distraction from pleasures and songstresses;
Indeed, it is more useful for me to avow my love of the Family of Muhammad than to spend my time with women.
Fill thy odes with them and empty for them a heart whose yearning you formerly stuffed with pleasures.
Cut the tie with him who desires others than them. And, in the love of them, may you reach a safe abode!

XLIV

I was informed that a dog of [the Banū] Kilāb reviled me, that a pure member of Kilāb cut short his prayers.
If I, a bold avenger, do not know the [Banū] Kilāb to be dogs,
Then my father belongs to Qais 'Ailān, my mother to those short, ugly women.

XLV

I saw az-Zūtatī—who to me was abominable and odious—in a gathering.

. . . .

XLI. Verses 2, 11, 12, are translated in Mas'ūdī, VI, 195; verses 37, 38, 42-43, in *Bad'*, V, 133. Abū'l-Faraj considers this the best poem and the best panegyric on the Family of the Prophet Muhammad (*Ag.*, XVII, 29). The Worshiper whose knees are calloused, in this context, is probably 'Alī Zain al-'Ābidīn, fourth Imām of the Twelvers, d. ca. 92/712. Ja'far is probably Ja'far as-Sādiq, sixth Imām of the Twelvers, d. 148/765. The problem of al-'Abarāt is discussed in *Buldān*, III, 603-604.

He said, "Ask me to recite what you wish." And I replied, "I ask you to recite silence."

XLVI

Ja'far ibn Muhammad ibn al-Ash'ath's [paternity] is for me no better than Ath'ath's.
In vain does he exert himself with the exertion of a viper which would not tarry if I rushed forth against it.
Were the inexperienced to know the disgrace he earned for his parent, [his efforts] would not be wasted.

XLVII

We attained the pleasures of life in Batyāthā,
When we were cheered thrice with the wine cup.
And thrice did I divorce my wife.

XLVIII

When a haughty person contends with us, life becomes angry with him and he becomes lame.
For our right hand dispenses generosity, and our swords dispense death.

XLIX

The calumniators have severed what was between us—we who need for our bond to be joined.
They saw a fault and boldly pounced on it. Forbearance did not hinder them, nor did they feel restraint.
They are men in whose absence I feel secure—[men] who betake themselves, day and night, after what is not encouraged.

L

My riding beast, accustomed to two cares—absence from home and the distance from the trough—spent the night in Qumm,
Among foreigners who, having taken up Arab customs, claim an [Arab] genealogy, and among Arabs who have assumed the customs of the foreigner.

LI

I welcome hoariness, for it is the mark of the chaste and the ornament of one who keeps aloof from sin.
My hoariness is as a string of shining pearls [set] in the crown of a most brilliantly crowned king.

LII

When he appears, he seems to be a ram. But by nature he is a ewe.
When you sit next to him, you think there is a barque in his scrotum.

LIII

She is the person who finds beautiful what you find beautiful, who finds ugly what you find ugly.

LIV

When the riders are impelled into [the desert] to live in celibacy, it [is to seek] forgiveness for their sins and to praise God.

. . . .

XLV. Verses are attributed to Muhammad b. abī Umayyah in *Bayān*, I, 404, and are addressed to ar-Raqāshī. Translated in Pellat, p. 101.

XLVI. Ja'far b. Muhammad b. al-Ash'ath was governor of Khurāsān in 171/787. See Ibn al-Athīr, VI, 79.

XLVII. Is translated in *Mahāsin*, Rescher, p. 53.

LV

The ugliness of Ibn Zayyāt's songstress exceeds that of the Devil.
She is black and large mouthed; her hair resembles the fringes of a saddlefelt.
If she appeared bareheaded in the morning, the dawn would turn black.

LVI

They are those who prefer death; a people chosen to command.

LVII

Because of its prolonged confusion, his soul, on the day of battle, was as one lying in ambush for him.

LVIII

I did not think that Time would give me relief, until I saw one satirized by no one.
I am amazed at one whose provision bag is filled with semen and does not give birth.
If you listen to him, in vain would you [try to] sell [your] lances, for he desires them without joints.

LIX

Praised be God! There is no need for self-constraint, patience, nor consolation when people of corruption die.
There died a caliph whom no one mourns; there has risen another in whom no one rejoices.
The former and the misfortunes which followed him have passed. Now that the latter has arisen, there is calamity and distress.

LX

He who is niggardly with his privy to his guest, how can he be generous [in other matters]?
Before this, we have never heard of or seen a privy for whose door one needed a key.
If you are hiding something therein, then, if you desire, I have something to add to it!

LXI

I am not a speaker of obscenities, but for what purpose do your servants serve you?

LXII

Her eyes are of dry dates and cheese; the rest of her countenance is [as] soup.

LXIII

O 'Abd al-Ilāh! hearken to my statement, for some statements contain truth.
As Iyād returned, you observed a darkness such as night brings to the world.
Tribes whose roots were cut, who have ceased to be, and whose very mention has, for a time, perished, have returned.
They were stuck and held in the sand just as the locust sticks its eggs [therein].
And if they were watered, they would rise and creep; when the spring rains pour on them, they multiply.
They are eggs of worms which open by splitting; some of them resemble ashes.
Tomorrow their despised brothers Jadīs and Jurhum will come; 'Ād will also return.
The lands and abodes will be so full of them that they will be unable to contain them.

. . . .

LV. Muhammad b. 'Abd al-Malik az-Zayyāt or Ibn az-Zayyāt, d. 233/847, vizier of the caliphs al-Mu'tasim and al-Wāthiq. See poem CI.

LVIII. Satirizes the poet Abū Sa'd al-Makhzūmī. See poems CXIII, CXIV, CXLIX, CCXIX, and CCXXV.

LIX. The verses are translated in Hammer, IV, 543.

LXI. Satirizes the caliph al-Mutawakkil.

I have not seen the likes of them who, having perished, have [again] returned, and having become few, have [again] multiplied.
Blood-letting and tyranny have deeply penetrated amongst them; they are the mob's paragon.
The Nabateans of the Sawād have become nomads, for the Sawād has become a waste.
If the Imām desired, he could set up a market and sell them just as manure is sold.

LXIV

O Valley of Khabr!—may the early morning [breezes] water you—where is the halting place of the tribe?
He chooses for his war companion, a horse resembling the swift eagle of the Sahrah.
Between the curtains of the litter is a veiled woman. When the singing cameler drives his camels, he takes away my heart.
[And I think of] a spear whose tip is blue like the tongue of the thirsty viper.

LXV

Al-Ma'mūn imposed on me the duty of clairvoyance. Did he not see yesterday the head of Muhammad [al-Amīn]?
We tower over the heads of men as mountains tower over the rocky hills;
We alight in inaccessible regions until [Tāhir] humbled a high mountain which had never been climbed.
Do not think my stupidity to be as the forbearance of my father, for the forbearance of the aged is not as the stupidity of the beardless youth.
I belong to people whose swords killed your brother and ennobled you with a throne.
They have raised your status after its prolonged obscurity; they have raised you from [being as] the lowest part of a mountain.
The seeker of revenge is wakeful. Therefore, desist tasting the spittle of the black viper.

LXVI

Avoid delaying payment, for delay is a bane for every hand.
If you postpone fulfilling a man's need, withhold it and do not [try] to be generous,
Since you will not find him thanking a hand forever weary with delay.

LXVII

Does it not occur in the vicissitudes of Time that the distant path returns them [home], and that, one day, absence is exchanged for closeness?
Yes. In its mutability [occur] all that I observe. But these [women] have, on purpose, neglected my share.
By God, I do not know by which of her noninjuring arrows I am struck,
Whether by [her] beautiful neck or by the place of the sash. [Yet] I suspect that her eyes are [only] for the black, curly haired one.

LXVIII

May God not bless a night which brought me near a bed companion [who felt] like the rubbing of one's hands with the fiber of a palm tree!
Touching her nude parts, my hands alighted on a peg.

. . . .

LXIV. Verse 4 was imitated by Abū Tammām, but according to al-Amidī he did not equal Di'bil's verse (*Muwāzanah*, p. 39).

LXV. Verses 1, 5-6, are translated in Ibn Hallikān, Slane, I, 508; verses 5-6, in Jarrett, p. 339; verses 1-3, 7, in *K. Baghdād*, p. 134.

LXVII. Addressed to al-'Abbās b. Ja'far b. al-Ash'ath. See note to poem XXXVI.

In her parts is a horn with which she strikes the side of her bedfellow, revealing her flaccid flesh.

LXIX

Without humiliation I am the guest's slave. And that is the only quality of the slave I possess.

LXX

Halting places of the tribe: Ghumdān, Nadad, Ma'rib, Zafār al-Mulk, and Janad,
The land of the Tubb'as, and of the Himyarite kings of Yemen. They are a mounted people [wearing] swords and armor.
They never entered a city without raising a written monument, which neither disappeared nor perished—
Monuments which are at the gates of China, Marv, India, and Sughd.

LXXI

They are a body of men who, if called to misfortune, bind nobility and life with iron.

LXXII

I said to many a companion who, wishing to be generous, was deterred from liberality by avarice:
"Do not fulfill the need of one whom you have tired with delay, lest you be afflicted with dispraise."
When I left him, it was as though I received a twisted heart cut from his back—
As though his limbs, by every noble act, were ripped out like the entrails on an iron spit.

LXXIII

Sālih's best feature is his face. Therefore, deduce the hidden from the obvious.
My eye contemplated his countenance, which induces one to charge his parent with adultery.

LXXIV

Abū Sa'd is a young poet who is known by his surname, not by his father's.
He searches in the tribe of Ma'ad for a father, who is unknown to the searcher and to the person asked.
May God's mercy be on a Muslim who directs one lost to another who is himself missing!

LXXV

I have found you a taster in love, [for] you do not persevere in one food [i.e., the lady is fickle].

LXXVI

I asked my father, who was acquainted with the abodes of the nomads and the city dwellers,
"Is Haitham of the tribe of Qais?" "Yes," he said, "just as Ahmad ibn abī Du'ād."
And if Haitham is of Qais, then Ahmad is without doubt of Iyād!
When Iyād rules a people, God has, indeed, become angry with his servants.

. . . .

LXVIII. Attributed in *Hamāsah* to Abū'l-Khandaq al-Asadī and also to Di'bil.

LXIX. This verse and three others are attributed in *Hamāsah*, p. 729, to Hātim at-Tā'ī. The verses are translated in Nicholson, p. 87. See Gaudefroy-Demombynes, p. 72, note 91, for the references regarding this verse.

LXX. Verse 1 is translated in Faris, p. 38.

LXXIII. Satirizes Sālih b. 'Atiyyah al-Adjam. See Tabari, III, 596, where he is mentioned as a *rāwī*.

LXXVI. Satirizes al-Haitham b. 'Uthmān al-Ghanawī and Ibn abī Du'ād. Al-Buhturī praises al-Haitham in Husrī, II, 217.

LXXVII

She said, after I reminded her, in despair, of our youth, "The habit of the ordinary man is broken."
"The exception, however, is the Imām, for the habit of his generosity is joined to his exceeding the excess [asked]."

LXXVIII

The matter most likely [to end in] corruption and loss is an affair managed by Abū 'Abbād.
He rages so against his companions that they appear as if they were at a bloody battle and a sword joust.
With his inkstand, he assaults his scribe who becomes anointed with blood and sprinkled with ink.
He is as one escaped from Dair Hizqil: one who, mad, drags the iron chains of his fetters.
O Prince of the Believers, fasten his bonds, for Baqiyyah, the blacksmith, is healthier than he.

LXXIX

Once, when Abū Khālid spent the night sitting, suffering from indigestion—
His stomach being too narrow for its children—he relieved himself of them, one by one.
Thus, from his excrement, the earth became filled with beetles which do not resemble their parents.

LXXX

How many are the people! No, on the contrary, how few they are!—and God knows that I do not lie—
My eye closes and opens upon a multitude, but I do not see a [generous] one.

LXXXI

[When] she dyes her palm cut from its wrist,
The henna is dyed with her blackness.
While the collyrium is on her slate pencil,
It is as though she were painting her eyes with part of her skin.
What most resembles her cheek is her buttock.

LXXXII

O, possessor of two right hands and one eye!
[Behold] two imperfections: one eye and one extra right hand.
[He is] niggardly in giving [and] of little use.
May God cause him to bite the clitoris of his mother!

LXXXIII

An expanse which the eye encompasses quicker than a flash.

LXXXIV

O Haitham, O Ibn 'Uthmān, of whom Nobility and Time boast.
Not only Mudar, [but also] Rabī'ah, and the other tribes of Yemen are proud of his courage.

LXXXV

If a forelock disturbs you, consider! For many a time does the aloeswood taste bitter through it is green.

. . . .

LXXVIII. Satirizes Abū 'Abbād Thābit b. Yahyā, vizier of al-Ma'mūn. See Tabarī, III, 1155; Zambaur, p. 6. *Ag.*, XVIII, 39, states that Baqiyyah was an inmate of Dair Hizqil, a mental hospital.

LXXIX. Satirizes Ahmad b. abī Khālid al-Ahwal, d. 210/825-26, vizier of al-Ma'mūn after al-Hasan b. Sahl. See poems CXX and CLXXX.

LXXX. The verses are translated in Hammer, IV, 545.

LXXXII. Satirizes Tāhir b. al-Husain, d. 207/822, founder of the Tāhirid dynasty of Khurāsān. See poems CLXIV and CLXXXIII.

LXXXVI

May God stop the laughter of Time if I laugh, while the family of Ahmad is oppressed and humbled.
They are scattered, exiled from the hearth of their homes as though they had committed an unpardonable sin.

LXXXVII

I went out early in the morning from Sāmarrā hastening to [fulfill] a need, and behold, I saw 'Umair.
So I did not tie the rein and said: "Go on, for your face, O 'Umair, is excrement, and more so."

LXXXVIII

Consider him and his wit. How he pretends to belong to Tayy, when he is well known [for not belonging]!
Woe to you whose heart becomes petrified, when one attributes to you a genealogy.
If "Tayy" is mentioned at a distance of a parsang, the light of your eye becomes darkened.

LXXXIX

I saw near us a house of a leader—a leader who neither visits nor is visited,
Who neither presents nor is presented with gifts; [indeed] this is not the way of neighborliness among the Arabs.

XC

Generosity knows that, from the time it made a compact with me, I have not betrayed it either in good or bad times.

XCI

Let not my needs cause you grief, O Abū 'Umar; for they but [give you food] for thought and excuses.
Of those needs which leave me, it is God who has facilitated their departure; of those which remain, [they do so] in accordance with Fate.

XCII

When you see the Banū Fadl in an abode, you do not know the male from the female.
The gown of their females is cut from the front; the gowns of their males are cut in the back.
They are experienced in turpitude, from infancy to old age.
They are experienced; yet, in old age, their amulets and [ties to their] nurses and weaning mothers remain unsevered.

XCIII

He has left al-Ahwāz and crossed beyond the Zāb in the land of Kaskar.
Ismā'īl, terrified by the swords and lances, fled from Zaid ibn Mūsā ibn Ja'far.
I saw him on the day he left his womenfolk, and lo! their shame, lo! what a pleasant sight.

XCIV

He came to us seeking trouble, and we requited him therewith.
We made him suffer loss. But since he was not satisfied, we added further to his loss.

XCV

We know of no tribe whether of Yamān, Bakr, or of Mudar,

LXXXVII. Satirizes the Kātib 'Umair. See Tabarī, II, 436, where is mentioned an 'Umair b. Ma'n al-Kātib ar-Rāwī.

LXXXVIII. Satirizes Ahmad b. Muhammad at-Tā'ī.

XCIII. Satirizes Ismā'īl b. Ja'far b. Sulaimān, governor of Basrah. Zaid b. Mūsā b. Ja'far was the brother of 'Alī ar-Ridā. See Tabarī, III, 986, 999; Mas'ūdī, VII.

But that they shared in their blood as the Maisir players share in the slaughtered camel.
[It is their habit] to kill, take prisoners, burn, plunder, and raid the peoples of Byzantium and Khazar.
I excuse the Umayyads, if they killed. But I do not excuse the Banū 'Abbās.
Sons of Harb and Marwān whose kindred are the Banū Mu'ait, patrons of rancour and fear.
Violating the tenets of Islām, they [*lit.* you] killed many a chieftan; were they able, they would [even] sanction Unbelief!
If you stop for a religious purpose, stop at the grave of the Pure One in Tūs.
At Tūs are two graves—the graves of the best and worst of men. [Therein lies] an admonition:
Impurity does not benefit from the grave of the Pure One nor does the Pure One take harm from the proximity of the impure.
Not so! Every man is a pledge for what his hands have acquired. So take or leave what you wish!

XCVI

Know, Abū 'Īsā, that I shun you not from hatred, from weariness,
Nor from ingratitude for your favors. Does anyone expect increase from ingratitude?
Rather, when I visited you—and you were overgenerous—I was unable to thank you.
If you increase your favors to me, I will increase my sullenness and you will not meet me until the Resurrection.
Henceforth, I will only come to you when I have an excuse; I will visit you once a month or [once every] two months.

XCVII

If you do not confer favors except [after having] accumulated gain, you will not bestow them till end of Time.
For which vase does not overflow when full? Which miser does not bestow in his abundance?
The nobleman is not he who gives solely in prosperity, but he who gives in hard and easy circumstances.

XCVIII

When he was a youth, I gave him my love, shared with him my wealth, and made my bosom his lodging.
Instead of a full life, he had only hope and despair, which left him poor.
His faults cannot be counted; the least of them transcends thought.
Were I to reveal some of them, I would awake in a sea made by the spit of his friends.
Here is my honor, and you may revile me while I am alive. But if I die, swear not to excrete on my grave.

XCIX

Our cooking pot with the camels' limbs spent the night singing openly with joy.

C

Beautiful white [women] were ordained for your desire—women who [rob you of your wits] with their eyes and chests.
Looking at their chests, you almost died. How would it have been if you looked at their waists?

CI

O he who manipulates and spreads out a paper scroll! Why this love for scrolls?
Herein is a resemblence to what rejoices

. . . .

XCV. Satirizes the caliph Hārūn, whose tomb is at Tūs. See Huber, pp. 1-20.
XCVIII. Satire of Di'bil's brother, Razīn.

you—length for length, roundness for roundness.
If you gathered wealth as you collect [scrolls], you would have accumulated houses [full] of dinars.

CII

Her body resembles the dog's iron collar, and her breast is flat as the lute.

CIII

O you with the knees of a goat ready for slaughter, ostrich-legged, round as the sweeper's basket, and whose head resembles the head of a male camel!
O you whom I compare with a roaring, shivering fever which cuts one's back.
Your temples have become hoary, your throat is dried out, and your breast is flat as the lute.
He who embraces her spends the night as though he were in a dungeon, covered with vermin and in an iron [dog] collar.
I kissed her and found the sting of her uvula like the sting of the wasp.

CIV

There are people who love you, showing a love without any shortcomings.
When you know him, his eye testifies to what he secretly thinks.
When you have considered the matter, you say, "I have confidence in this person, and he is a source of great wealth."
But when you ask him for a fourth of a farthing, his love is overtaken by death.

CV

O Nasr, you embalmed him with camphor and lifted him to the forsaken abode.
Why did you not embalm him with some of his sour wine, so that it might diffuse into the adjacent graves?

CVI

A river which no one crossed, except him who was fearful of his sins or who cared to risk his life.
And it became, to one who became prosperous through your favors, as though it were spanned by vaulted bridges.

CVII

He made his lances and swords muzzles for the breached frontier passes.

CVIII

A face like the ugly face of the ogre: large-mouthed, evil-eyed, and camel-lipped.

CIX

A people who, eating, hide their conversation and secure themselves against one cleaving to their door.
Their neighbor does not seek the benefit of their fire, and their hand does not desist from taking what belongs to their neighbor.

CX

O you with the countenance of the scarecrow, depart and favor me with your prolonged absence.
Your face and my union with you have injured me with wounds which resist the surgeon's probe.
[She has] a defective chin, a thick nose, and a forehead [flat] like the beam of the moneychanger.
Throughout my protracted night with her I cried, "O avenge him who seeks the light of day!"

CIII. See Wright, I, 179, where *hummā* is given as feminine.

Her shape resembles a scorpion, her little finger a washer's beetle.

CXI

Rebelling against God, we committed foul acts until we came across Yahyā and Dīnār.
Two foolish barbarians whose fruit is not cut (*i.e.*, remain uncircumcized), and who have long prostrated themselves before the sun and fire.

CXII

Resolution, courage, fear of God, and the bestowing of gifts [so] vied for priority in him that they became discordant.

CXIII

They wrote the deed—of which you are aware—against you and sprinkled sand over you.

CXIV

O Abū Sa'd, O date basket, fornicator of sister and wife.
If you saw him squatting, you would think him an arch of a bridge;
If you saw the penis in his buttock, you would say, "A shank in a stock";
If you saw him chewing it, you would say, "Butter with sugar";
If you saw him smelling it, you would say, "Musk with ambergris."
The servant sends forth his falcon, and he is his perch;
There is, forever, a rider in his behind.

CXV

If one killed or injured Ibn Tauq, the Banū Taghlib, or their kindred,
They would not receive a dirham for blood money nor dung for their blood price.
Their blood is without a seeker, and is unretaliated as the blood of a virgin.
Their faces are white, but their genealogy is black; in their ears are copper rings.

CXVI

The Banū 'Amr are a wonder; their description transcends understanding.
Their father's complexion is brown, but theirs is reddish.
I think that, when he came to their mother, he brought a reddish color in his semen.

CXVII

He soils his wide, long beard, wetting it as one wets dough.
O what a white, greasy beard! It is as though you used it for eating meat cooked with sour milk.

CXVIII

Every day, Abū Sa'd raids the genealogies.
One day he belongs to Tamīm; another day, to Fazārah.

CXIX

I saw Abū 'Imrān generous with his honor, whereas his bread is most guarded.
Sated, he yearns for his wives; while they, vehemently hungry, long for bread.

. . . .

CX. The poem is translated in Rückert, II, 369. See *Verhältnisse*, p. 325, for usage of *yā* plus *la* where *la* is uncombined with following word.

CXI. Satirizes Dīnār b. 'Abd Allāh, one of al-Ma'mūn's generals who was sent against an 'Alid rebellion in the Yemen in 207/833.

CXV. Satirizes Mālik b. Tauq at-Taghlibī, d. 259/872 (*Fawāt*, II, 177). See poems CLXXXVII, CCXXVI, and CCXXVII.

CXVI. Verses 1-2 are translated in *Gefährte*, p. 279.

CXX

Were you not as one of your middle-sized scribes, who discharges [his] needs stretching out his neck,
You would have never breakfasted on a weaned, milk-fed camel, nor on fried colocasia.
Or [were you not] as the noble Ibn Mas'adah, whose origin [lies] in the Registry of the Banū 'Abbās,
Who, in the morning, appears before his guests seeking food like the dog who eats in people's houses.

CXXI

I was afflicted with a hermaphrodite who resembled a staff; she was a greater thief and viler than the magpie.
She loves women, refuses men, and keeps company with the vilest rabble.
When she decks herself out, she has the face of an ape and the complexion of the spotted eggs of the Qatā.
[Her] breast droops over her chest like the waterskin of the herder whose flocks have become thirsty.
Her thigh is like the cloven foot of the male gazelle and yellower than apricots.
The gap between her thighs permits the camel's litter to pass without bumping.
The ankle of her shank is thinner than the ankle of the locust.
The warts on her face resemble bits of currants.
Above her mass of hair is a tuft which resembles the feathers of a white pigeon.

CXXII

His face is a complete abomination and resembles the remains of the desolate abode, whose inhabitants have departed.
Were your buttock as narrow as your chest and your chest as wide as your posterior, you would be the most perfect man walking.

CXXIII

O Abū Nadīr, leave our company, for you are a waste to whoever associated with you.
You are like the ass which is restive when I approach and which darts away when I intend its good.
Sparing no effort, I brandished you. Would that you were a sword! But [in truth] I only brandished a stick.

CXXIV

I said, "Tears overflow my eye, which has an aversion for sleep."
And she said, "This is but little suffering for one smitten by languid eyes."
I replied, "Does your heart incline for my master or for him who is afflicted in his intestines?"

CXXV

When I could not stand his guidance, I forsook him and shut off my love,
Saying to [another] soul, "Mourn him when the long journey absents him or because the connection is cut."
[As for myself], I neither cried over him nor experienced grief in my intestines when we separated.

. . . .

CXX. Satirizes Ahmad b. abī Khālid—see note to poem LXXIX—and 'Amr b. Mas'adah, d. 215/217, one of al-Ma'mūn's viziers and uncle of Ibrāhīm b. al-'Abbās as-Sūlī. See Ibn Hallikān, Slane, II, 410-14. The poem is translated in *K. Baghdād*, p. 103.

CXXI. Poem, in *Hamāsah*, p. 822, is attributed to Abū'l-Ghatammash al-Hanafī. It is translated in Rückert, II, 371-72.

CXXIII. Satirizes Abū Nadīr b. Humaid at-Tūsī, brother of Abū Nahshal. See note to poem XXXI.

CXXIV. Translated in Hammer, IV, 546.

CXXVI

O troops, do not despair; be satisfied, do not rage;
For you will be given melodies of Hunain, which delight the beardless youth and the hoary.
Your leaders will be given melodies of Ma'bad, which can be neither bound nor put in one's purse.
This is how a caliph, whose Qur'ān is a lute, provides for his leaders!
He signed a deed which provides for your sustenance and he has made firm resolution. Therefore, be not displeased.
Ibrāhīm's investiture is ominous; the people will be slaughtered or afflicted with drought.

CXXVII

I have never seen a row like the row of the ninety crucified Zutt.
They seem as though they were dipped in tar. [One of them], on his beam by the river bank, resembles
A slumberer in a deep sleep who is stretching without snoring.

CXXVIII

Bring to the Imām a message from one far away.
[And say], "When one does not bribe Ibn Wahb, he writes with faulty pens."

CXXIX

The muadhdhin Sālih and his guests captured an ironclad [warrior], who slipped on the battlefield.
[Thus] they sent their sons and daughters: pluckers and scalders,
Who litigated [over him] as though they had bound a great Khan or put to flight the squadrons of the Nā'it tribe.
Biting him, they broke their teeth; [climbing] the wall, they bruised their skulls.

CXXX

The dog who had been extolled has now become humiliated. There is no benefit in a dog!
He attained the goal before which all heights fall short.
Verily, the end of all things is that they fall after soaring.
[Therefore] say to Yahyā ibn Aktham, "What you feared has occurred."
May God curse pride which is followed by humiliation!

CXXXI

O men, the head of the son of Muhammad's daughter and his executor is raised on a spear.
Yet the Muslims, seeing and hearing, are neither afflicted with grief nor shamed.
I kept awake sleepy eyelids, and an eye without slumber I made sleep.
Eyes, looking at you, became anointed with blindness; the announcement of your death rendered deaf every listening ear.
There is no meadow but that it desires to be your bed and the furrow of your grave.

CXXXII

She said, after his absence had worn on, and the circle of her eye was [filled] with blood and tears,
"It is high time that they return, before my

. . . .

CXXVI. Satirizes Ibrāhīm b. al-Mahdī, d. 224/839, countercaliph in Baghdād in 202 A.H. Verses 1-2 are translated in Hammer, IV, 540-41. See poem CL.

CXXVIII. Satirizes al-Hasan b. Wahb, who was secretary to Ibn az-Zayyāt and director of the chancery office; al-Hasan was a patron of Abū Tammām. See poem CLVII.

CXXX. Satirizes Yahyā b. Aktham, d. 242/857, judge in the periods of al-Ma'mūn and al-Mutawakkil. See poem CCIX.

CXXXI. Praises al-Husain b. 'Alī, d. 61/680.

death, from the journey to their home-land!"

And I said, unable to control the tears that expressed what my heart felt:

"Understand! how many are the houses whose affairs are disordered? How many are the scattered groups who return re-united?"

Such are the vicissitudes of Time. For every man there is [a time] of barrenness and luxury.

CXXXIII

Ziyād said, "Stop, once, with your friends at the [deserted] abode." And I said, "What have I to do with this?"

Pass around the cup at the loss of one's beloved; many a time have I drunk at the absence of my beloved and at the dis-tress of losing one's family.

No cup reached me but that I drank it, but that I watered the earth with a cup of tears.

CXXXIV

Salīm's guests [sit] at ease amid drink and meat which is not [denied] them,

While 'Amr and his guest both spend the night awake—'Amr surfeited, and the guest hungry.

CXXXV

We brought him to intercede for [our] need; yet he himself needed an intercessor for [his own] admission.

CXXXVI

When the stranger stops at Homs, you see difficult obstacles put before him.

They are extolled because of the noble qualities of 'Īsā's family, who raised them to the rank of mountains.

There, the profligate wears silk, while 'Īsā is [in their eyes] as rotten garments.

A mule's penis directed itself to the buttock of the Ash'ath; another found its way into the harem of Abū Sanā'.

Thus he is no creator of nobility. Rather, he squanders it, for his name is Abū Dayā'.

CXXXVII

They only accept thanks for favors which are found praiseworthy.

CXXXVIII

O Abū Makhlid! we were bound by love; our passions and hearts were as one.

You, who do not protect me, I protected with love. And I was anxious lest I cause you pain.

After you turned away, you made me dis-trust my heart and I feared everyone.

You adulterated our love until its roots crumbled; you neglected [our] tie so that it split apart.

You had lodged in my heart a treasure of love which, for a long time, remained inaccessible.

Do not upbraid me; I have no desire for you. You are torn to pieces, and I find no patch for you.

Consider yourself my right hand which, hav-ing become gangrened, I have cut off. I suffered my heart to bear its loss, and it has taken courage.

CXXXIX

My eyes fixed on lightning, extinguished, then blinding—lightning whose course is as the eye's bloodspot;

. . . .

CXXXIII. See Wright, II, 150, for con-struction: *mā lī wa lī.*

CXXXVI. See Wright, II, 112; 132, for construction of *huwa minnī* with accusative.

CXXXVIII. Satirizes the poet Muslim b. al-Walīd. Verses 4-7 are translated in Ibn Halli-kān, Slane, I, 508, and Hammer, IV, 539. See poems CXLII, CLXX, and CLXXV.

Whose flash, stretching from Khaffān, settled the cares of my heart and disappeared.

CXL

Since the past has passed, be men of wit!
And go on. Today we will make merry, for I will sell my boot.

CXLI

O Abū Dulaf! by your hand, God has well distributed most of his gifts.
Never have His two [recording angels] written "No" in His Book, though "No" is written in other books.
Abū Dulaf gave while the wind blew. And though it stopped, he did not stop [giving].
What does an old man do with a virgin who can be likened to a walnut between the jaws of a toothless dotard?
If he wishes to break it with his teeth, it breaks his gums; yet its breaking is a joy for one dying of passion.

CXLII

[Its author is one] who has in his harem a thousand excrescences which are higher than the idol Manāf.

CXLIII

You promised [me] the shoe, but you reneged. It is as though you desire insult and blame.
If you do not give me a sh̲oe, then be that which results when the letter after the "Nun" is mispronounced [*i.e.*, a bastard].

CXLIV

I rammed [my] satire down the vile man's throat. And when he tasted it, he loathed its vileness.

CXLV

I wonder at Ibn al-Husain's fireship, for it travels without sinking.
It is between two seas: one beneath her and another above her.
It is a greater wonder that her planks, touched by his hand, do not grow leaves.

CXLVI

The man who bestows gifts [only] when another intercedes with him, and expects my thanks, is indeed stupid.
Thank him who intercedes for your needs, for he guards you from displeasure while he himself is disgraced.

CXLVII

An ass seeing a lion became frightened, so that it turned away braying.

CXLVIII

With your deceptive promises you placed me in a surging, heaving sea.
When you awaited the foe—your decline having become conspicuous as the piebald horse—
You swore that your love for me was pure and that your tie to me was unbreakable.
You thought God's earth too narrow for me, whereas it is not;
You regarded me as the vile mushroom and tread me under foot.

CXL. Translated in K. *Baghdād*, p. 137.

CXLI. Praises Abū Dulaf al-Qāsim b. 'Īsā b. Idrīs al-'Ijlī, d. 225/840-41, general of al-Ma'mūn and al-Mu'tasim. Verses 1-3 are translated in Ibn Hallikān, Slane, II, 504.

CXLIII. Pun is achieved by changing *n'l* (shoe) to *nghl* (bastard) through the addition of one diacritical point.

CXLV. Attributed in Ibn Hallikān, Slane, I, 651, to Muqaddis b. Saifī and addressed to Tāhir b. al-Husain. The poem is translated in Ibn Hallikān, Slane, I, 651, and in Hammer IV, 548.

Out of hatred you set me up as a target, and the foe cast their eyes upon me.
All this for no crime other than my trusting you, when you said, "Trust me,"
And for a love which my soul inclined to you without reproach or flattery.
If I ever ask you to fulfill my need, fasten therewith the bolt to the lock.
Our friendship stands on a crumbling edge which is undermined by water. Therefore, sell it as one sells wornout garments;
Prepare for me manacles and a pillory, and bind my hands to my neck.
I spared you from what you would not like. [Therefore] let me be gone on the paths of the land.
Moreover, throw me in a dark pit if, after today, I return amongst the fools.
How long, how wide is the world! And what a wonderful guide am I for the paths of travel!

CXLIX

He is an enemy traveling in the guise of a friend; he shares your morning and evening meals.
He has two faces: his external one is that of a cousin; his hidden one is that of a son of an old adulteress.
Outwardly he rejoices you, while secretly he wrongs you. So [behave] the sons of the road.

CL

Knowledge, judgment, and hoariness of crown have wiped away the bloom of the comely youth.
Holding office in an auspicious government was the greatest impediment to frivolity.
Thus, I do not travel now, day or night, with the haughtiness of the beloved nor with the humiliation of the lover.
Ibn Shiklah and his party have overrun Irāq, and every heedless fool runs to [join] him.
If Ibrāhīm is entrusted with the caliphate, then it befits Mukhāriq after him;
Likewise it befits Zulzul and Māriq.
That cannot be; nor can it happen that one profligate receive the caliphate from another profligate.

CLI

Do you see Time making us happy by letting us meet and by uniting the lover with his beloved?

CLII

I saw before me a gazelle showing her girdle.
She was short, stout, and rolled in her gait as a ball.
When her forearm is exposed, it seems like the end of a spoon.
She pencils her eyebrows with ink and ties a pillow to her buttock.
The nostrils of her flattened nose are small as the fruit of the pistachio tree.
One of her breasts is like an acorn; the other is like a filled waterskin.
Her chest, above which rattles her necklace, is thin and bony.
When she shows her gums, you think them the wormlike marks on a galled leg.

CLIII

In one year you have robbed the tribe of 'Ijl of two pudendas. You have corrupted them without repairing your lineage.

. . . .

CXLVIII. Verses 4-5, 9, 11, 14, are translated in Hammer, IV, 547; see Kazimirski, II, 261, and Lane, p. 2428, for *fāqa bi qarqarah* derivation.

CXLIX. Attributed to Abū Sa'd in *Ag.*, XVIII, 54.

CL. Verses 4-7 are translated in Ibn Hallikān, Slane, I, 18. Mukhāriq, Zulzul, and Māriq were singers of the time. Ath-Tha'ālibī and Ibn ash-Shajarī cite verse 5 as an example of ***kināyah*** (*Fiqh*, p. 323; Ibn Saj., *Amālī*, I, 59).

If you proposed marriage to Tauq and his family, their acceptance would not add to your merit.
Have intercourse with whomever you desire and procure whatever lineage you wish. For, as regards lineage, you are the son of Ziryāb.
If God wished to humiliate a people who married you for your gold,
This necessitated His joining nab' wood to your willow or gharab tree.
If you kept silent and did not propose to pure Arabs, you would not be caught in this self-inflicted suffering.
And if you counted the Arab families who would be pleased with your proposals, you would find Fazārah of 'Ukl amongst them.

CLIV

This is a present from a servant whom you have clothed in rich garments. Accept, therefore, what is easily given.

CLV

Where is youth? Where did it depart? No! where can it be sought? No! it has perished.
Do not be surprised, O Salmā, at a man who cries while the hoariness of his hair laughs.
O Salmā! there is no defect in hoariness, which spares neither rabble nor king.
He resisted the seduction of loving a woman [*lit.* moon], the path to whom he found common to all.
Seeking her, he turned from another; for love, he trod before her prickly thistles.
O would that I knew how you, my two friends, fare this day when my blood is shed!
Do not punish anyone for my suffering, for my heart and eye were accomplices [in forfeiting my life].

CLVI

The face of Time laughs because al-Ma'mūn, the Hāshimite, restored Fadak [to the 'Alids].

CLVII

Who will convey to the Imām of Guidance a verse revealing a secret?
This is [condition of] the "Wing of the Muslims" which the appointment of the weaver has clipped.
The mules of the mail service are bringing prostitutes to Ibn Wahb.

CLVIII

What will I say to my companions when I come, emptyhanded, from the generous bestower of gifts?
If I said, "He gave," I would be lying. If I said, "The Emīr was niggardly," it would be unseemly.
You are too famous for nobility for me to attribute to you what you did not do.
Choose, therefore, what I shall say. For, though I am not asked, I have to inform them.

CLIX

Her inner nature is disposed to generosity; her external countenance, to kisses.

. . . .

CLV. Verses 1, 2, 6, 7, are translated in Hammer, IV, 541, 549. Verses 2, 6-7, are translated *ibid.*, 550. Verse 2 was plagiarized, according to al-Asma'ī, from al-Husain b. al-Mutair (Ag., XVIII, 3), and according to Abū Hiffān, from Muslim b. al-Walīd. However, Abū Hiffān regards Di'bil's verse as the more excellent (Ag., XVIII, 32). Qudāmah b. Ja'far cites verse 2 as an example of the figure *takāfu'* (*Naqd*, p. 86). Cf. *Qānūn*, p. 436, where the same verse is cited as an example of the figure *tibāq*. *Literary Theory*, p. 37, note 287, points out that the two figures are the same. See Lane, 132, for usage of *ayyah*.

CLVII. The term *Janāh al-Muslimīn* refers to the mail service (*al-Barīd*).

CLVIII. Addressed to 'Abd Allāh b. Tāhir.

CLX

The people of Qumm were annihilated and dwindled away; where they had settled now settles burnt debris.
In destitution, they extolled generosity. But in prosperity, they became sullen.

CLXI

Did you not see the calamity [wrought by Time] upon the family of Barmak and Ibn Nahīk? [Did you not see] the vicissitudes of past ages?
They were a family planted and secure as the palm tree, but they were cut down as herbs.

CLXII

Do you close an empty pot, lest one eat thereof?
This [is the] pot you safeguard! Why a lock on a privy?
But you are niggardly with everything, even with your excrement.

CLXIII

O Muttalib, you will find sweet the poison of the viper and will look forward to death.
If I am cured of you, you will be reviled; if I am freed from you, what will you do?
If you come to Irāq, pages, which Di'bil has chosen, will greet you in
An embellished book between whose folds are insults which do not disappear.
You have humbled men, but what harm came to them? You attempted to ennoble a people, [but] they were not ennobled.
Which one of them is the ornament among the crowd? Is it 'Atiyyah, Sālih the squint eyed,
The eggplant seller, or 'Āmir the keeper of the singing pigeons?
Egypt has loaded you with insults, and Mosul spits in your face.
On the day the heroes meet, you will sip insults which, in comparison, make the colocynth sweet.
While ends of lances shook in the bodies of our youth, you, riding hard, escaped.
When you were the commander of battle, their lot was death.
On the morning of encounter, you supplied the heads; your foe, the sword.
Routed, on the day of clamor, your battle cry is "Hasten! hasten!"
The defeats of you, the inexperienced, are famous; whoever shoots an arrow therein hits the mark.
It is your nature that, when war rages, the first to escape is found between the two of you.
You are last when battle is joined, but first [to flee] when routed.

CLXIV

O possessor of two right hands and two titles; O you in whom is beneficence and bestowing of favors!
Are you pleased that one such as I stand, forsaken and humiliated, at your door?
From among all that one hopes for, including love and benefits,
I would prefer to be greeted amongst the five or six [you notice] when you are surrounded by company.
From none but you would I be happy to receive but that! Is that what pleases a wise man?
If you are occupied with business, then [know that] I, too, am busied.
Peace be with you, for I am a man who departs when a land becomes too constrained for him.

CLXI. Translated in Mas'ūdī, VI, 405.
CLXIII. Verses 5, 8, 13, 16, are translated in Hammer, IV, 544. This poem is cited in Azdī, p. 96, as an example of *tamlīt*.
CLXIV. Translated in Hammer, IV, 547-48.

CLXV

How can I please my guest, who eats little
  and is annoyed by my stratagems?
I fear that my continued saying "Eat" will
  abash him, whereas if I desist, he will
  leave [thinking] me niggardly.

CLXVI

When she saw hoariness in my hair, she
  turned away with the courtesy of one
  departing on a journey.
I humbly sought union with her, but hoariness winked at her not to.

CLXVII

I counsel and give sincere advice to Fadl
  when I say, directing my words to him,
"Verily, there is a lesson in the affair of Fadl
  ibn Sahl, if Fadl ibn Marwān takes
  warning";
"Moreover, there is an admonition in the
  affair of Fadl ibn Yahyā, if he reflects
  thereon."
Therefore, remain composed when tried by
  an event, and do not forgo doing good
  and the taking of benefits.
For you have become a guardian to the government, and have taken the place of the
  three Fadls.
And I have not seen previously verses of an
  excellent poem whose entire rhyme is
  "Fadl."
Recited, no defect is [found] among them;
  except that my excellent advice is wasted.

CLXVIII

Your spear rose with happiness—a spear to
  which is tied the standard of auspicious
  kingdom.
It quivers above the two rows [of camels] as
  though it were taking flight—[as though]
  the wings of a falcon were severed for it.
The miser gains his honor by deception, for
  it [is actually gained] by the generosity
  of your hands and smiling countenance.
If he but knew that your bestowing is a
  swift [river] from which no small streams
  flow!

CLXIX

God knows that nothing rejoices me like
  the guest's coming for lodging.
I so prolong my welcome that you regard
  me as his guest and him as the owner
  of the house.

CLXX

O strutter, tell me, how do you compare
  with a man? For you are neither known
  or unknown.
As for satirizing you, your honor is beneath
  it; as for praising you, it would be too
  much.
Go. You are devoid of honor. You glorified
  in it, but you are humbled.

CLXXI

[She is] ugly, so wide-mouthed that laughter
  reveals her liver; she is hook-nosed [when
  viewed] from the side; wide-eyed from
  the front.
She has a mouth whose corners meet at the
  nape of the neck. It is as if her lips were
  cut from an elephant.

CLXXII

He is ruled by the desire of anyone who
  petitions him.

. . . .

CLXVI. Praised by 'Alī b. al-Jahm (Ibn 'Asāk., *Tar.*, V, 230).

CLXVII. Addressed to al-Fadl b. Marwān. Al-Fadl b. Sahl, d. 203/818, was vizier of al-Ma'mūn. See Ibn Hallikān, Slane, II, 475. Al-Fadl b. Yahyā al-Barmakī, d. 192-93/808.

CLXVIII. Translated in Hammer, IV, 548.

CLXXIII

Black eyebrows [extending] like ropes to beards which resemble feedbags.
Countenances which are sullen, coarse, without beauty and elegance.

CLXXIV

I asked him regarding his father, and he said, "Dīnār is my uncle."
I replied, "Who is Dīnār?" And he said, "The governor of al-Jibāl."

CLXXV

Do not pay any attention to Ibn Walīd, for he will bore you after three days.
Through his friendship is of long standing, it becomes as sun annulled by shade.

CLXXVI

When you conquer them, give them poison to drink; [but now] mix honey for them with your tongue.

CLXXVII

You sent me a sacrificed ewe—and it was fitting that you do so—
But it was defective as though you pastured her on rue.
And if God accepted her as an offering, then Glory be to your Lord! for how equitable is He?

CLXXVIII

The mutual bestowing of gifts gives birth to union in the hearts of men.
[It] implants love and passion in the mind and clothes them, when they appear, in elegance.

CLXXIX

They announced my death. But it is an act of him who rejoices at my misfortune and of a foe mortally wounded [by my satire].
They hold that if a poet experiences evil, his poetry dies. Far from it! The lifespan of a poem is long.
I shall finish with a verse which people will praise—a verse which will have many bearers among the Transmitters:
The bad poem dies before its author, but the excellent one lives, though its author dies.

CLXXX

We thank the caliph for supplying Ibn abī Khālid with food.
Sending him food, he prevented his harming other Muslims.
He used to divide his affairs, but [now] he has taken his affair on himself.

CLXXXI

You began with good actions, then doubled, tripled, and quadrupled with continuous benefits and generosities.
You facilitated my affairs, attended to my needs, thwarted my reviler, and presented me with favors.
Thus if we requite [him] fully, he was entitled to our love. But if we fall short, our love is not to be doubted.

CLXXXII

Your farewell is like the departure of life; your absence is like the absence of rain.
Peace be with you! From how many of

. . . .

CLXXIII. Satirizes Nasr b. Mansūr b. Bassām, d. 227/841, controller of land taxes under al-Fadl b. Marwān. He was the grandfather of the poet al-Bassāmī. See Marin, p. 19.

CLXXVI. Translated in Hammer, IV, 548.

CLXXX. Verses 1-3 are translated in K. *Baghdād*, p. 103, and verses 1-2 in Jarrett, p. 341.

your fulfilled promises and kindnesses do I ruefully separate myself?

CLXXXIII

Tāhir has left us three remarkable [things] which render the mind light-witted:
Three brothers, of one father and mother, claim different origins.
One says, "My people is Quraish"; this is refuted by clients and those of pure stock.
Another traces his genealogy to Khuzāʻah [though it is] a clientship old and well known.
The third inclines to [claim] the family of Chosroe, but he is regarded as a foreigner.
Their genealogies have swarmed over us; [in fact], however, each of them is a bastard.

CLXXXIV

O marvel at a fine poet who traces his ancestry to Tayy!
I came upon him reviling, out of ignorance, my mother. And, paying him no mind,
I said, "Bravo! As far as I know, his mother is noble and pure."
And, by God, I lied regarding his mother as he lied regarding mine.

CLXXXV

O come buy from me the kings of Mukharrim. I will sell al-Hasan and the two sons of Rajā' for a dirham.
Moreover, I will throw Rajā' into the bargain and will offer Dīnār without any regret.
Though all of them charge me with vices, yet Yahyā ibn Aktham cannot charge me with his.

CLXXXVI

When she dyes her palm, it seems as the bloody claw of a falcon.

CLXXXVII

All people, joyful and grieved, exert themselves to satisfy his needs.
Mālik spends his day busy with his genealogy, repairing ruins beyond repair.
He constructs, between Tauq and ʻAmr ibn Kulthum, empty, ruined houses.

CLXXXVIII

Tell the Imām of the Family of Muhammad what he who defends and is compassionate toward you says:
"You denied showing favor to Sālih ibn ʻAtiyyah, the Cupper."
Favors in his case are not beneficial; they are the detriment of Islām.
[Therefore], beat the foe's army with his face—a face which is an army of plague and pleurisy.

CLXXXIX

Rather, they are [Satan's] suggestions, for he neither gives nor refuses from avarice or nobility.

CXC

He is a singer who bequeaths anxiety to his companions,
So that he who is deaf is best off.

CXCI

What he spends of his wealth he regards as gain; what he saves, as loss.

CXCII

If you balance the deliberate, [swift] generosity of Talhah at-Talhāt with the nig-

. . . .

CLXXXII. Regarded as an imitation of a verse by al-Qutāmī (Ibn ʻAsāk., *Tar.* V. 230). See Qutāmī, p. 7.

CLXXXIV. Satirizes the poet Abū Tammām.

gardliness of Muttalib, and then judge [between them],
You will pronounce Khuzā'ah devoid of avarice and nobility, for you will perceive neither quality.

CXCIII

Prudence did not leave a track of the man whose saddle came to rest, during the night, at Aswān.
I alighted at a place which the eye cannot reach. [Even] the specter [undertaking such a journey] would fail to attain it.

CXCIV

Believe his oath when, with effort, he says, "No, by the round cake!" For that shows its good faith.
It would surprise me, if his zeal for cakes were [equaled by his zeal] for his harem.
If you want to make him anxious, assault his bread, for it is his flesh and blood.

CXCV

Preserve your love for Abū Muqātil, when you eat his food.
[To eat] a piece of bread is [to eat] one of his bones.
Thus you see him frightened in his sleep, lest a guest alight.
So when you pass his house, conceal your bread from his servant.

CXCVI

Whoever honors ar-Raqāshī sends him the utmost [of his desire];
[Yet] he receives, in exchange for his generosity and compassion, the accusation that his brothers violate his harem.

CXCVII

At times you suppose him neglectful of generosity. But how well does he know what he is doing!

CXCVIII

A soft, green, variegated meadow wherein blossom all sorts of flowers.
When the winds dally with it, it laughs and arches as the bending drinker.
My companions compared its blossoms with the silk garment of Chosroe and the turban of Yemen.
And I said, "You are far off. It compares with the courtyard of al-Hasan,"
A nobleman who regards money only for the giving, the treasury only for the acquiring of glory.

CXCIX

When they separated, after concealing him in a vile grave, I said to the vile [person] interred:
"Go to the Fire and to chastisement, for your character is that of the Devil.
"You did not die until you insured the investiture of one who [likewise] will harm Muslims and Religion."

CC

O my two friends of Ka'b, help your brother in his adversity, for the nobleman is he who helps.
Do not become miserly as Ibn Qaz'ah, who is grieved for fear that one may expect his generosity.
If you go to him after a few days delay, he closes his door. Thus you meet him only if you await him in hiding.

. . . .

CXCIII. Translated in Ibn Hallikān, Slane, III, 178. Verse 2 is translated in Hammer, IV, 542. Verse 2 was imitated by Abū'l-'Alā' al-Ma'arrī (Wāhidī, p. 24).

CXCV. Verses 1-3 are translated in Ibn Hallikān, Slane, IV, 74, and are attributed to Abū Muhammad al-Yazīdī.

CC. Verses 1-2 are translated in *Literary Theory*, p. 45, where Ibn Qaz'ah is identified with Abū' l-Mughīrah 'Ubaid Allāh b. Qaz'ah, brother of al-Malawī, a follower of Ibrāhīm an-Nazzām, the Mu'tazilite theologian, d. between 835 and 845 (note 352).

CCI

Unwillingly, I left Ahmad, over whom was placed a heavy stone building.
I lodged him in a poorly furnished house; yet, in spite of myself, I am niggardly thereof.
Were it not for the consolation of the Prophet and his Family, tears from my eye would pour over him.
He is my soul. But near it, in the interior of my heart, lies hidden the Family of Muhammad.
The inheritance of the Prophet has injured them, and death has shared their inheritance.
The wolves of the Umayyah have destroyed them; poverty and barrenness advance uninterruptedly towards them.
The Banū 'Abbās have damaged the Faith, so that a tyrant and one whose belief is suspect pass judgment.
They named one of their caliphs Rashīd (*i.e.*, the rightly guided), yet he was not rightly guided. Likewise, they bear the names of al-Ma'mūn and al-Amīn.
From their guidance did not result beneficent rule, nor were those charged with security pious.
Their rightly guided one leads [others] into error. And his two children [al-Ma'mūn and al-Amīn], to the former occur misfortunes, and before the latter, excesses.
O remote grave at Tūs, may the night clouds pour forth rain upon you.
I do not know whether you were poisoned by drink, and I weep over you, or whether [you died] from natural causes, which would make your death easier to bear.
Whether I say, "Drink or natural death," he [still] deserves my tears.
O what a wonder! They call you ar-Ridā (*i.e.*, the one with whom one is pleased), whereas stern looks and frowns greet you.
Do you wonder at fools who choose different guideposts of God's religion, which is, however, clear beyond doubt?
Through your favor, a sign regarding them has reached me. But what is certain here?

CCII

O my two friends, what can I expect tomorrow from a man who broke off with me today when he is powerful?
Verily is he a miser who is niggardly with such speech as would close the breach [of my need].

CCIII

Were it not for Huwayy of the house of Lihyān, the penis of the wornout stranger would not have risen.
In his drawers is an inkwell into which those far and near [dip their] cotton.

CCIV

You have presented him with a jaded, crippled [hackney], which is fit neither for riding nor for sale.
You mounted a poet on a cripple; he will repay you with a crippling poem.
O Fadl, [beware of] loss and blame. What did you hope to obtain with this deceit?

CCV

In happiness, the one most worthy of your munificence is he who consoled you in grief.
In comfort, the noble remember those who frequented them in [their] crude dwellings.

. . . .

CCI. Mourns 'Alī ar-Ridā and his son Ahmad.

CCII. Attributed in *Ag.* to Di'bil's father, 'Alī.

CCIII. Satirizes Huwayy b. 'Amr as-Siksikī. See *Waraqah*, p. 87, where reference is made to 'Amr b. Huwayy as-Siksikī.

CCIV. Addressed to Yahyā b. Khāqān. He was the father of 'Ubaid Allāh, vizier of al-Mutawakkil. See Ibn al-Athīr, VII, 27.

CCVI

I offered to men for sale a panegyric not worth their money—abominable, repugnant, and ineloquent.
Thus, I did not escape from them but as the leg of the gnat moves from the jar of milk.

CCVII

I spent the night with a band of the Banū Makhzūm in a place where the spade would not desire [to dig] the mud.

CCVIII

O what a curious report is warbled in the two horizons!
O 'Ijl, you became affiliated with Ibn abī Du'ād, without expecting that he would acquire two [women].
Desiring extreme haste, they sold you cheaply, hastily, for credit,
The adulterated goods of one who lost his capital—goods which are sold for date stones.
One could question who was careless [in the transaction], if they erred with one [woman].
But the pairing of the two [women] points to the corruption of both sides.
May God curse money [earned] by the pudenda of a woman! even [money earned] through marriage to Dhū Ru'ain.
When he acquires new wealth and struts in his garments,
He assumes a surname and traces his origin to Abū Du'ād. However, his real name is the son of two adulterers.
Therefore, send him back to Faraj, his father, and to Dhiryāb—the vilest parents.

CCIX

Amongst monstrosities, I saw two judges who are the talk of the East and the West.
They share the same degree of blindness as they share the cases of the two regions.
And you would suppose that the one, shaking his head examining inheritances and debts,
Were covered with a wine cask whose tap, consisting of a single eye, were open.
Indeed, Yahyā's death is an omen of the times, since the cases are tried by two blind [judges].

CCX

O you who are generous with your tongue [but] not in deed, would that the generosity of your palm were like that of your tongue!
You have repeatedly slapped the eye of Mihrān; fear, therefore, the Lord.
You have rendered him blind in one eye. Leave him the other, and do not let him ramble among the blind.

CCXI

Were I afflicted by a Hāshimite whose maternal uncles are the Banū 'Abd al-Madān,
I would have borne his hatred. But come and see who plagues me.

CCXII

They were unable to listen, but we listened and endured the grinding of teeth;
For the sound of the guest's mastication is to me more beautiful than the tune of the songstress with her lute.

CCXIII

O lady in the litter, desist from reproaching [me], [for] the past forty years provide you with sufficient blame.

. . . .

CCVIII. Cf. *Mu'jam*, p. 239, for usage of Dhū Ru'ain in a poem of 'Amr b. abī 'l-Habar. See also Nicholson, p. 25, for story of Dhū Ru'ain and the Yemenite king 'Amr.

CCX. Translated in Hammer, IV, 547.

Do not the events of the nights, which render white the forelocks and the plaits, grieve you?
Is the inexperienced one ashamed of the leaders of my people? Madīnah was [also] ashamed of us.
And if the People of Israel are of you, and you boast of the Persians,
Do not forget those who were transformed into swine and despised apes.
At 'Ailah and at the (Persian) Gulf are their ancient, unerased traces.
Al-Kumait sought revenge, but we are satirized for [offering] our help!
Nizār knew well that my people boast of their aid to prophecy—
A people who left written [records] at the gates of Marv and China;
Who named Samarqand for Shamr and settled there the inhabitants of Tubbat;
And who melted the idol of the West [standing] above the sand, making its [metal] flow as [the water] of a ship's channel.

CCXIV

God disgraces them, helps you against them, and heals the hearts of a believing people.

CCXV

My most beloved possession and treasure are the singers who, though modest,
Are mindful of my every lament over encampment and hoariness.

CCXVI

We killed with the noble al-Qasrī their al-Walīd, the Prince of the Believers.
And for Yazīd we killed Marwān. That is our judgment on tyrants!
And with our Ibn Simt we killed al-Amīn Muhammad ibn Hārūn.
Everyone [else] kills rabble; we make the killing of caliphs [a part of] our religion.

CCXVII

I love the hoariness which visits me as much as I love the guest stopping [at my door].

CCXVIII

O for days spent with Muttalib—days so well watered that they were a meadow and a paradise!
All generosity, except yours, is constraint; I am pleased with no one but you.
You have repaired me with your generosity. No, you have corrupted me, for you left me displeased with the benefits [of others].

CCXIX

Abū Sa'd in his jesting,
Frailty of mind, faith, and intellect,
Continually prostrates himself
To a viper gliding in his behind.
And he plants his neighbor's cucumber in his fig (*i.e.*, he practices sodomy).

CCXX

O Khuzā'ah, when one boasts, be silent and put your hands over your mouths.

. . . .

CCXIII. Di'bil's rejoinder to the famous poem of al-Kumait b. Zaid, d. 126/743. See Mas'ūdī, VI, 35-46. Verses 1-8 are translated in Mas'ūdī, VI, 44-45. Verse 1 is translated in Margoliouth, p. 193. See *Abhandlungen*, pp. 12-14, for a discussion of the use of *za'īnah* in all types of poetic motifs.

CCXIV. Highly favored for matching a similar verse of Abū Nuwās (Ibn al-Mu'tazz, *Tab.*, p. 94).

CCXVI. Al-Qasrī is Khālid b. 'Abd Allāh b. Yazīd; he was governor of Kūfah in 737 A.D. Al-Walīd is al-Walīd b. Yazīd b. 'Abd al-Malik, d. 744; Marwān is Marwān b. Muhammad b. Marwān, d. 750; Yazīd is Yazīd b. al-Walīd b. 'Abd al-Malik, d. 744.

CCXVIII. Praises al-Muttalib b. 'Abd Allāh b. Mālik. The verses are translated in Ibn Hallikān, Slane I, 509; *Ahbār*, p. 105; Hammer, IV, 539.

You sew—when it is not time for mending
—and rend of the orifices of buttocks.
Boast only of sodomy. For, when one boasts,
your boast is of buttocks.

CCXXI

Until calamity overtook her, Baghdād was
the home of kings.
Gone is the joy of a government, which was
transferred to another land.
He who sees Sāmmarā is not rejoiced. Nay!
she is a sorrow for whoever sees her.
May my Lord hasten her shame and the
humiliation of him who built her!

CCXXII

Khuzā'ah filled the ampleness of the earth,
but the passage of Time has shorn her
of her adherents.
Abū Qāsim is buried in Balqa'ah, and the
winds blow its dust over him.
They blow, knowing there is no blowing in
him—though when he vied with them,
they sometimes became weary.
He showed hospitality to the Fates when
they alighted at his abode, for, in days
gone by, he used to receive them as his
guests.

CCXXIII

You reanimate spears for hurling—spears
which came thirsty to the pool of Fate.
If people adorn their swords with silver,
you return your swords adorned with the
hearts [of the foe].
The report of your endeavors does not
perish. Though the remembrance of
others ceases, the [renown of your] efforts
endures.

CCXXIV

When I saw the sword fall upon Ja'far and
the caliph's herald call out Yahyā's [fate],
I lamented the world, and I became certain
that the nobleman's end is that he, one
day, abandon this world.

CCXXV

He is as their prey, which they chase away
with disgrace;
They wrote the deed against him, and he
became a sign among men.
If he approaches, they say, "Rubbish comes."

CCXXVI

I fear not the penalty [given to] one who
says that your mother is an adulteress.
O adulterer son of an adulterer who is the
son of an adulterer [born] of an adulteress!
You are traced back to adultery over all the
past years,
And you will be so traced in the years to
come.

CCXXVII

In the remotest and nearest regions of the
earth, I asked regarding you, O son of
Mālik!
But no one knew a genealogy for you until
I said, "The sons of the adulteress."
Then they replied: "Forgo the house on the
right! There! That is their house—the
second one."

CCXXVIII

Sitting with him, you gave him the seat of
honor [and] leaned on him for protection;
Traveling with him, you made him precede

CCXX. Attributed in *Waraqah* to Razīn al-'Arūdī.

CCXXII. Praised by al-Mubarrad (*Ag.*, XVIII, 34).

CCXXIII. Bewails the fate of Ja'far b. Yahyā al-Barmakī, who in 803 was killed by order of the caliph Hārūn.

CCXXVII. Verses 1-2 are translated in Hammer, IV, 543.

while remaining behind with her who
  awaits [him];
When you behaved gently toward him, you
  found him easygoing and secure;
When you became his intimate, you found
  him proud, shrewd, and vehement in his
  opinions.
Therefore, praise God for his friendship
  and ask Him for his good health.

CCXXIX

I love you with a love which, were it con-
  tained by your namesake, the high, strong
  mountain Salmā, . . .

CCXXVIII. Praises Mu'ādh b. Sa'īd al-Hamīrī.

4

THE POET AS A CRITIC

THE SECOND CENTURY of Islām, particularly after the establishment of the ʿAbbāsid caliphate in 132/750, had as a leading intellectual and literary activity the collecting, sifting, and examining by Muslim scholars of the works of Arabic poets. Attention first was centered on the tribal *Dīwāns*, which consisted of poems, by one author or by several, together with anecdotes of the occasions which prompted them. As the scholars began to lose interest in the tribal life of the desert, regard for the tribal *Dīwāns* declined and became chiefly confined to the members of the particular tribe. The compilers of poetry then selected out of these works the pieces which had won wider recognition and which, because of their merit and historical interest, might become valued by society at large. Such anthologies, in which were gathered the best specimens of the tribal poetry, together with the definitive editions of the *Dīwāns* of the Master Poets (*Fuhūl*), contributed to the eventual oblivion of the tribal *Dīwāns*, of which only the *Dīwān* of the Hudhailites has survived.[1]

Along with the compilation of anthologies, Muslim scholars of the second and third centuries of Islām began composing works which dealt with the lives as well as the work of poets. These studies can be divided into works which treat only the life and poetry of a single poet, those which deal with a class of poets, and those which examine the poets of a region or of a tribe. Prior to and contemporaneous with the *Book of Classes* of Ibn Saʿd (d. 230/845), appeared a series of "class" (*tabaqāt*) works, most of which have not survived.[2] In general, these have as their titles one of the following: "the accounts of the poets (*Akhbār ash-Shuʿarāʾ*)," "the classes of the poets (*Tabaqāt ash-Shuʿarāʾ*)," "the book of poets (*Kitāb ash-Shuʿarāʾ*)," or "the book of poetry and the poets (*Kitāb ash-Shiʿr wa'sh-Shuʿarāʾ*)." They contain little biographical information. Usually only the poet's name, origin, genealogy, and period —rarely the dates of his birth and death— are given. Furthermore, they show little concern with the development of the poet's literary and intellectual career.[3] Despite this biographical sparseness, the notices regarding the poets are rich in anecdotes, especially stories which involve the selections chosen by the author.

The value of these works to modern scholarship lies in the uniqueness of the texts which they preserve, for these "class books" laid the foundation for all later essays in literary history, which attained its perfection in the *Kitāb al-Aghānī*. They provide also the basis for textual comparison with later compilations and for the study of the formation of the classical ideal of the ninth century. Similarly, they are the precursors of the later, more systematic treatment of Arabic rhetoric and aesthetics, and they reflect the literary conflict between the ancients and the moderns.[4] Yet only three have survived: *Tabaqāt ash-Shuʿarāʾ* of al-Jumahī (d. 230/845), *Kitāb ash-Shiʿr* of Ibn Qutaibah (d. 276/889), and *Tabaqāt ash-Shuʿarāʾ al-Muhdathīn* of Ibn al-Muʿtazz

(d. 296/908). Di'bil's *Book of the Poets,* of which a reconstruction has been attempted below on the basis of the material found in extant literary sources, falls between the works of al-Jumahī and Ibn Qutaibah, and so invites comparison with them.

The *Tabaqāt* of al-Jumahī has a somewhat cursory and digressive introduction, which begins with a discussion of poetic criticism (pages 3-4), the gist of which can be stated as follows: To poetry are peculiar a certain craft and skill, which are comprehended by the specialist of this branch of knowledge just as other arts are comprehended by their specialists; thus the value of gems is not known by their description and weight but rather by the inspection by the jeweler; likewise, two horses or two slaves, whose descriptions are similar and who have externally the same virtues, can only be distinguished by the skilled trader; moreover, should a nonexpert try to oppose the decision of the experts and assert that he approves of a certain piece of poetry irrespective of the experts' opinion, he would be in the position of one who approves of coins which the money changer deems counterfeit. Next follows a brief passage on the reliability and unreliability of the transmitters of poetry (page 4), and then an essay on the beginnings of the Arabic language (page 5). Next the founders of Arabic linguistics and their followers are treated in some detail (pages 6-7). The poet al-Farazdaq (d. 110/728) and his dealings with the philologian Ibn abī Ishāq then come in for discussion,[5] concluding with the philological criticism of poetic errors (pages 8-9). At this point al-Jumahī gives the scheme for the organization of his text. He divides the Master Poets into two major groups: those of the Jāhiliyyah and those of Islām. Each division comprises ten classes, with each class containing four poets. For each poet, al-Jumahī quotes "evidentiary" verses (*hujjah*), cited as models of correct Arabic (pages 9-10). Poetry in the Jāhiliyyah was the storehouse of the Arabs' knowledge. With Islām and the death of many poets in the Muslim conquests, much of this poetry was lost; what remained was but a small fraction of what had existed. To make up for this loss, poetry was therefore attributed to poets like Tarafah and 'Abīd (pages 10-11). Al-Jumahī then discusses the origin of Arabic poetry, giving examples of old poetry, naming the first poet to compose a *qasīdah,* and illustrating the transfer of preeminence in poetry from poets of one tribe to those of other tribes during the Jāhiliyyah (pages 11-13). He deals with the problem of the forging of poetry by later transmitters (*rāwīs*) and the difficulty of its discovery if this had been done by Bedouin Rāwīs, citing the example of Hammād ar-Rāwiyah (pages 14-15). Lastly, the scheme for the organization of the *Tabaqāt* is repeated (page 15). Although they are not listed in the introduction, between the two major divisions of Jāhiliyyah and Islamic poets appear sections on the elegiac poets; the poets of the Arabian cities and regions of Madīnah, Makkah, at-Tā'if, and al-Bahrain; and the Jewish poets of Madīnah.

It is quite apparent that at this stage—and this was still true for the later Ibn Qutaibah—criticism of poetry was largely subjective. The classification of the poets, opinions on their relative standing in a given genre, and appreciations of random individual lines out of context did not offer a unified critical theory based upon aesthetic principles.[6]

. . . .

[1] *Dīwāns,* p. 332-33.

[2] See Ibn al-Mu'tazz, *Tab.,* p. XVIII, and Bräu, pp. 12-15, for a list of such works.

[3] Ibn al-Mu'tazz, *Tab.,* p. XVIII; Gaudefroy-Demombynes, pp. xxvii-xxviii.

[4] Von Grunebaum, p. 135; *Criticism,* p. 51; *Abhandlungen,* p. 166.

[5] Ibn abī Ishāq is mentioned among the founders of the grammatical school at Basrah. Ibn Hallikān, Slane, I, 666.

[6] Bräu, p. 8; Trabulsi, pp. 7-9, 63-66.

Another significant feature of this early criticism is the influence of the literary tradition which ascribed superiority in linguistic purity and originality to the Jāhiliyyah poets.[7] In al-Jumahi's work it is seen in the chronological division. But the endeavor to give the newer poetry its due, in spite of the prejudices of the philologians, was not long in coming. This reaction, significantly, had perhaps its earliest direct expression in the *Kitāb ash-Shi'r wa'sh-Shu'arā'* of Ibn Qutaibah, who was one of Di'bil's students.[8]

Ibn Qutaibah is concerned with the education of the secretaries (*Kuttāb*) of the governmental bureaus of the 'Abbāsids. In composing the *Kitāb ash-Shi'r*, he is not just assembling an anthology; he is also giving instructions which are essential for the secretary's employment.[9] Moreover, Ibn Qutaibah wishes his students to honor the tradition of Islām and the tradition of the Arabic language. He clearly expresses his purpose and method in the introduction to his work:

> This is a book which I have composed on the poets. I have spoken of their times, merit, the circumstance which inspired their verses, their tribes, the names of their ancestors, those known by a surname or by a patronym, of that in their history which is worthy of merit and of appreciation, of the errors which the critics have raised against their expressions and their thoughts, of what the ancients were the first to say and of what the moderns have borrowed from them.
>
> I have also dealt with the divisions and the categories of poetry, the points which render poetry preferred and beautiful, and of other matters which I have inserted, in an introductory manner, in this first section.
>
> I have been especially interested in the celebrated poets who are known to men of letters, and whose verses furnish *hujjah* for the study of the rarities of language, grammar, the Qur'ān, and the Tradition of the Prophet. As regards those poets who are obscure and not famous, whose verses are without sale in the market place of poetry, those who are only known to the specialists, there are but few mentioned, since I know only a few of them and have but little information regarding them. I know in effect (O reader) that you have no need for me to cite names without accompanying them by an account, a date, a genealogy, a curious fact, or by an admirable or strange verse.[10]

The remainder of the introduction treats the following topics: the divisions of poetry (pages 6-13), the *qasīdah* (pages 13-14), the types of poets (pages 15-17), poetic inspiration (pages 17-19), reasons for admiring a poem (pages 19-24), the natural and the studied poet (pages 24-29), errors of prosody (pages 29-31), and errors of syntax (pages 31-35). The content is better organized than the introduction of al-Jumahī's *Tabaqāt*, but the anecdotes are for the most part common to both works—a fact which reflects the existence of a common literary tradition.[11]

The text includes poets from the Jāhiliyyah to Ibn Qutaibah's own day and follows a loose chronological order, but a section devoted to the poets of the tribe of Hudhail is interposed.[12]

In the arrangement of his materials, Ibn Qutaibah seems to have followed a pattern used by his mentor; there is little evidence

7 *Abhandlungen*, pp. 135-40.

8 *Ibid.*, p. 155.

9 Gaudefroy-Demombynes, p. xi. Cf. Ibn Qutaibah's *Adab al-Kātib*, which is a compendium of Arabic stylistics.

10 Gaudefroy-Demombynes, p. 2.

11 *Ibid.*, p. xxxviii. Cf. Trabulsi, pp. 70-73.

12 *Si'r*, pp. 413-25.

that Di'bil used in his book a class arrangement similar to that of al-Jumahī's *Tabaqāt*. Indeed, the lack of such an organization suggests that the original title of Di'bil's work was *Kitāb ash-Shu'arā'*—as the earliest transmitters give it—and not *Tabaqāt ash-Shu'arā'*, as it is generally referred to in later works.[13]

Like the works of al-Jumahī and Ibn Qutaibah, Di'bil's book had an introduction dealing with the criticism of poetry, the purpose of studying poetry, and the inspiration for the various poetic motifs: "Abū 'Alī Di'bil b. 'Alī al-Khuzā'ī satirized the rulers and the caliphs whereas he did not attack their poets, except when absolutely necessary. In the beginning of his book, which he composed regarding the poets, he cautioned one against attacking even an insignificant poet, for he said that many a verse is current through the tongue of such a poet."[14]

In addition to this reference, the following statements are more appropriate to an introduction than to the body of the text:

> You see two horses which are free of any defect and in which are found markings of beauty and speed. However, one of them is superior to the other by a difference which is only discernible to men of long study and experience. This is equally valid respecting two girl slaves, beautiful and free from defect. Yet, one experienced in such matters can distinguish between them so that there is a marked difference in their value. If the slave trader were asked by what means he preferred the one over the other, he would not be able to come up with a satisfactory explanation which would explain the difference. Rather, he knows it instinctively and by long study. Similar is the case respecting poetry. Sometimes two verses are beautiful, yet the one learned in the poetic craft knows which is the more beautiful if their motifs are the same, and which of the two verses expresses the motif better, if the motifs are different. This very subject has been mentioned by Di'bil and Muhammad b. Sallām al-Jumahī in their books.[15]

> Di'bil said in his book dealing with the praise of the poets that no one lies but that they call him a liar—except the poet, for his lies are considered beautiful; he is forgiven, and no blame is attached to him. Moreover, it is not long before they say, "How well have you done!" And it is also stated therein that the royal and common person when he sends his son to school orders his teacher to teach him poetry and the *Qur'ān*. He joins poetry to it, not because poetry is a pastime, nor because poetry has a particular nobility, rather because poetry is one of the most excellent fields of instruction. Thus he orders the teacher to teach him poetry because through it one obtains access to the salons of the great, mastery of proverbs, and insight into ethics. Furthermore, his lasting fame will be due to his poetry. For it should be noted that Imru'-u'l-Qais was the son of the sons of kings, and his family had more than thirty kings among them. Yet, they and the memory of them perished, while he will be remembered until the Resurrection. For that which preserved his memory was his poetry.[16]

> Di'bil said in his book that he who wishes to eulogize should be motivated by desire;

. . . .

[13] *Waraqah*, p. 123; Sūlī, *Abū Tammām*, p. 244; *Kāmil*, p. 122; *Muwāzanah*, pp. 8-9; *'Umdah*, I, 93; *Ta'rīh Baghdād*, II, 342; Ibn 'Asāk, *Tar.*, V, 227; *Irshād*, IV, 194. The first reference to *Tabaqāt* is found in *Fihrist*, p. 161. However, al-Āmidī and al-Marzubānī, contemporaries of Ibn an-Nadīm, make no reference to *Tabaqāt*. See *Ta'rīh Baghdād*, IV, 143.

[14] *Muwāzanah*, p. 6.

[15] *Ibid.*, pp. 167-68.

[16] *Latā'if*, p. 25.

> he who aims to satirize should be motivated by disgust; he who intends to compose amatory verses should be motivated by love and passion; he who desires to remonstrate should be motivated by his patron's procrastination in rewarding.[17]

In comparing Di'bil's viewpoint with that of al-Jumahī and Ibn Qutaibah, one is struck by his concern with the practical aspects of poetry. Though poetry is to him, as it is to both the others, the storehouse of knowledge, it is also the means for getting on in the world. Therefore, the poet must know the tricks of the trade and the proper inducements to produce the desired results. One is almost tempted to regard the introduction as a primer for the practicing poet. In any case, the qualitative distinction between Di'bil, al-Jumahī, and Ibn Qutaibah can readily be felt, and reflects Di'bil's personal status as a practicing poet.

The text of Di'bil's *Kitāb ash-Shu'arā'* included poets from the Jāhiliyyah to Di'bil's contemporaries.[18] However, it should be pointed out that there are very few Jāhiliyyah poets in the reconstruction, chiefly because many of the available sources using Di'bil's book are restricted in subject. Ibn al-'Asqalānī's *Isābah* deals with the contemporaries of Muhammad, Ibn al-Jarrāh's *Kitāb 'Amr* deals with the poets named 'Amr, and his *Kitāb al-Waraqah* contains only modern poets. It may be, also, that later authors preferred to use other works dealing with the Jāhiliyyah poets. Di'bil seems, from the evidence on hand, to have been chiefly interested in the minor poets of the Islamic period.[19]

The poets were arranged according to chronology and geography, as the following references suggest:

> Di'bil mentioned him in the *Classes of the Poets* amongst the people of Hijāz and said that his activity covered both the Jāhiliyyah and Islamic periods.
>
> Di'bil mentioned him in the *Book of the Poets of Baghdād.*
>
> Di'bil mentioned him among the poets of Baghdād.
>
> Di'bil mentioned him among the poets of Yamāmah.
>
> Di'bil mentioned him among the poets of Basrah.
>
> Di'bil mentioned him in accounts of the poets of Basrah.[20]

Such an arrangement was usual for the period. Between the two major divisions of al-Jumahī's *Tabaqāt*, for example, was a section on the poets of the Arabian cities. This dual system was followed by "class books" dealing with nonreligious and religious subjects.[21]

The problem of ascertaining whether or not certain poets, concerning whom Di'bil gives information, were listed in Di'bil's *Kitāb ash-Shu'arā'* is difficult of solution, for an oral tradition as well as a written record existed. Other complicating factors are the different terminology and usages of the authors citing Di'bil as their source and the infrequent crediting of Di'bil as the authority by later authors.

In Ibn al-Jarrāh's *Kitāb al-Waraqah*, for

. . . .

[17] *'Umdah*, I, 79.

[18] *Mu'jam*, p. 227.

[19] Goldziher points out that Ibn al-Mu'tazz was primarily interested in the postclassical poets and that the list of poets cited in his *Fusūl at-Tamāthīl fī Tabāshīr as-Surūr* shows how far the modern poets had become accepted at the time of the author, who died in 908. *Abhandlungen*, pp. 166-67.

[20] *Isābah*, IV, 75 (cf. I, 370, 511; II, 163); *Mu'talif*, pp. 67-68 (Brockelmann suggests that this book is part of the *Kitāb ash-Shu'arā'*. *GAL Suppl.*, I, 122.); *Ta'rīh Baghdād*, XIV, 262; *Mu'talif*, pp. 120, 168; *Hamāsah*, p. 465; *Isābah*, III, 257.

[21] See the *Tabaqāt* of Ibn Sa'd, al-Jumahī's contemporary.

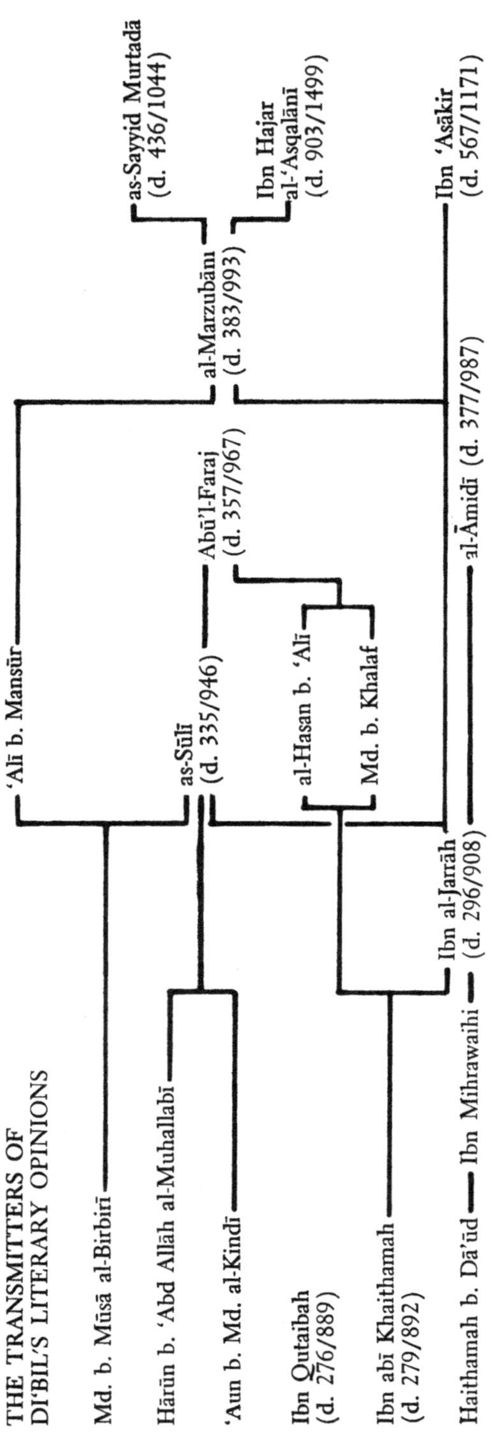

example, references to poets having Di'bil as the ultimate source of information appear in the following forms:

Di'bil said (*qāla Di'bil*).

Ibn abī Khaithamah said on Di'bil's authority (*qāla Ibn abī Khaithamah 'an Di'bil*).

Ibn abī Khaithamah said [that] Di'bil said (*qāla Ibn abī Khaithamah qāla Di'bil*).

Di'bil recited [his verses] in the *Book of the Poets* (*anshada lahu Di'bil fī Kitāb ash-Shu'arā'*).

Di'bil recited [his verses] and mentioned (*anshada Di'bil wa dhakara*).

Di'bil recited [his verses] (*anshada Di'bil* or *anshada Di'bil lahu*).

Ibn abī Khaithamah recited [his verses] on Di'bil's authority (*anshada Ibn abī Khaithamah 'an Di'bil*).

Di'bil mentioned (*dhakara Di'bil*).[22]

The reference *anshada lahu Di'bil fī Kitāb ash-Shu'arā'* suggests that all other references introduced with *anshada lahu Di'bil* also refer to the *Kitāb ash-Shu'arā*. This is

[22] *Waraqah*, pp. 7, 37, 46, 84, 85, 88-90, and 101; 4, 36, 91; 13; 123; 59, 82; 10; 48, 50, 53, 77, 83, 97, 98, and 118; 3, 4, 67, 87. *Dhakara*, *qāla*, and *anshada Di'bil* appear in regard to 'Amr b. Huwayy as-Siksikī, p. 88. It should be pointed out that the *qāla* and *dhakara* references cite Di'bil's anecdotes or opinion regarding a poet, whereas *anshada* refers to Di'bil's citing the poet's verses. A similar situation exists in Ibn al-Jarrāh's *Kitāb 'Amr*, where we find the following usages: p. 67, *dhakara Di'bil;* pp. 53, 62, *anshada lahu Di'bil;* p. 71, *dhakarahu wa anshada lahu;* p. 50, *haddathanī Ahmad (b. abī Khaithamah) 'an Di'bil;* p. 64, *akhbaranī Ahmad (b. abī Khaithamah) 'an Di'bil;* p. 47, *anshadanā Ahmad (b. abī Khaithamah) 'an Di'bil;* p. 64, *anshadanī Ahmad (b. abī Khaithamah) 'an Di-'bil.*

supported by the cases of the poets Tālib and Tālūt. Whereas the *Kitāb al-Waraqah* has simply, "Di'bil recited [these verses] of Tālib" and "Di'bil recited [these verses] of Tālūt" (*anshada Di'bil li Tālib* and *anshada Di'bil li Tālūt*),[23] the *Ta'rīkh* of Ibn 'Asākir has regarding each of these poets: "Di'bil mentioned him in the *Classes of the Poets* and recited his verses" (*dhakarahu Di'bil fī Tabaqāt ash-Shu'arā' wa anshada lahu*).[24]

In the case of *anshada* [*nī*] *Ibn abī Khaithamah 'an Di'bil,* there is evidence suggesting that poets so mentioned were also listed in the *Kitāb ash-Shu'arā'*. For in regard to the poet al-Mumazziq, the *Kitāb al-Waraqah* states: "Ibn abī Khaithamah recited [his verses] on Di'bil's authority," but al-Āmidī's *Mu'talif* has "Di'bil b. 'Alī recited his verses" (*anshada lahu Di'bil b. 'Alī*).[25] Additional support comes from the case of Muhammad b. Umayyah b. abī Umayyah and 'Alī b. abī Umayyah; for while the *Kitāb al-Waraqah* has: "Ibn abī Khaithamah recited [their verses] on Di'bil's authority," a collation of this reference with the accounts in the *Tabaqāt* of Ibn al-Mu'tazz, Ibn Rashīq's *'Umdah*, and the *Ta'rīkh Baghdād* shows that the entire Umayyah family was listed in Di'bil's *Kitāb ash-Shu'arā'*.[26]

Similarly, regarding the reference *qāla Ibn abī Khaithamah qāla Di'bil,* there is external evidence to suggest that accounts so referred to were in Di'bil's text. The poet Ibn abī Subaih is so listed in the *Kitāb al-Waraqah,* but in the *Fihrist* the identical account is introduced by *qāla Di'bil.*[27]

It is interesting to note that relative to certain poets, for example al-Mustahill b. al-Kumait, Abū Dil' as-Sindī, and Abū'l-'Udhāfir, there are dual references.[28] From this is would seem that Ibn al-Jarrāh used the *Kitāb ash-Shu'arā'* for certain information and then possibly obtained additional material from Ahmad ibn abī Khaithamah.

Al-Marzubānī, for a second example, has a reference in his *Mu'jam* which, like Ibn al-Jarrāh's *anshada* or *anshadanī Ibn abī Khaithamah 'an Di'bil,* offers some uncertainty, namely, *qāla fī riwāyat Di'bil* ("The poet said in Di'bil's transmission").[29] Though one is inclined to assert from the evidence that Di'bil's book is the source for the references in this form,[30] yet relative to those poets named 'Amr the situation becomes less certain, for it appears that the greater part of the information regarding these poets is the *Kitāb 'Amr* of Ibn al-Jarrāh. Thus, for the poet 'Amr b. abī al-Habar there is: "He says in Di'bil's transmission (*yaqūlu fī riwāyat Di'bil*),"[31] and in the *Kitāb 'Amr*: "Ahmad [Ibn abī Khaithamah] recited his verses on Di'bil's authority (*anshada Ahmad 'an Di'bil lahu*)."[32]

. . . .

23 *Waraqah,* pp. 89-90.

24 Ibn 'Asāk., *Tar,* VII, 46-47.

25 *Waraqah,* p. 98; *Mu'talif,* p. 186. In *Mu'talif,* pp. 120, 169, al-Āmidī refers to Di'bil's *Kitāb*.

26 *Waraqah,* pp. 48-50; Ibn al-Mu'tazz, *Tab.,* pp. 152-53; *'Umdah,* II, 236; *Ta'rīh Baghdād,* II, 85.

27 *Waraqah,* p. 13; *Fihrist,* p. 49. Cf. *Fihrist,* p. 44, for the use of *qāla Di'bil* regarding Abū Ziyād al-Kilābī.

28 *Waraqah,* pp. 77-78, "*anshada lahu Ibn abī Khaithamah 'an Di'bil*" and "*anshada Di'bil lahu aidan*"; pp. 90-91, "*qāla Ibn abī Khaithamah 'an Di'bil*" and "*qāla Di'bil*"; p. 4, "*qāla Ibn abī Khaithamah 'an Di'bil*" and "*qāla Di'bil.*" Cf. pp. 85-86, where Ibn al-Jarrāh uses Di'bil and Ibn abī Khaithamah as separate authorities: "*qāla Di'bil huwa Kūfī wa anshada lahu fī'l-Mahdī . . . wa anshadanīhā Ahmad b. abī Khaithamah 'an Abī Shaikh 'an Sa'īd b. Yahyā al-Umawī.*"

29 *Mu'jam,* pp. 371, 376.

30 *Ibid.,* p. 365: "*Dhakarahu Di'bil wa qāla,*" also pp. 272, 434, 478: "*Dhakarahu Di'bil.*" See *Isābah,* I, 93, and III, 455: "*Dhakarahu al-Marzubānī wa naqala 'an Di'bil.*" Cf. *Isābah,* II, 23, and *Mu'jam,* p. 240.

31 *Mu'jam,* p. 239.

32 *K. 'Amr,* p. 56. The verb *dhakara* is frequently used to indicate materials drawn from written records used on their own authority and the verbs *qāla, akhbara* usually signify oral trans-

Another difficulty is illustrated by the cases of six poets named 'Amr who are cited in the *Mu'jam* without reference to *Di'bil.* However, when their accounts are collated with those of the *Kitāb 'Amr,* Di'bil appears as the authority.[33]

A much less difficult problem is the determination of a date of final composition. Fortunately, a reference exists to Muhammad b. 'Abd Allāh b. Ja'far b. az-Zayyāt (d. 233/847) which says: "Di'bil mentioned him in the *Tabaqāt ash-Shu'arā'* and cited a poem of his in which he mourns Abū Tammām."[34] Since the death date of Abū Tammām is 231/846, the final date of composition is probably close to the death date of Di'bil, 246/860.[35]

mission, even when the author or teacher dictated his materials from memory or from a written copy to his pupils, his fellow scholars, or professional copyists. There was a widespread custom of citing an authority by name rather than by title, even when the existence of the particular authority's work was unquestioned and its use general. See *OIP,* pp. 22-24.

[33] The poets are 'Amr b. al-Hasan b. Hānī, 'Amr b. 'Āmir, 'Amr b. Zaid, 'Amr b. Mabradah, 'Amr b. Huwayy, and 'Amr b. abī Bakr al-'Aduwī. See respecting them *Mu'jam,* p. 232, *K. 'Amr,* p. 62; *Mu'jam,* p. 233, *K. 'Amr,* p. 64; *Mu'jam,* p. 228, *K. 'Amr,* p. 64; *Mu'jam,* p. 240, *K. 'Amr,* p. 62; *Mu'jam,* p. 218; *K. 'Amr,* p. 71; *Mu'jam,* p. 220; *K. 'Amr,* p. 67.

[34] *Ta'rīh Baghdād,* II, 342. Di'bil also cited Ahmad b. abī Du'ād (d. 240/854) in his *Kitāb ash-Shu'arā'*. *Ibid.,* IV, 143.

[35] Cf. Ibn al-Mu'tazz, *Tab.,* p. XVII, for the method of computing the date of the *Tabaqāt.*

5

THE BOOK OF THE POETS

I

'Umdah, I, 79

في حد الشعر وبنيته

قال دعبل في كتابه من أراد المديح فبالرغبة ومن أراد الهجاء فبالبغضاء ومن أراد التشبيب فبالشوق والعشق ومن أراد المعاتبة فبالاستبطاء فقسم الشعر كما ترى هذا الاقسام الاربعة وكان الرثاء عنده من باب المدح على ما قدمت الا انه جعل العتاب بدلا منه

II

Laṭā'if, p. 25

قال دعبل في كتابه الموضوع في مدح الشعراء انه لا يكذب أحد الا اجتواه الناس فقالوا كذاب الا الشاعر فانه يكذب ويستحسن كذبه ويحتمل ذلك له ولا يكون عيبا عليه ثم لا يلبث ان يقال أحسنت وفيه ان الرجل الملك او السوقة إذا صير ابنه في الكتاب أمر معلمه ان يعلمه القرآن والشعر فيقرنه بالشعر ليس لان الشعر لهو ولا كرامة للشعر لكنه من أفضل الآداب فيأمره بتعليمه اياه لانه توصل به المجالس وتضرب فيه الامثال وتعرف به محاسن الاخلاق ومشاينها فتقدم وتحمد وتهجى وتمدح واى شرف أبقى من شرف يبقى بالشعر وفيه ان امرأ القيس

كان من ابناء الملوك وكان من اهل بيته وبني ابيه اكثر من ثلاثين ملكا فبادوا
وباد ذكرهم وبقي ذكره الى القيامة وانما امسك ذكره شعره

III

Muwāzanah, p. 6

وكذلك كان ابو علي دعبل بن علي الخزاعي يهجو الملوك والخلفاء ولا يعرض لشاعرهم الا ضرورة
وقد حذر في اول كتابه الذي الفه في الشعراء من التعرض لشاعر ولو كان من أدون الناس صنعة في
الشعر وقال رب بيت جرى على لسان مفحم قيل فيه رب رمية من غير رام فسارت به الركبان

IV

Muwāzanah, pp. 167-68

الا ترى انه قد يكون فرسان سليمان من كل عيب موجود فيهما سائر علامات العتق والجودة
والنجابة ويكون احدهما افضل من الآخر بفرق لا يعلمه الا اهل الخبرة والدربة الطويلة
وكذلك الجاريتان البارعتان في الجمال المتقاربتان في الوصف السليمتان من كل عيب قد
يفرق بينهما العالم بامر الرقيق حتى يجعل في الثمن بينهما فضلا كبيرا فإذا قيل له فللنخاس
من اين فضلت انت هذه الجارية على اختها ومن اين فضلت انت هذه الفرس على صاحبه لم
يقدر على عبارة توضح الفرق بينهما وانما يعرفه كل واحد منهما بطبعه وكثيرة دربة وطول ملابسته
فكذلك الشعر قد يتقارب البيتان الجيدان النادران فيعلم اهل العلم بصناعة الشعر ايهما اجود
ان كان معناهما واحدا اوايهما اجود في معناه ان كان معناهما مختلفا وقد ذكر هذا
المعنى بعينه محمد بن سلام الجمحي وابو علي دعبل بن علي الخزاعي في كتابيهما

V

Aǧ., IX, 21; Ibn Ḫallikān, I, 12

ابراهيم بن العباس الصولى

قال محمد بن داود قال حدثنا ابن ابراهيم قال سمعت دعبل يقول لو تكسب ابراهيم بن العباس بالشعر لتركنا في غير شيء

VI

Waraqah, p. 89 Wāfir

ابراهيم بن هشام بن يحيى الغسانى

وانشد دعبل لابراهيم بن يحيى الغسانى الدمشقى يرثى عمرو بن حُوَىّ

فَلَوْ كَانَ ٱلْبُكَاءُ يكون حقًّا ... على قَدْرِ الرَّزَايَا بِالعِبَادِ
لَكَانَ بُكَاكَ بَعْدَ أَبِى حوىّ ... يُقِلُّ وَلو جَرَى بدمِ ٱلفُؤَادِ
مَضَى وَأَقَامَ مَا دَجَتِ الليالى ... لَهُ مَجْدٌ يَحُلُّ عَلَى ٱلبِعَادِ
فَإِن يكُ غَابَ وَجْهُ أَبِى حوّى ... فَأَوجُهُ عُرْفِهِ غُرٌّ بَوَادِى

VII

Taʾrīḫ Baghdād, IV, 143; Ibn Ḫallikān, I, 27

احمد بن ابى دؤاد

قال محمد بن عمران وقد ذكره دعبل بن على الخزاعى في كتابه الذى فيه أسماء الشعراء وروى له ابياتا حسنا

VIII

Waraqah, p. 59 Wāfir

احمد بن اسحاق الخاركى

واحمد بن اسحاق - وذكره ذلك دعبل انشد له يهجو ابا ذفافة ابراهيم بن سعيد بن سلم الباهلى

أَرَدْتُ به الهجاءَ فَأَدْرَكَتْنِي ... عَلَى ٱلأَشْعَارِ حَيْطَةُ وَرَافَهْ

IX

Waraqah, p. 51 Ḫafīf

احمد بن أميّة بن ابى أمية

ومن قوله انشده دعبل

خَبَّرَتْ عن تَغَيُّرِى ٱلأَتْرَابَا ... وَمَشِيبِى فَقُلْنَ باللهِ شَابَا

نَظَرَتْ نَظْرَةً إِلَىَّ وَصَدَّتْ ... كَصُدُودِ ٱلمَخْمُورِ شَمَّ ٱلشَّرَابَا

X

Waraqah, p. 123 Ṭawīl

احمد بن سيف ابو الجهم

وانشد دعبل لابى الجهم احمد بن سيف فى كتاب الشعراء

أَعَاذِلُ لَيْسَ البُخْلُ منى سَجِيَّةً ... ولكن رَأَيْتُ الفَقْرَ شَرَّ سَبِيلِ

XI

Waraqah, p. 88 Sarī'

احمد بن محمد بن فضالة

وانشد دعبل لاحمد بن فضلة الشامى فى ابى حوى

قد عَلِمَتْ سكسكُ فى حَربها ... بأنَّه يضربُ بالسيف

ويطعنُ القِرْنَ غَدَاةَ ٱلوَغَى ... ويحضر الجَفْنَةَ لِلضَّيْفِ

ويملأُ الأَعساس من فارس ... حُلَّ بماء المُزْن فى الصَّيف

ويُؤمِنِ الخائفَ حتّى يُرَى ... كأنَّه من ساكنى الخَيْفِ

عَنَيْتُ عمرو بْنَ حوىٍّ ولم ... أَبْغِ سوى القَصْدِ بلا حَيْفِ

XII

Waraqah, p. 80 Ṭawīl

جرير بن يزيد بن خالد

ولجرير بن يزيد بن خالد شعر انشد له دعبل

أَيا رَبِّ قد نَزَّهْتَني مذ خلقتني　　عَنِ ٱللُّؤْمِ وَٱلأَدْناسِ في العُسْرِ وَٱليُسْرِ
وأَبْلَيْتَني ٱلحُسْنَى قديمًا وَحِطْتَني　　وَبَصَّرْتَني أَمْري وَعَرَّفْتَني قَدْري
فَيا رَبِّ لا تجعلْ عَلَيَّ لِكاشِحٍ　　وَلا لَئِيمٍ نِعْمَةً آخِرَ ٱلدَّهْرِ

XIII

Waraqah, p. 101 　 Hazaj 　　 اسمعيل بن معمر القراطيسي

وقال دعبل انه مدح الفضل بن الربيع فلم يثبه فقال

أَلا قُلْ لِلَّذي لَمْ يَهْـ　　ـدِهِ اللّٰهُ إلى نَفْعي
لَئِنْ أَخْطَأْتُ في مدحِـ　　ـكَ ما أخطأتُ في مَنْعي
لَقَدْ أَنْزَلْتُ حاجاتي　　بِوادٍ غَيْرِ ذي زَرْعِ

XIV

Mu'talif, p. 118 　 Tawil 　　 ذو الاصبع الكلبي

انشد له دعبل يهجو حكيم بن عياش حين هجا بني اسد بكلب وكان حكيما اعور من كلب

اذا جئتما أَرضَ ٱلعراقِ فَبلِّغا　　بها ٱلأَعورَ الكلبي عني ٱلقوافِيا
اترضى لكلب دقّة غير عذلها　　بِدُودانَ لا شِمْتَ ٱلسَّحابَ الغوادِيا
فَهاجَ الذَّرى لا دَرَّ دَرُّهُ بالذَّرى　　وهاجَ قَبيلًا ينكرون ٱلمَخازِيا

XV

'Umdah, I, 59 (n.e. 76) 　　 امرو القيس

وقال ما يجتمع على واحد الا ما روى عن النبى صلى الله عليه وسلم في امرئ القيس انه اشعر الشعراء وقائدهم الى النار يعني شعراء الجاهلية والمشركين قال دعبل بن على الخزاعي وَلا يَقودُ قَوْمًا إِلَّا أَميرُهم

XVI

'Umdah, I, 60 (n.e. 77) Basīṭ امرو القيس

روى الجمحي ان سائلا سال الفرزدق من أشعر الناس قال ذو القروح قال حين يقول ماذا

قال حين يقول

وَقَاهم جدُّهم ببني أبيهم وبالأَشْقَيْن ما كان العِقَابُ

واما دعبل فقدمه بقوله في وصف عقاب

وَيْلُمِّهَا من هواء الجوّ طالبة ولا كهذا في الارض مطلوبُ

وهذا عنده اشعر بيت قالته العرب

XVII

'Umdah, II, 236 (n.e. 290) بيت أميه الكاتب

وبيت أمية الكاتب ذكرهم دعبل وهم أمية واخوته علي ومحمد والعباس وسعيد ومن اولاد

هؤلاء ابو العباس بن أميه و اخواه علي وعبد الله وابن عمهم محمد بن علي بن ابي امية

XVIII

Iṣābah, I, 82; 136; Šir, p. 461 Ṭawīl انس بن زنيم الكناني

ومن هذه القصيدة قوله

فما حملت من ناقة فوق رحلها أعفّ وأوفى ذِمّةً من محمد

قال دعبل بن علي في طبقات الشعراء هذا أصدق بيت قالته العرب

Iṣābah, I, 136

ذكره دعبل بن علي في طبقات الشعراء وقال انه القائل أصدق بيت قاله الشعراء في المديح

XIX

Iṣābah, I, 93 اوس بن ثعلبة التيمي

وذكر المرزباني في معجم الشعراء ونسبه كذلك ولكن قال زور بن عمرو بن اوس بن وديعة

ونقل عن دعبل انه شاعر مخضرم

XX

Iṣābah, I, 175 Ṭawīl

بشر بن ربيعة

وقال دعبل في طبقات الشعراء بشر الخثعمي صاحب جبانة بشر يقول لعمر فذكر البيتين

الاولين وبعده

تَذَكَّرْ هَدَاكَ اللهُ وَقْعَ سيوفنا ببابِ قديس والقلوبُ تَطِيرُ

اذا ما فَرَغْنَا مِن قِرَاعِ كَتِيبَةٍ دَلَفْنَا لأُخرى كالجبالِ تسير

غَدَاةَ يَوَدُّ القومُ لو ان بعضهم يُعَارُ جَنَاحَيْ طائِرٍ فيطير

قال وكان سعد بن ابي وقاص حين اجتبى الخراج فضلت فضله فكاتب عمر فأمره ان يفرقها في قراء

القرآن ففعل فلما كان العام الماضي كتب الى عمر انهم كانوا سبعة فصاروا الآن سبعين فكتب اليه فرقها

في اهل البلاء والنكاية في العدو فكتب بشر الخثعمي الى عمر بهذا الشعر فكتب الى سعد ان الحقه باهل البلاء

وقدمه ففعل

XXI

Aġ, XVIII, 43-44 Rajaz

بكر بن خارجة

قال لي [علي بن عبد الله بن سعد] دعبل وقد انشده قصيدة بكر بن خارجة في عيسى الحيراء النصراني

زُنَّارُهُ في خَصْرِهِ معقود كأنه من كَبِدِي مَقْدُود

فقال والله ما اعلمني حسدت احدا على شعر كما حسدت بكرا على قوله: كأنه من كبدي مقدود

XXII

Aġ, XIII, 51-52; Sir, 401 Basīṭ

ثابت قطنة

اخبرني وكيع قال حدثني احمد بن زهير قال حدثني دعبل بلغني ان ثابت قطنة قال هذا البيت وخطر

بباله فقال

لَا يعرفُ الناس منه غير قطنته   وما سواها من الانساب مجهولُ

وقال هذا البيت سوف اهجى به او بمعناه وانشده جماعة من اصحابه واهل الرواية وقال اشهدوا انى

قائله فقالوا ويحك ما أردت ان تهجو نفسك به ولو بالغ عدوك ما زاد على هذا فقال لا بد من ان

يقع على خاطر غيرى فاكون قد سبقته اليه فقالوا له اما هذا فشر قد تعجلته ولعله لا يقع

لغيرك فلما هجاه حاجب الفيل استشهدهم على انه قائله فشهدوا على ذلك

فقال يرد على حاجب

هَيْهاتِ ذلك البيتِ قد سبقتُ به   فَاطْلُبْ له ثانيا يَاحاجبَ الفيل

XXIII

Šír, pp. 261-62 Ṭawīl

جميل بن معمر العذرى

وقال كثير قال لى جميل خذ لى موعدا من بثينة قلت له هل بينك وبينها علامة فقال لى عهدى بها

وهم بوادى الدوم يرحضون ثيابهم فاتيتهم فاجد اباها قاعدا بالفناء فسلمت فرد وحادثته ساعة

حتى استنشدنى فانشدته

فقلت لها يا عز ارسل صاحبى   على نأى دار والموكّل مرسَلُ

بان تجعلى بينى وبينك موعدا   وان تأمرينى بالذى فيه أفعلُ

وآخر عهد منكِ يَومَ لقيتنى   بأسفل وادى الدَّوم والثوب يُغْسَلُ

وضربت بثينة جانب الخدر وقالت اخسأ فقال لها ابوها مَهْيَم يا بثينة قالت كلب يأتينا اذا نوم الناس
من وراء هذا الرابية فأتت جميلا فاخبرته انها واعدته وراء الرابية اذا نوم الناس قال ابو محمد هكذا
حدثنا دعبل بن علي الشاعر

XXIV

<u>Waraqah</u>, p. 46

ابو الجنوب وابو السمط ابنا مروان بن سليمان بن ابي حفصة

قال دعبل كل من قال الشعر من آل ابي حفصة بعد مروان واخوته وولده وولد ولده فمتكلف
وقد جهدنا ان نجد لهم بيتا نادرا فلم نجده

XXV

<u>Ag.</u>, XIII, 49-50; <u>Šiʿr</u>, p. 401 Basīṭ

حاجب بن ذبيان المازني

اخبرني محمد بن خلف وكيع قال حدثني احمد بن زهير بن حرب عن دعبل بن علي قال كان يزيد بن
المهلب يقوم الى ثابت قطنة ان يصلي بالناس يوم الجمعة فلما صعد المنبر ولم يطق الكلام قال
حاجب الفيل يهجوه

ابا العلاء لقد لُقّيتَ مُعضِلةً — يومَ العَروبةِ من كَربٍ وتَخْنيقِ
اما القرآن فلم تُخلَقْ لمُحكَمِه — ولم تُسَدَّدْ من الدنيا لتوفيق
لما رَمَتْك عيون الناس هِبْتَهم — نكِدتَ تشرقُ لما قُمتَ بالريقِ
تلوي اللسانَ وقد رُمْتَ الكلامَ به — كما هوى زَلِقٌ من شاهقِ النيقِ

XXVI

<u>Iṣābah</u>, I, 370

الحارث بن قيس الكندي

ذكره دعبل بن علي في طبقات الشعراء وقال مخضرم وانشد له شعرا من قصيدة تائية

XXVII

Ibn ʿAsak, <u>Tar.</u>, IV, 172-73 Sarīʿ

الحسن بن رجاء ابن ابي الضحاك

وذكر ابن الجراح ان ابن ابى خيثمة انشده عن دعبل للحسن بن رجاء

مُستَشعِرُ الهمّ له جُنّة　　تقيه من عادية الدهر
ما ذا ينالُ الدهرُ من ماجدٍ　　له عليه عُدّةُ الصبر
هل هو إلّا فقدُ خُلّانه　　وفقدُ ما يملكه من وَفر
ما سرّ حرًّا حظُّه في الغنى　　من حظّه في الحمد والأجر

XXVIII

ʿUmdah, II, 236 (n.e. 240)　　بيت حميد بن عبد الحميد

كان حميد شاعرا وبنوه اصرم وابو عبدالله وابو نصر وابو نهشل شعراء ذكرهم دعبل

XXIX

Iṣābah, I, 411　Ṭawīl　　خالد بن غلاب

أبلغ أبا المختار عنّي رسالةً　　وقد كنتُ ذا قربى لديك وذا سَمَر
وما كان لي يوما اليك جنايةٌ　　فتجعلني ممّن يُؤْلو في الشعر

XXX

Waraqah, p. 10.　Ibn al-Muʿtazz, Ṭab., p. 116　Ṭawīl　　ابو خالد الغنوىّ

وانشد دعبل لابى خالد الغنوىّ يهجو البطين

وإنّ حِرًا أدّى البطينَ بزحرةٍ　　ولم يتفتّق قطرُه لرحيبُ
وإنّ زمانًا أنطقَ الشعرَ مثلَه　　وأدخلَه في عدّنا لعجيبُ
ويُحشَرُ يومَ البعث أمّا لسانُه　　فعيٌّ وأمّا دُبرُه فخطيبُ

1a Ibn al-Muʿtazz. اذى زبزجرة 1b Ibid. تنفق أقطاره 3a Ibid. المحشر
Poem is introduced by ومن البطين يقول ابو خالد no source is mentioned.

XXXI

Ibn al-Muʿtazz, Tab., p. 64 Ramal

خلف الاحمر

قال دعبل قال خلف الاحمر قال وقد تجارينا في الشعر تابط شرا وذكرنا قوله

إِنّ بالشِّعْبِ الذى دُونَ سَلع كَقَتِيلًا دَمُهُ مَا يُطلّ

انا والله قلتها لم يقلها تابط شرا

XXXII

Mu'talif, p. 120 Basīṭ

ابو ذويب النميرى

ذكره دعبل فى شعراء اليمامة وانشد له

ستتركِ أُمّك دينارا وقد كذبت بَلْ أَنتَ فِى القوم فَلْسٌ غير دينار

XXXIII

Iṣābah, I, 511

ربيعة بن مقروم

وذكره دعبل فى طبقات الشعراء وقال مخضرم حبسه كسرى ثم ادرك القادسية وانشد له فى ذلك شعرا

XXXIV

Iṣābah, I, 509

ربعى الذهلى

ذكره دعبل بن علي في طبقات الشعراء وقال شهد القادسية وانشد له شعرا في قومه من بني سدوس

XXXV

Iṣābah, IV, 75   Ṭawīl

ابو الرميح الخزاعي

ذكره دعبل بن علي في طبقات الشعراء في اهل الحجاز وقال مخضرم وهو الذي رثى الحسين بن علي

بتلك الابيات السائرة

مَرَرْتُ على أَبْيَاتِ آلِ محمّدٍ   فلم أَرَها كعهدِها يَوْمَ حَلَّتِ

فلا يُبْعِدُ اللهُ البُيُوتَ وأَهلَها   وإِنْ أَصْبَحَتْ مِن أُهلِها قَدْ تَخَلَّتِ

XXXVI

Waraqah, pp. 37-38   Ramal

زرزر الرفاء

قال دعبل له شعر صالح وانشد لزرزر يهجو رزين العروضي

سَلَحَتْ أُمُّ رزين   ذاتَ يومٍ في طحين

فَسَأَلْنَاهَا فَقَالَتْ   ذَا خَمِيرٌ لِلْعَجِين

XXXVII

Iṣābah, II, 107   Ḫafīf

سالم بن مسافع بن دارة

وقال دعبل بن علي في طبقات الشعراء وانشد له يخاطب عيينة بن حصن الفزاري وكان قد ارتد في خلافة ابي بكر ثم عاد الى الاسلام وقال لابي بكر قصتي وقصة الأشعث واحدة فما بالكم اكرمتموه وزوجتموه ولم تفعلوا ذلك بي وكان ابو بكر زوج الأشعث اخته فاجاب سالم بن دارة عن ذلك بقوله

يا عيينة بن حصن آل عَدِى   انت من قومك الصميم صَمِيمُ

لست كالأشعث المعصب بالتا   ج غلامًا قَدْ سَادَ وهو فطيم

جَدُّهُ آكل المرار وقيس   خطبه في الملوك خطب عظيم

ان تكونا أُتيتما خطبَ العُذْ   رِ سواكما تقدّ الأديم

كَفَلَهُ هَيْبَةُ الملوك وللأشـ   ـعث إن حان حادث وقديم

ان للأشعث بن قيس بن معدى   كرب عِزّةٌ وانت بهيم

XXXVIII

Iṣābah, II, 102   Ṭawīl

سيان الكوفى

ذكره دعبل بن على الخزاعى فى طبقات الشعراء وقال كانت له صحبة وكان يلى السجن بالكوفة فى خلافة عثمان قال دعبل فى ترجمة ابيه الازدى لما ضرب جندب بن زهير الازدى الساحر بين يدى الوليد بن عقبة حبسه الوليد فقال فى ذلك ابياتا منها

أَمِنْ ضربة السحار يحبس جندب   ويقتل أُصحاب النبى الأُوائل

قال وكان جندب لما بلغه عمل الساحر اشتمل على سيف ودخل على الوليد فقال للساحر انت تقتل رجلا ثم تحييه قال نعم فضربه بالسيف فقتله فامر الوليد بسجنه فسأله السجان فيم سجنت فأخبره فأطلقه فقدم المدينة فأخبر عثمان فكتب عثمان الى الوليد ان لا سبيل له عليه فكف عنه وقتل السجان واسمه سيان وكانت له صحبة ففى ذلك يقول الشاعر ما قال

XXXIX

Hamāsah, p. 724   Kāmil

شبيب بن البرصاء

بَكَرَ ٱلعَوَاذِلُ بِٱلسوادِ يلمنني   جَهْدًا يَقُلْنَ أَلَا ترى مَا تَصْنَع

قال دعبل هجي لشبيب بن البرصاء

XL

Azdī, p. 186; Ag, III, 47   Rajaz

ابو الشمقمق

وذكر دعبل بن علي قال كان لابي الشمقمق على بشار مائتا درهم في كل سنة فأتاه ابو الشمقمق في بعض السنين فقال له هلم الجزية يا ابا معاذ فقال ويحك او جزية هي قال نعم هو ما تسمع فقال له بشار يمازحه انت أفصح او أحكم مني قال لا فلم اعطيك قال لئلا اهجوك قال لئن هجوتني لاهجونك قال ابو الشمقمق او هكذا هو قال نعم فقال لا بد لك فقال ابو الشمقمق

1 اني اذا ما شاعر هجانِيَهْ   2 ولجّ في القول له لسانِيَهْ

3 أُدخلته في است أمّه علانِيَهْ   4 بشار يا بشار يابن زانيهْ

واراد ان يقول يا ابن الزانيه فوثب اليه بشار وامسك فاه ثم قال اراد والله ان يشتمني ثم دفع اليه مائتي درهم قال لا يسمع هذا منك الصبيان

Ag.

ونسخت في كتاب هرون بن علي ايضا حدثني عبيد الله بن ابي الشيص عن دعبل قال

XLI

Waraqah, p. 53   Wāfir

شويس ابو فرعون الساسى

ومن قوله انشدنيه احمد بن زهير عن دعبل وقال ابو العيناء قاله في عمر بن حبيب القاضي

كفاني الله شرَّك يا ابن عمي   فأَمَّا الخير منك فقد كفاني

XLII

Waraqah, pp. 3–4   Ṭawīl

ابو الصلت مولى بني سُليم

وفيه [ابو الغذافر] يقول ابو الصلت مولى بني سليم وكان اعرابيا ذكر دعبل انه صار الى البصرة ثم الى بغداد وكان ابوه يعمل التنانير فيما زعموا

وكان اسمه فيما مضى ناك امك   يسمّى به في كل بدوٍ وحاضرِ

فلما اكتسى رِيشًا وعادَ جَنَاحُه   تسمّى بِوَرْدٍ وآكتنى بغذافرِ

XLIII

<u>Waraqah</u>, pp. 90-91 Sarīʿ

ابو الصلح السندى

وقال دعبل هو مولى لآل جعفر بن ابى طالب ونزل بغداد ومات بها وكانت له اشعار فصاح ملاح

وقال ابن ابى خيثمة عن دعبل كان شرط شعره أربعة آلاف درهم فاتى انسانا من الكتاب فمنعه فقال

ما فعل المرءُ فهو أهلُه   كلُّ فتى يشبِهه فعلُه

ما أحد أعجزُ من عاجز   يعجز عن سنّتِنا فَضْلُه

XLIV

<u>Waraqah</u>, pp. 89-90; Ibn ʿAsāk, <u>Tar.</u>, VII, 46-47 Kāmil

طالب وطالوت

قال دعبل لهما شعر صالح وانشد دعبل لطالب فى ابى جعفر المنصور

أُذكرْ لِقومٍ فَضْلَهم ووفاءَهم   لكم وكن يا ابن الكِرام وَصُولا

يَا ابن الكرام إنّى من عُصْبَةٍ   مُتَسَرْبِلِينَ مِنَ الحديدِ شَلِيلا

خَرَجوا لِدَعْوتِكم فلم يأْلُوا فَقَدْ   رَفَعَتْكُم فوق الأَنَامِ طَوِيلا

وانشد دعبل لطالوت فى قتل عتبة بن محمد بن ابان بن حوى السكسكى وكانت قيس قتلته

أَبعدَ السكسكى فَتى يمانٍ   تَجِمُّون الجِيادَ وتحمدونا

وقد فَرَشَتْ لنا أسياقُ قَيْسٍ   بِذات الأفك مُفْتَرَشًا كَنِينَا

فَجُدِّلَ بين أظهرِهِم صريعًا   سَلِيبًا رَاكِبًا مِنه الجَبِينَا

يُنادي الأقربين وأين منه — وأين وأين منه الأقربونا

فيا يمنَ الكُماةُ ثِبُوا فأطفوا — مقالَ العارِ واطّلبوا الدّيونا

فقد نمتم وليس أوانُ نومٍ — ولم يَنَمْ العُداةُ الكاشحونا

وأغمدتم سيوف الحرب حتّى — كرينَ معًا وضرّين الجفونا

أيا مضر التي قلّت وذلّت — أتاكِ الموتُ فابتدري الحصونا

وكوني كالّتي دفنت بنيها — لتحييهم فماتوا أجمعينا

طالوب بن الازهر الكلبي شاعر ذكره دعبل في طبقات الشعراء وانشد له في قتل عتبة بن محمد Ibn ʿAsāk.

طالوت بن الازهر الطائي دمشقي شاعر انشد له دعبل في ابي جعفر المنصور.. زعم Ibn ʿAsāk.

المرزباني ان طالوت هذا والذي قبله واحد وفرق دعبل بينهما وجعلهما اثنين كل واحد منهما اخ لآخر ودعبل أقدم واعلم بذلك

XLV

ʿUyūn, II, 195 Ṭawīl

الطرماح بن حكيم

اخبرنا دعبل بن علي قال أهجى بيت قيل قول الطرماح في تميم

تميمٌ بطرقِ اللؤم أهدى من القطا — ولو سلكت طرقَ المكارم ضلّت

XLVI

ʿUmdah, II, 111; *Muʾtalif*, p. 149; *Muwaššaḥ*, p. 75 Ṭawīl

ابو الطمحان القيني ذ في باب المديح

وقال دعبل بل قول ابي الطمحان القيني

أَضَاءَتْ لهم أحسابهم ووجوههم دُجَى الليل حَتَّى نَظَّمَ العِقْدَ ثاقِبُه

Mu'talif does not mention Di'bil. In Muwaššah verse is cited by Di'bil as one of category اكذب الابيات

XLVII

Waraqah, p. 10 Ṭawīl

ابن ابى عاصم الشامى

وانشد دعبل لابن ابى عاصم الشامى فى البطين

وَقُلْتَ مَعَدٌّ إذ عَرَفْتَ لنا الرِّبا وكَهْلانُ صِنْوا نَبْعَةٍ شُكرانى

وأَمْلَتَ من هذا وذاك سفاهةً تدانَى أمرٍ ليس بالْمُتَدانى

فَبُلِّغْ عُبيدا إذْ تَخَوَّنَه الثرى وَلَا تَنكِهِ مِن نَكْبَةِ الحدثان

أَلَمَّ بنا ضُبْعًا فصادفَ مَعْشَرًا أقاموا له إذ حَلَّ سُوقَ طِعان

XLVIII

Waraqah, p. 67; Mu'jam, p. 272

عاصم بن محمد المدينى المبرسم

مولى العمريين وهو ينتمى الى لخم وكنيته أبو صالح ذكر دعبل انه ابن ابى عاصم الأسلمى

وكلاهما قد مدح الحسين بن زيد وكان عاصم المبرسم يصحب الحسن وينقطع اليه

وكان خبيث اللسان كثير الهجاء

Mu'jam وذكر دعبل انه ابن ابى عاصم الاسلمى وكلاهما قد مدح الحسين بن زيد الحسينى

وعمال المدينة للمنصور

XLIX

Waraqah, p. 24 Wāfir عامر بن عمارة بن خريم المرى ابو الهيذام

ومن قول ابى الهيذام انشده دعبل

يقولون الحديدُ أشدُّ منى ونقد يُثْنَى الحديدُ وما ثُنِيتُ
تَحِنُّ ٱلأَرْضُ إِنْ نُودِيتُ بِٱسْمِى وَتَنْهَدُّ الجِبَالُ إِذَا كُنِيتُ
وكم من شَامِتٍ بِى يَوْمَ أُنْعَى ومِنْ باكٍ عَلَىَّ إِذَا نُعِيتُ

L

Muʿjam, p. 304 Kāmil عباءة البصرى

يقول فى رواية دعبل

يا ابنَ ٱلمهلّبِ مَا تَرَى وأَشِرْ بِرَأْيِكَ يا عُقيلْ

LI

1-2 Waraqah, pp. 97-98. 1 Muʾtalif, p. 186 Basīṭ عباد المخرق

ومن قول عباد انشدنيه ابن ابى خيثمة عن دعبل

أَنَا المخرِّقُ أَعراضَ اللِئَامِ وقد كان المُمَزِّقُ أَعراض اللئام أَبِى
لَنْ أَهْجُوَ ٱلدهرَ إِلَّا مَنْ له حَسَبٌ وَلَسْتُ أَمْدَحُ إِلَّا ثاقِبَ ٱلحَسَبِ

Muʾtalif قال [دعبل] وابن عباد بن الممزق ويعرف بالمخرق وله اشعار كثيرة وهو القائل

LII

Dīwān al-Maʿānī, I, 269 العباس بن الأَحْنَف

اخبرنا ابو احمد عن الصولي عن هارون بن عبد الله المهلبي قال كنا عند دعبل فذكر العباس بن

الاحنف فقال بيده قليل ولا أعرف أحسن من شعره في الشعر

LIII

Ibn al-Muʿtazz, Ṭab, pp. 152-53 Kāmil عبد الله بن ابي أمية

حدثنا احمد بن علي البصري قال حدثنا ابو خالد الجزري قال ذكر دعبل بن علي الشاعر ان هذا البيت

اهل بيت شعر وان محمد بن ابي أمية وابنه عبد الله بن ابي أمية وابنه العباس بن ابي أميه وابن ابنه

عبد الله بن ابي أمية وهو ابو حلتيشة كلهم شعراء وأشعرهم عبد الله بن ابي أميه وهو القائل

هذي الرِقاق لدى الفراق ملأتها   بالجِدّ في طوعي وفي إكراهي

ضحِكَ الفراقِ بكاءُ صَبٍّ مُذنِبٍ   وبكاؤه ضَحِكُ الضعينِ الواهي

LIV

Waraqah, pp. 83-84 Ṭawīl عبد القدوس وعبد الخالق

انشدني ابن ابي خيثمة عن دعبل لعبد القدوس

نَدًى تَحكُمُ الأموالُ فيه ونَجدةٌ   تَحكُم في الأعداء بالأسرِ والقتلِ

وَكَم أضغَنَت في يَومِ بَدرٍ نفوسَنا   نفوسًا دُرِيّاتِ الصُدورِ مِنَ الدَجلِ

فأنتَ مَتَى نَشَّت آستَنثَرتَ مُنافِقًا   ببغضَتِهِ إيّاكَ نَجِيَّ ذي فَضلِ

وانشد عن دعبل لعبد الخالق يمدح الله عز وجل Ḥafīf

اِفتَخَحَتْ الغَنِيَّ عَن مدح النا   سِ بِصدقِ المديحِ والأحكامِ

بكلام أَشَادَ إِعظامَه النا ... سُ وقالوا قُلْ يا صَدُوقَ الكلام

فَرَجَوتُ آلنجاةَ مِن كَبْوَةِ النا ... رِ وَفَوزًا بالدارِ دارِ المُقام

ربِّ إِنّي ظلمتُ نَفْسي فَأَفْرَط ... تُ وأنت الغَفُور للظلّام

فَآعْفُ عنّي يا مالكَ آلعَفْوِ وآغفِرْ ... لي رُكُوبي هَوْلَ الذنوبِ العظام

كَذَبَ آلعَادِلُون باللهِ مالِلّـ ... ـه نِدٌّ وَمَا لَه من مُسَام

LV

Aġ., XVIII, 115 Basīṭ

عبد الله بن أيوب التميمي

اخبرني أحمد بن عبيد الله بن عمار عن محمد بن داود بن الجراح قال قال دعبل كان للتميمي ابن يقال له حيان ومات وهو حديث السن فجزع عليه وقال يرثيه

أَوْدَى بِحيّانَ مالَمْ يَتْرُكِ الناسا ... فَآمنح فُؤَادك من أحبابك اليَاسَا

لمّا رَمَتْهُ المَنَايَا اذ قَصَدْنَ له ... أَصَبْنَ منّي سَوَادَ آلقَلْبِ والراسا

وإِذْ يَقُولُ لِيَ آلعُوّادُ إِذْ حَضَرُوا ... لا تَأْسَ أَبْشِرْ أبا حيّان لا تأسا

فَبِتُّ أَرْعَى نجومَ آلليلِ مكتئبًا ... أخالُ سُنَّتَه في الليلِ قرطاسا

LVI

Kāmil, p. 112 Basīṭ

عبد الله بن الزبير الاسدي

وقال عبد الله بن مخروية ايضا ذكر دعبل في اخبار الشعراء له ان هذا الشعر لعبد الله بن الزبير الاسدي

أَنّى يكون أخًا أَوْ ذا مُحافظةٍ ... مَنْ كُنتَ في غَيْبِهِ مُسْتَشْعِرًا وَجَلا

إِذَا تَغَيَّبَ لَمْ تَبْرَحْ تَظُنُّ بِهِ   سُوءًا وَتَسْأَلُ عَمَّا قَالَ أَوْ فَعَلَا

LVII

Iṣābah, III, 91   عبد الله بن سبرة الجرشي

وذكر قصة دعبل بن علي في طبقات الشعراء وذكر له قصة اخرى وهي ان امرأة من جيرانه عبث بها عطّار يقال له فيروز فلما اضجرها قالت لو ان عبدالله بن سبرة بقربي ما طمعت في فبلغته مقالتها وهو في غزاة ارمينية فترك مركزه وقدم الشام فدخل على المراة فاستخبرها فذكرت قصتها فقال أرسلي اليه وكمن في جانب البيت فجاء فلما دخل عليها ودنا منها وثب عليه عبد الله بن سبرة فقتله ورجع الى مكانه من غزاته ولم يعلم بذلك أحد

LVIII

Waraqah, pp. 13-14; Fihrist, p. 49   Wāfir   عبد الله بن عمرو بن ابي صبيح

قال ابن ابي خيثمة قال دعبل حضر محمد بن عبد الملك الفقعسي دارا فيها وليمة وحضرها ابن ابي صبيح الاعرابي وكان بدويا نزل بغداد ومات بها وكان شاعرا مجيدا فازدحما على باب الدار فغلب ابن ابي صبيح ودخل قبل محمد فقال ابن ابي صبيح

أَلَا يَا لَيْتَ أَنَّكِ أُمَّ عمرو   شَهِدْتِ مقاومي كَيْ تعذريني

وَدَفْعِي مَنْكِبَ ٱلْأَسَدِيِّ عَنِّي   عَلَى عَجَلٍ بِنَاجِيَةٍ زَبُونِ

بِمَنْزِلَةٍ كَأَنَّ ٱلْأُسْدَ فيها   رَمَتْنِي بِٱلحواجب وٱلعُيُونِ

وَكُنْتُ إِذَا سَمِعْتُ بِجَيِّ خَصْمٍ   مَنَعْتُ الخصم أَنْ يَتَقَدَّمُونِي

Fihrist

ابن ابي صبيح عبد الله بن عمرو بن ابي صبيح المازني اعرابي بدوي نزل بغداد وبها مات كان شاعرا فصيحا أخذ عنه العلماء وله مع الفقعسي اخبار طويلة قال دعبل حضر الفقعسي دارا فيها وليمة وحضرها ابن ابي صبيح الاعرابي وازدحما على الباب فغلب ابن ابي صبيح ودخل قبل محمد وقال

LIX

Waraqah, pp. 85-86 Ramal

عتّاب بن عبد الله بن عنبسة

قال دعبل هو كوفيّ وانشد دعبل له في المهدي انشدنيها اسحاق النخعي والمبرد ولم يسميا قائلها وانشدنيها أحمد بن ابي خيثمة عن ابي شيخ عن سعيد بن يحيى الأموي

يا امين الله قد قلت لكم   قول ذي دين ورأي وحسبْ
من يقل غَيْرَ مقالي فلقد   قال زورًا وتعدّى وكَذَبْ
عبدُ الشمس كان يَتْلُو هاشما   وهما بَعْدُ لِأُمٍّ ولِأَبْ
ثم ما فرّق حتى آدمٍ   بيننا الرحمن في جِذْمِ النسبْ
5 لكم الفضلُ علينا ولنا   بكم الفضل على كلّ العربْ
فَأَبْدَ بالأقربِ منا إنّما   عَصَبٌ نأتيك مِن دون عَصَبْ
لا تُنَادِي من بعيدٍ إنّما   يهتِفُ الهاتفُ منا مِنْ كَثَبْ
القرابات شَديدٌ وُدُّها   عَقْدُها أَوْكَدُ من عَقْدِ الكَرَبْ
فصِلُوا الأرحامَ مِنّا واحفظوا   عبدَ شمسٍ عمَّ عبدِ المطّلبْ

LX

Mu'jam, p. 254 Madīd

عثمان بن عامر بن عمرو بن كعب ابو قحافة

وهو القائل في رواية دعبل

اذهبي يا لهو فاستمعي خبّريه بالذي فعلا وسليه في ملاطفه كم وصلناه منها وصلا

LXI

Murtaḍā, II, 39-40 Kāmil

عقيل بن عُلَّفة

إني ليَحمَدُني الخليلُ إذا آجتَدَى مَالي وَيكرهني ذوو الأضغانِ

وَأَبيتُ تَخلِجُني الهمومُ كأنّني دَلْوُ السقاةِ تُمَدُّ بِالأشطانِ

وأَعيشُ بِالبَلَلِ القليلِ وَقَدْ أرى أنَّ الرموسَ مَصَارِعُ الفتيانِ

واخبرنا ابو عبيد الله المرزباني قال حدثني علي بن المنصور قال اخبرني محمد بن

موسى عن دعبل بن علي قال قال لي عقيل بن علفة وذكر الابيات الثلاثة وزاد فيها

وَلقَدْ عَلِمْتُ لَئِنْ هلكتُ ليَذْكُرَنْ قَومِي إذَا عَلَنَ آلنجيّ مَكَاني

LXII

Waraqah, p. 50 Munsariḥ

علي بن ابي أمية

وانشد ابن ابي خيثمة عن دعبل لعلي بن أمية قال ابو عفان مما لمحمد وهذا مشهور من

قول علي انشدنيه جماعة عن ابي خشيشة

يَا ريحُ مَا تَصْنَعِينَ بِالدِمَنِ كَمْ لكِ مِن مَحْوِ مَنْظَرٍ حَسَنِ

مَحَوتِ آثارَنا وأَحْدَثتِ آ ثارا بِرَبْعِ الحبيبِ لم تكن

LXIII

Mu'jam, p. 283; Aǵ, XVIII, 30 Basīṭ علی بن رزین الخزاعی

وعلی هو القائل فی روایة ابنه دعبل

قَدْ قُلْتُ لَمَّا رایتُ الموتَ یطلبنی　　یَا لَیْتَنِی درهمٌ فِی کیسِ میّاحِ

فَیَا لَهُ درهما طَالَتْ سلامته　　لا هالکا ضیعةً یوما ولا صاحِ

Aǵ, XVIII, 30 Ṭawīl اخبرنی الحسن بن علی الخفاف قال حدثنی محمد بن القاسم

بن مهرویه قال حدثنی ابی قال اخبرنی دعبل بن علی قال قال لی ابی علی بن رزین ما قلت

شیأ من الشعر قط الا هذه الابیات

خلیلیّ ماذا أرتجی من غدا مرئ　　طوی الکشح عنی الیوم وهو مکین

وان امرأ ضنّ منه بمنطق　　یسدّ به فقر امرئ لضنین

LXIV

Mu'jam, p. 220; K. 'Amr, p. 67; Bräu, p. 29 Ṭawīl عمرو بن ابی بکر

وکان عمرو بن مسعدة یقوم بأمره فی ایام المأمون وکان محمد بن یزداد یحمل علیه فقال

یمدح عمرا یغمز علی ابن یزداد ولم یکن عمرو وزیرا

لَشَتَّانَ بَیْنَ ٱلْمُدَّعِینَ وِزَارَةً　　وَبَیْنَ الوَزِیرِ ٱلحقِّ عمرِو بْنِ مَسْعَدَهْ

فَهَمُّهُمُ فِی النَاسِ أَنْ یَجْبَهُوهم　　وَهَمُّ أَبِی الفضلِ ٱصْطِنَاعٌ وَمَحْمَدَهْ

فَأَسْکَنَ رَبُّ النَاسِ عمرا جِنَانَهُ　　وَأَسْکَنَهُم نَارًا مِنَ ٱلنَارِ مُوصَدَهْ

In K. 'Amr the account is introduced by ذکر دعبل أن

LXV

Muʿjam, p. 239; K. ʿAmr, p. 56; Bräu, p. 33 Wāfir عمرو بن ابي الحبر

يقول في رواية دعبل

تهدّدني كأنّك ذو رعين بأنعم عيشة أو ذو نواس

فكم قد كان قبلك من نعيم ومالك كان في الأقوام راسي

تبدّل بعد نزوته وأضحى تنقّل من أناس في أناس

K. ʿAmr انشدنا له احمد بن زهير عن دعبل

LXVI

Muʿjam, p. 232; K. ʿAmr, p. 62; Bräu, 36 Wāfir عمرو بن حسان بن هانئ

انشدني ابن ابي خيثمة عن دعبل لعمرو

ألا يا امّ عمرو لا تلومي إذا اجتمع الندامى والمدام

أفي تأبيدنا لهما إساءٌ تأوّه طلّتي ما إن تنام

In Muʿjam have no mention of Diʿbil.

LXVII

1-6 Waraqah, p. 88. 1, 2, 3, 5 K. ʿAmr, p. 71; Muʿjam, p. 218.
1-2, 5 Bräu, p. 38 Ṭawīl

عمرو بن ذُوَيّ السكسكي

ذكر دعبل انه كان صديقه وانه شاعر وابنه نوح شاعر قال دعبل وكان ابن حوى جوادا شربنا ولى الري سنين وانشد له

هلمّ اسقنيها لا عدمتك صاحبا ودونك صفو الراح إن كنت شاربا
إذا أسرت نفس المدام نفوسنا جنينا من اللذات فيها الأطايبا
أيا كوكبا لا يمسك الليل غيره بربّك لا تخبر علينا الكواكبا
ويا قمر الليل المفرّق بيننا تأخر عن الإمساء بالله جانبا
ويا ليل لولا ان تشوبك غدرة بنا ما تبدلنا بك الدهر صاحبا
دعوت حفاظا باسمها طرف ناظري وكان لها عيننا على مراقبا

Mu'jam

عمرو بن حوى السكسكي ابو حوى من اهل دمشق كان على عهد الرشيد والمأمون وهو من ولد ابن حوى قاتل عمار بن ياسر رضى الله عنه بصفين تقلد عمرو الري ثلاث سنين وهو القائل

K. 'Amr

عمرو بن حوى السكسكي ابو حوى من اهل دمشق كان على عهد الرشيد والمأمون وذكر دعبل انه صديقه وكان ينزل عليه ايام مقامه بالشام وانه وابنه نوح بن عمرو كانا شاعرين حسنين وكانا يتقلدان للسلطان اعمالا وهو من ولد ابن حوى قاتل عمار بن ياسر بصفين وانشد له دعبل

LXVIII

Waraqah, p. 56; Mu'jam, p. 219 Hazaj

عمرو الخاركي

انشد له الجاحظ ودعبل

إذا لامَ على المُرِدِ   نَصيحٌ زادَني حِرصا

ولا والله يا قوم   فلا أُقلِعُ أو أُخصى

Muʿjam does not mention source.

LXIX

K. ʿAmr, p. 64; Bräu, p. 39   Ṭawīl   عمرو بن دويرة البجلي

اخبرني ابن ابي خيثمة عن دعبل وذكر ابو طالب بن سواد

There follows a long account in which the poet defends before Ḫālid his brother, who is falsely accused in a matter of love.

أخالِدُ قد واللهِ أُوطِئتَ عَشوةً   وما العاشقُ المظلومُ فينا بسارِقِ

أقرَّ بما لم يأتِهِ المرءُ أنّهُ   رأى القطعَ خيرًا من فضيحةِ عاتِقِ

ومثلُ الذي في قلبِهِ حلَّ قلبَها   فكُن أنتَ تَخلو اليومَ عن قلبِ عاشِقِ

ولولا الذي قد خِفتَ من قطعِ كفِّهِ   لأُلفيتَ لي أمرَ الهوى غيرَ ناطِقِ

إذا مُدَّتِ الغاياتُ في سَبقِ للعُلى   فأنتَ ابنَ عبدِ اللهِ أوّلُ سابِقِ

LXX

K. ʿAmr, p. 53; Bräu, p. 41   Kāmil   عمرو الوكّال النعمان

انشد له دعبل

عَضَّت بنو هندٍ بأيرِ أبيهِمِ   هل كنتَ إلّا عاقدًا لمُجيرِ

إذ خيلُهم تَردي على فُضولِها   ورِجالُهم في الكوكبِ المسحورِ

LXXI

K. ʿAmr, p. 64; Bräu, p. 68, Muʿjam, p. 228 Basīṭ عمرو بن زيد بن هلال

انشد له دعبل

أَبْلِغْ لَدَيْكَ أَبَا النعمان مَغْتَبَةً   فَهَلْ لَدَيْكَ لِمرءٍ حَوْلَ مُغْتَتَبِ

Muʿjam does not mention Diʿbil as source.

LXXII

Iṣābah, III, 119 عمرو بن شزبى بن بشر

ذكر دعبل فى طبقات الشعراء انه بعد ان قتل الثلاثة وكانوا من عسكر على طلب البراز
فبرز له على فقال له من انت فقال على بن ابى طالب قال والله ما احب أن اقتلك وما
احب ان تقتلنى فرجع عنه فسأله عمار عن رجوعه فاخبره فقال له انا له فقال له على خذ
مغفرى فاجعله على رأسك ثم امكنه من ضربة فى رأسك فاذا فعل فاقصد رجله فانى رأيتها
مكشوفة ففعل فسقط فجره عمار برجله حتى أتى به عليا فقال له استبقنى يا أمير المؤمنين
لعدوك فقال لو لم تقتل الثلاثة لفعلت اضرب عنقه يا عمار ففعل

LXXIII

Muʿjam, p. 240; Iṣābah, II, 232 ابو الاسود الدؤلى

اسمه فى رواية دعبل وعمرو بن شبّة عمرو بن ظالم بن سفيان الكنانى

LXXIV

K. ʿAmr, p. 47; Bräu, p. 48 Ṭawīl عمرو بن العاص بن وائل السهمى القريشى

انشدنا ابو بكر أحمد بن ابي خيثمة عن دعبل لعمرو

مُعَاوِيَ لا أُعْطِيكَ دِينِي وَلَمْ أُصِبْ   بِهِ مِنْكَ دِينًا فَانْظُرَنْ كَيْفَ تَصْنَعُ

فَإِنْ تُعْطِنِي مِصْرًا فَأَرْبِحْ بِصَفْقَةٍ   أَخَذْتَ بِهَا شَيْخًا يَضُرُّ وَيَنْفَعُ

LXXV

K. ʿAmr, p. 64; Bräu, p. 48; Muʿjam, p. 233   Mutaqārib عمرو بن عامر

انشد أحمد عن دعبل له

أَرِقْتُ لِلَوْعَةِ هَمٍّ سَرَى   فَبِتُّ أُرَاعِي النُّجُومَ الْمُثُولَا

إِذَا قُلْتُ وَلَّتْ تَدَاعَتْ لَهَا   غَيَاطِلُ تُؤْيِسُنِي أَنْ تَزُولَا

Muʿjam does not mention Diʿbil as source.

LXXVI

K. ʿAmr, p. 68; Muʿjam, p. 216   Ṭawīl عمرو بن عبد الرحمن بن الحلق ابو هشام

حدثنا ابو بكر عن دعبل علي قال كان ابو هشام يعبر الجسر على دجلة بمدينة السلام فلقيه عليه ابو نبيقة الحسين بن الرواس مولى خزاعة وكان شاعرا فتكلما وعاتبه ابو نبيقة على هجائه آل المهلب ثم اتخذا وتلاطما فدفع ابو نبيقة اباهشام فرمى به الى الدجلة فبادر اليه قوم من الملاحين واصحاب الزواريق فاخرجوا و تشبث به وكان على احد الجانبين المسيب بن زهير الضبي وعلى الآخر نصر بن مالك الخزاعي فقال ابو نبيقة ارفعونا الى نصر وقال ابو هشام ارفعونا الى المسيب ففرق الناس بينهما فقال ابو نبيقة

فَمَنْ مُبْلِغٌ عَلْيَا خزاعة أنني   قذفت بعبد الباهليين في الجسر

قذفت به كي يغرق العبد عَنْوَةً   فَجَاشَ به مِنْ لُؤْمِهِ زَبَدُ الْبَحْرِ

Muʿjam does not cite source which is the K. ʿAmr.

LXXVII

K. ʿAmr, p. 64; Bräu, p. 54 Kāmil عمرو بن غراد الزيادى

انشد له احمد بن زهير عن دعبل

قَصَبٌ يُهَزْهِزُهُ ٱلرِّيَاحُ كَأَنَّهُم عِنْدَ ٱلْهِيَاجِ نَعَامُ وَادٍ مُجْدِبِ
يَرِقُونَ حَتَّى يَكْشِفُونَ لِسَوْءَةٍ فَصَفُونَ فِي عَقْدِ ٱلْأُمُورِ ٱلْخُيَّبِ

LXXVIII

K. ʿAmr, p. 62; Bräu, p. 58; Muʿjam, p. 240 Ṭawīl عمرو بن مبردة

انشد له دعبل

نَهَيْتُكُمْ أَنْ تَحْمِلُوا هُجَنَاءَكُم عَلَى خَيْلِكُم يَوْمَ ٱلرِّهَانِ فَتُدْرَكُوا
فَتَنْتَشِرُ كَفَّاهُ وَ يَسْقُطُ سَوْطُهُ وَتَخْدَرُ سَاقَاهُ فَمَا تَتَحَرَّكُ
وَهَلْ يَسْتَوِي ٱلْمَرْءَانِ هٰذَا ٱبْنُ حُرَّةٍ وَهٰذَا ٱبْنُ أُخْرَى ظَهْرُهَا مُتَشَرِّكُ
فَأَدْرَكْنَهُ خَلَاتُهُ فَٱخْتَزَلْنَهُ أَلَا إِنَّ عِرْقَ السَّوْءِ لَا بُدَّ مُدْرِكُ

LXXIX

Waraqah, p. 7; K. ʿAmr, p. 66; Bräu, p. 65; Ibn al-Muʿtazz, Ṭab, p. 220; Muʿjam, p. 220 Basīṭ عمرو بن نصر القصافى

قال دعبل قال القصافى الشعر ستين سنة لم يقل الا هذا البيت فى الإبل

خُوصٌ نَوَاجٍ إِذَا صَاحَ ٱلْحُدَاةُ بِهَا رَأَيْتَ أَرْجُلَهَا قُدَّامَ أَيْدِيهَا

K. ʿAmr اخبرنى ابن ابى خيثمة عن دعبل قال القصافى

Ibn al Muᶜtazz قال لي الحسين بن دعبل سمعت ابي دعبل بن علي بن رزين يقول

عمرو القصافي مولى لبني ربيعة بن كلب بن سعد بن زيد مناة بن تميم وقال الحسين سمعت ابي

يقول كان عمرو القصافي يقول الشعر ستين سنة ولم يقل بيتا جيدا غير بيت واحد وهو

Muᶜjam وقال دعبل قال القصافي الشعر ستين سنة فلم يعرف له بيت الا قوله

LXXX

Muᶜjam, p. 227 عمرو بن حميل الهذلي حجازي

ذكره دعبل ايضا

LXXXI

K. ᶜAmr, p. 50, Bräu, p. 68 عمرو بن يثربي الضبي

حدثني ابن ابي خيثمة عن دعبل ان اسمه عمرو بن يثربي وكان عثمان بن عفان استقضاه على البصرة

إنْ تنكروني فانا ابن يثربي

LXXXII

Muᶜjam, p. 244 عمير بن ضابئ بن الحارث البرجمي

وهو وابوه ممن سكن الكوفة وهما شاعران ذكرهما دعبل

LXXXIII

Muᶜjam, p. 245 ابو قلابة الهذلي

اسمه في رواية دعبل عويمر بن عمرو وقال الزبير بن بكار اسمه الحارث بن صعصعة بن

كعب بن طابخة بن لحيان جاهلي قديم حجازي

LXXXIV

1-2 Iṣābah, III, 123. 3-7 Muᶜjam, p. 269 Ṭawīl عياض الثمالي

ذكره دعبل بن علي في طبقات الشعراء وذكر له قصة مع شرحبيل بن السمط حين بايع معاوية
بصفين وابيات في ذلك يقول فيها

وَمَا ذَا علمتم ان نطاعن دونهم   عَلِيًّا بأَطرافِ المثقفة السمر
يَهُونَ عَلَى عُلْيَا لُؤَيّ بن غالب   دِماءُ بَنِي قحطان في مُلكهم تجرِي
فان ابن حرب ناصِبٌ لك خُدْعةً   تكون علينا مثل راغية البكر
فإنْ نَالَ مَا نَرْجُوهُ كَانَ مُلْكُنَا   هَنِيئًا لهُ والحربُ قَاصِمَةُ الظَّهْر
وإنّ عَلِيًّا خَيْرُ مَنْ وَطِئَ الحَصَى   من الهاشميين المَدَاريكِ للوتر
له في رِقابِ النّاسِ عَهْدٌ وذِمّة   كعهدِ أبي حفص وعهدِ أبي بكر
فَبَايِعْ وَلَا ترجعْ إلى العقب كافرا   أُعيذك باللهِ العزيز مِنَ الكفر

<u>Mu'jam</u> does not cite Di'bil as source.

LXXXV

<u>Mu'jam</u>, p. 267 Basīṭ

عيينة بن اسماء بن خارجة

وهو القائل واتى صديقا له فعضه كلب على بابه في رواية دعبل و عمر بن شبة

لو كنت احمل خمرا حين جئتكم   لم ينكرْ الكلب أني صاحبُ الدار
لكن أُتيت وريح المسك تفد مني   والعنبرُ الوردُ مشبوبا على النار
فأنكرَ الكلب ريحي حين خالطني   وكان يعرف ريحَ الزفتِ والقارِ

LXXXVI

<u>Mu'talif</u>, pp. 67-68 Ṭawīl

عصين بن براق

ذكره ابو علي دعبل بن علي الخزاعي في كتاب شعراء بغداد وقال انه هاجر اليها واقام بها حتى مات ولم ينسبه ابو علي الى قبيلته وانشد له

وَلَوْ أَنَّ مَا بِي بِالْحَصَى فُلِقَ الْحَصَى وَبِالرِّيحِ لَمْ يُسْمَعْ لَهُنَّ هُبُوبُ
وَلَوْ أَنَّنِي أَسْتَغْفِرُ اللهَ كُلَّمَا ذَكَرْتُهُ لَمْ يُكْتَبْ عَلَيَّ ذُنُوبُ

قال ابو القاسم الآمدي وهذان البيتان في قصيدة ابن الدمينة الطويلة وانشد له ايضا

أَرُوحُ وَلَمْ أُحْدِثْ لِلَيْلَى زِيَارَةً لَبِئْسَ إِذًا رَاعِي الْمَوَدَّةِ وَالْوَصْلِ
تُرَابٌ لِأَهْلِي لَا وَلَا نِعْمَةٌ لَهُمْ لَشَدَّ إِذًا مَا قَدْ تَعَبَّرَنِي أَهْلِي

LXXXVII

1-7 <u>Waraqah</u>, p. 36. 1, 3-4, 7 <u>Mu^cjam</u>, p. 312 Basīt الفضل بن العباس

قال ابن ابي خيثمة عن دعبل له اشعار كثيرة وذكر انه ولي بلخ وطخارستان من كور خراسان فغزا كابل وكان له بها أثر حسن فقال في ذلك

إِنَّا عَلَى الثَّغْرِ نَحْمِيهِ وَنَمْنَعُهُ بِنُصْرَةِ اللهِ وَالْمَنْصُورُ مَنْ نُصِرَا
كَمْ وَقْعَةٍ بِحِمَى إِسْكِينَ مُشْعَلَةٍ وَبِالْمَنُوجَارِ أُخْرَى تَقْدَحُ الشَّرَرَا
يَا أَهْلَ كَابُلَ هَلَّا عَاذَ عَائِذُكُمْ بِالْبُدِّ يَمْنَعُ مِنَّا مَنْ بِهِ انْتَصَرَا
لَوْ كَانَ يَدْفَعُ ضَيْمًا عَنْكُمُ لَدَرَا عَنْهُ الْقِسِيَّ الَّتِي غَادَرْنَهُ كِسَرَا
تُصِبْنَا نِقْمَةٌ لِلَّهِ بَالِغَةٌ رِضْوَانُهُ فَاصْبِرُوا لَا تَهْلَعُوا ضَجَرَا
بِاللهِ يَطْلُبُ ثَأْرَ الدِّينِ طَالِبُنَا وَبِالرَّسُولِ وَبِالْفُرْقَانِ إِذْ نُشِرَ

لا تمنع الواردينَ الوِرْدَ ما نَهَلُوا   الى اللقاء ولكن تَمْنَع الصَّدَرَا

Mu'jam does not mention Di'bil as source.

Note in *K. War* has لا يوجد في معجم البلدان اسكين ولا المنوحار وقد تكون محرفة عن منوقان

LXXXVIII

Mu'talif, p. 168; *Hamāsah*, p. 465; *Iṣābah*, III, 257   Rajaz

القلاح العنبري

ذكره دعبل في شعراء البصرة وذكر انه هرب له غلام يقال له مقسم فتبعه يطلبه ونزل بقوم فقالوا له من انت فقال

1 انا القلاح جئتُ أبغي مقسما   2 أُقسمُ لا أَسأمُ حتّى يسأما

Iṣābah في اخبار شعراء البصرة *Hamāsah* has only ذكره دعبل في شعراء البصرة no verse.

LXXXIX

Iṣābah, III, 261   قيس بن المشكوح

وجزم دعبل بن علي في طبقات الشعراء بان له صحبة وذكر ان سعد بن ابي وقاص في فتوح العراق أُمّر قيس بن المشكوح وكان عمرو بن معد يكرب من جنده فغضب عمرو من ذلك

XC

Iṣābah, IV, 163   ابو قيس بن سمي الكندي

ذكره دعبل بن علي في طبقات الشعراء وقال مخضرم وانشد له شعرا وسطا

XCI

Mu'talif, p. 169   Basīṭ   كثير بن كثير السهمي

انشد له دعبل بن علي في كتابه في محمد بن علي بن الحسين بن علي

هٰذا الّذى تَعرِفُ آلبطحاءُ وَطْأَتَهُ | وَآلبيتُ يعرفُه والحِلُّ وَآلحَرَمُ
هٰذا آبنُ خَيرِ عِبادِ اللّٰهِ كلّهِم | هٰذا التّقيُّ النّقيُّ الطاهِرُ العَلَمُ
إذا رَأتْهُ قريش قالَ قائلُها | إلى مَكارِمِ هذا يَنتهى الكَرَمُ
وَكادَ يُمسِكُهُ عِرفانَ راحتِهِ | رُكنُ الحَطيمِ إذا ما جاءَ يَستلِمُ

XCII

ʿUmdah, II, 115 (n.e. II, 136); Muʿjam, p. 342 Kāmil كعب بن مالك

وقال دعبل بن على أفخر الشعر قول كعب بن مالك

وَبِبئرِ بدرٍ إذ يردّ وجوههم | جبريل تحت لِوائنا ومحمّد

وهو القائل ويقال انه افخر بيت قالته العرب Muʿjam

XCIII

Aġ, XII, 6 Madīd كلثوم بن عمرو العتابى

قال دعبل ما حسدت احدا قط على شعر كما حسدت العتابى على قوله

هَيبَةُ آلإخوانِ قاطِعَةٌ | لِأخى آلحاجاتِ عن طَلَبِهِ
فإذا ما هِبتَ ذا أَمَلٍ | ماتَ ما أمّلتَ مِن سَبَبِهِ

XCIV

Muʿjam, p. 348 Ṭawīl الكميت بن زيد

وله فى رواية دعبل

لَعَمرى لَقَومُ آلمرءِ خَيرُ بَقِيَّةٍ | عَليهِ وإن عالَوا بِهِ كُلَّ مَركَبِ

إِذَا كُنْتَ فِي قَوْمٍ عِدًى لَسْتَ مِنهم   فَكُلْ مَا عُلِفْتَ مِن خَبِيثٍ وَطَيِّبِ

وَإِن حَدَّ نَيْلُ النفسِ إِنَّكَ قَادِرٌ   عَلَى مَا حَوَتْ أَيْدِي الرِّجَالِ تَجَرَّبِ

XCV

مالك بن الشرعبي   Mu'jam, p. 365

ذكره دعبل وقال هو كثير الشعر

XCVI

مالك بن عوف بن سعد بن يربوع   Iṣābah, III, 332; Mu'jam, p. 361

قال دعبل له اشعار كثيرة جياد مدح فيها النبى وغيره

وقال دعبل لمالك بن عوف اشعار جياد   Iṣābah

XCVII

محمد بن اسمعيل بن يسار   Mu'jam, p. 414   Basīṭ

قال دعبل ابن اسمعيل بن يسار هو القائل ولم يسمه

رَاحَ الشَّقِيُّ عَلَى رَبْعٍ يُسَائِلُهُ   وَرُحْتُ أَسْأَلُ عَن خَمَّارَةِ الْبَلَدِ

تَبْكِي عَلَى طَلَلِ الْمَاضِينَ مِن أَسَدٍ   فنكت أُمَّكَ قُلْ لِي مَنْ بَنُو أَسَد

وَمَنْ تَمِيمٌ وَمَنْ عُكْلٌ وَمَنْ يَمَنٌ   لَيْسَ الْأَعَارِيبُ عِنْدَ اللّٰهِ مِنْ أَحَد

XCVIII

محمد بن أمية بن ابى أمية   Waraqah, p. 48   Ramal

وانشد ابن ابى خيثمة عن دعبل وغيره عنه

رُبَّ وَعْدٍ مِنْكَ لَا أَنْسَاهُ لِي   وَاجِبُ الشُّكْرِ وَإِنْ لَمْ تَفْعَلِ

أَقْطَعُ الدهرَ بِظَنٍّ حَسَنٍ   وَأُجَلِّي غَمرةً مَا تَنجَلِي

وَأَرَى الايامَ لَا تُدْنِي الذى   أَرتَجِي مِنكِ وَتُدنِي أَجَلِي

كُلَّما أَمَّلْتُ يَوْمًا صَالِحًا   عَرَضَ المكروهُ لِي فِي أَمَلِي

XCIX

__Ta'rīh Baghdād__, II, 85   محمد بن ابى اميه الكاتب

من ظرفاء كتّاب البغداديين وشعراءهم وهو محمد بن ابى أمية بن عمرو مولى بن أُميه بن عبد شمس واصله من البصرة وله اخوة واقارب كلهم شعراء فمنهم أمية وعلي والعباس وسعيد بنو امية ذكرهم دعبل بن علي هكذا وقال في موضع آخر أصبنا آل ابى أُميه الكاتب شعراء كلهم منهم شيخهم أمية ومحمد ابنه وابنه علي بن امية وابنه عبد الله بن امية وابنه ابو العباس بن امية واخوه علي بن ابى أمية كان شاعرا ومحمد بن ابى أمية وسعيد بن ابى أمية وقد اختلط اشعارهم واختلفت الروايات ايضا في انسابهم الا ان محمد بن أُميه اشعرهم ذكرا وأكثرهم شعرا وأحسنهم قولا والباقون اشعارهم نزرة يسيرة جدا

C

__Mu'jam__, p. 434   محمد بن ابى الحارث

ذكر دعبل ان له اشعارا كثيرة حسانا ملاحا

CI

Ibn Hallikān, II, 306   Wāfir   محمد بن ابى محمد اليزيدى

وكان محمد أُسنهم وأشعرهم وهو القائل فيما رواه دعبل بن علي المقدم ذكره من جملة ابيات

أَتَظْعَنُ وَالَّذِى تَهْوَى مُقِيمٌ   لَعَمْرُكَ إِنَّ ذَا خَطَرٌ عَظِيمٌ

إِذَا مَا كُنْتَ لِلحِدْثَانِ عَوْنًا   عَلَيَّ مَعَ ٱلزمانِ فَمَنْ أَلُومُ

سَقِيتُ بِهِ فَمَا أَنَا عَنْهُ سَالٍ   وَمَا هُوَ إِذْ شَقِيتُ بِهِ رَحِيمُ

CII

Waraqah, p. 82   Ṭawīl   محمد بن عبد الله بن كناسة

وقال ابن كناسة انشده دعبل وذكر انه مرّ بجذع مصلوب عتيق فقال يعرض بامرأته

أَيَا جِذْعَ مَصْلُوبٍ أَتَى دُونَ صَلْبِهِ   ثَلَاثُونَ حَوْلًا كَامِلًا هَلْ تُبَادِلُ

فَمَا أَنْتَ بِٱلْحِمْلِ ٱلَّذِي قَدْ حَمَلْتَهُ   بِأَعْرَضَ مِنِّي بِٱلَّذِي أَنَا حَامِلُ

CIII

Tarīḫ Baghdād, II, 342; Ibn Ḫallikān, II, 71   محمد بن عبد الله ابو جعفر ابن الزيات

وقد ذكره دعبل بن علي في كتاب طبقات الشعراء واورد له شعرا يرثي به أبا تمام الطائي

Ibn Ḫallikān   وقد ذكره دعبل بن علي في كتاب طبقات الشعراء

CIV

Waraqah, p. 118; Mu'jam, p. 427   Kāmil   محمد بن مخلد بن قيراط

انشد احمد بن زهير عن دعبل له

كَمْ مِنْ مَضِيقٍ بِٱلْفَضَا   ءِ وَمَخْرَجٍ بَيْنَ ٱلأَسِنَّهْ

تَخْطِي ٱلنُّفُوسُ عَلَى ٱلعِيَا   نِ وَقَدْ تُصِيبُ عَلَى ٱلمَظِنَّهْ

In Mu'jam the verses are reversed and there is no mention of Di'bil.

CV

Mu'jam, p. 478

مخارش الاموى مولى زياد الفقيمى

ذكره دعبل بن على

CVI

Isābah, III, 455

مخارق بن شهاب بن قيس

ذكره المرزبانى ونقل عن دعبل انه شاعر اسلامى وابو ابضا شاعر

CVII

Mu'jam, p. 370 Ramal

مرداس بن حذام الأسدى

وله فى رواية دعبل وتروى لغيره

رب ندمان كريم خيمه ماجد الجدين من فرعى مضر

قد سقيت الكأس حتى هزّها ومشت فيه سمادير السكر

يقرن الظهر مع العصر كما تقرن الحقة بالحق الذكر

CVIII

Mu'jam, p. 383 Kāmil

مرة بن عمرو الخزاعى اسلامى

يقول فى رواية دعبل

ذهب الرجال المكرمون ذوو الحجى والمنكرون لكل أمر منكر

وبقيت فى خلف يزين بعضهم بعضا ليدفع معور عن معور

CIX

Waraqah, pp. 77-78; Mu'jam, p. 479 Ṭawīl

المستهلّ بن الكميت

انشد له ابن ابى خيثمة عن دعبل

يعدون لى مالا منهم يحسدوننى وذو آمال قد يغرى به كل معدم

وَلَوْ حَسَبُوا مَالِي طَرِيفِي وَتَالِدِي   وَقَرْضِي وَفَرْضِي لَمْ يَكُنْ نِصْفَ دِرْهَمِ

وانشد دعبل له ايضا في بني العباس

إِذَا نَحْنُ خِفْنَا فِي زَمَانٍ عَدُوَّكُمْ   وَخِفْنَاكُمُ إِنَّ الْبَلَاءَ لَرَاكِدُ

CX

Muʿjam, p. 470   Wāfir

مسروق بن حجر بن سعيد

يقول في رواية دعبل

أَلَا مَنْ مُبْلِغٌ عَنِّي شعيبا   أَكُلَّ الدهرِ عِزُّكُم جَدِيدُ

CXI

Muʿjam, p. 376

مسعود بن علية الكوفي

قال دعبل كان شاعرا محسنا

CXII

Muʿjam, p. 383   Ṭawīl

المفضل بن قدامة

يقول في بيعة ابن الزبير في رواية دعبل

دَعَا ابنُ الْمُطِيعِ لِلْبِيَاعِ فَجِئْتُهُ   إِلَى بَيْعَةٍ قَلْبِي لها غَيْرُ عَارِفِ

فَنَاوَلَنِي خَشْنَاءَ حِينَ لَمَسْتُهَا   بِكَفِّي لَيْسَتْ مِنْ أَكُفِّ الْخَلَائِفِ

مُعَوَّدَةً حَمْلَ الهوادي لِقَوْمِهَا   وَلَيْسَ أَخُوهَا بِالشُّجَاعِ الْمُسَايِفِ

CXIII

Muʿjam, pp. 383-84   Ṭawīl

المفضل بن المهلب بن ابي صفرة الازدي

يقول بعد وقعة العقر في رواية دعبل

أَرى الشمسَ يَنفي الهمَّ عنّي طلوعُها   وَيأوي إليَّ الهمُّ حِينَ تغيبُ

هَلِ ٱلمَوتُ إن جِذنا بِسَفكِ دِمائِنا   مُطهّرُنا مِن عَثرةٍ وَذُنوبِ

وَما هِيَ إلّا وَشنةٌ تُورِثُ السَنا   لِعَقبِكَ ما حَنّت رَوائِمُ نِيبِ

وَما خَيرُ عَيشٍ بَعدَ فَقدِ مُحَمّدٍ   وَفَقدِ يَزيدٍ وَالحَرونِ حَبيبِ

CX IV

1-10 Muwaššah, p. 327. 1, 3, 5-6, 8-10 Muwāzanah, p. 29. 1, 3-8 Ṣūlī, Abū Tammām, pp. 200-201; Aġ, XV, 107. 1-8 Ibn ʿAsāk, Tar., IV, 25-26 Ṭawīl

مكنف ابو سلمى المزني

حدثني محمد بن موسى بن حماد قال كنت عند دعبل بن علي انا والعمردي سنة خمس وثلاثين بعد قدومه من الشام فذكرنا ابا تمام فجعل يثلبه وزعم انه سرق الشعر ثم قال لغلامه يا نفنف هات تلك المخلاة فجاء بمخلاة فيها دفاتر فجعل يمرها على يده حتى اخرج منها دفترا فقال اقرءوا هذا فنظرنا فاذا في الدفتر قال مكنف ابو سلمى من ولد زهير بن ابي سلمى وكان هجا ذفافة العبسي بابيات منها

إنَّ الضُراطَ بِهِ تَصاعَدَ جَدُّكم   فَتَعاظَموا ضُرطًا بَني ٱلقَعقاعِ

قال ثم رثاه بعد ذلك فقال

أَبَعدَ أَبي العباسِ يُستَعذَبُ الدهرُ   وَما بَعدَهُ للدهرِ حُسنٌ وَلا عُذرُ

وَلَو عُوتِبَ المِقدارُ والدهرُ بَعدَهُ   لَما أَعتَبا ما أَورَقَ السَلَمُ النضرُ

أَلا أَيُّها الناعي ذُفافةَ ذا النَدى   تَعِستَ وَشُلَّت مِن أَنامِلِكَ العَشرُ

أَتَنعى لَنا مِن قَيسِ عَيلانَ صَخرةً   تَفَلَّقَ عَنها مِن ٱلجِبالِ ٱلصَدى الصَخرُ

إذا ما أبو العباس خلّى مكانه — فلا حملت أنثى ولا نالها طهر

ولا أمطرت أرضا سماء ولا جرت — نجوم ولا لذّت لشاربها الخمر

كأنّ بني القعقاع يوم وفاته — نجوم سماء خرّ من بينها البدر

توفّيت الآمال بعد وفاته — وأصبح في شغل عن السفر السفر

يعزّون عن ثاو تعزّى به العلا — ويبكي عليه البأس والمجد والشعر

وما كان إلّا مال من قلّ ماله — وذخرا لمن أمسى وليس له ذخر

ثم قال سرق ابو تمام اكثر هذه القصيدة فادخلها في شعره وحدثني محمد بن موسى بهذا الحديث مرة اخرى ثم قال فحدثنى الحسن بن وهب بذلك فقال لي أما قصيدة مكنف هذه فانا اعرفها وشعر هذا الرجل عندي وقد كان ابو تمام ينشد نيه وما في قصيدته شيء مما في قصيدة ابي تمام ولكن دعبل خلط القصيدتين اذ كانتا في وزن واحد وكانتا مرثيتين ليكذب على ابي تمام

1a Aǧ; Ṣūlī الشعر 1a Muwāzanah; Muwaššah يستعتب 1b Ibid.; علي
Ibn ʿAsāk. عتب 2a Ibn Asak. اغننا 3a Ibid. زفافة ; Aǧ; Ṣūlī والندى
3b Ibn ʿAsāk. شكت 4a Ibn ʿAsāk; Muwaššah فتى 5b Ibid. مسها
7a Aǧ. يوم مصابه 7b Ibn ʿAsāk. جرت 9a Muwāzanah ثاو

CXV

Waraqah, p. 98. Muʾtalif, p. 186 Wāfir المهزق ابو عباد المخرق

انشدني ابن ابي خيثمة عن دعبل لابيه المهزق

إذا ولدت حليلة باهليّ — غلاما زيد في عدد اللئام

وَعِرْضُ ٱلبَاهِلِيِّ وَإِنْ تَوَقَّى　　عَلَيْهِ مِثْلُ مِنْدِيلِ ٱلطَّعَامِ
وَلَوْ كَانَ الخَلِيفَةُ بَاهِلِيًّا　　لَقَصَّرَ عَنْ مُسَامَاةِ الكِرَامِ
إِذَا ٱزْدَحَمَ الكِرَامُ عَلَى المَعَالِي　　تَنَحَّى البَاهِلِيُّ عَنِ ٱلزِّحَامِ

__Mu'talif__ انشد له دعبل بن علي الخزاعي

CXVI

__Muʿjam__, p. 366

المنذر بن حرام بن عمرو بن زيد

قال دعبل والمبرد أعرق الناس في الشعر آل حسان فمنهم يعدون ستة في نسق كلهم شاعر سعيد بن عبد الرحمن بن حسان بن ثابت بن المنذر بن حرام

CXVII

__Waraqah__, p. 24　　Wāfir

ابو المنيب الكلبي

وفيه [ابو الهيذام] يقول ابو المنيب الكلبي انشده دعبل

فَمَهْلًا يَا بَنِي ٱلقَيْنِ بْنِ جَسْرٍ　　وَلَا يَغْرُرْكُمْ مِنَّا السَّرَابُ
يُمَنِّيكُمْ أَبُو ٱلهَيْذَامِ نَصْرًا　　وَيُسْلِمُكُمْ إِذَا ٱخْتَلَفَ ٱلضِّرَابُ

CXVIII

__Muwaššah__, p. 74　　Wāfir

مُهَلهِل بن ربيعة

حدثني محمد بن موسى البربري عن دعبل قال أكذب الابيات قول مُهَلهِل

فَلَوْلَا الرِّيحُ أُسْمِعَ أَهْلُ حَجْرٍ　　صَلِيلَ البِيضِ تُقْرَعُ بِالذُّكُورِ

CXIX

__Iṣābah__, III, 536　　Ṭawīl

النعمان بن نضلة الانصاري

ذكره دعبل بن علي في طبقات الشعراء وقال ولاه عمر فشرب الخمر وقال

مَنْ مُبْلِغُ الحَسْنَاءَ أَنَّ حَلِيلَهَا ... بِمِيسَانِ يَسْقِى فِى زُجَاجٍ وَحَنْتَمِ

لَعَلَّ أَمِيرَ المُؤْمِنِين يَسُوؤُهُ ... تَنَادُمُنَا فِى الجَوْسَقِ المُتَهَدِّمِ

فقال عمر اى والله وعزله

CXX

__Waraqah__, p. 84

آل النعمان بن بشير

قال دعبل وآل النعمان بن بشير حظ وافر من الشعر اشعار السدد وابراهيم وابان وبشير

بنى النعمان

CXXI

__Waraqah__, p. 17 Ramal

هارون الرشيد

قال ابو بكر ومن قوله انشدنيه جماعة من الناس وانشد ايضا دعبل

إِنَّ سِحْرًا وضياء وَخَنَث ... هن سحر وضياءٌ وَخَنَثْ

أَخَذَتْ سِحْرُ وَلَا ذَنْبَ لَهَا ... ثُلُثَىْ قَلْبِى وترباها الثُلُثْ

CXII

__Kāmil__, p. 98 Wāfir

ابو المهوس الاسدى

ولمذكر دعبل انه لابى المهوس الاسدى

إِذَا مَا مَاتَ مَيْتٌ مِنْ تَمِيمٍ ... فَسَرَّكَ أَنْ يَعِيشَ فَجِئْ بِزَادِ

بِخُبْزٍ أَوْ بِتَمْرٍ أَوْ بِلَحْمٍ   أَوِ الشَّيْءِ الْمُلَفَّفِ فِي الْبِجَادِ

تَرَاهُ يُنَقِّبُ الْبَطْحَاءَ حَوْلًا   لِيَأْكُلَ رَأْسَ لُقْمَانَ بْنِ عَادِ

CXXIII

ورد بن سعد العمّى ابو العُذافر   Waraqah, p. 4   Ṭawīl

قال ابن ابى خيثمة عن دعبل ان ابا العذافر اتصل بعلى بن عيسى ابن ماهان وصحبه الى خراسان فوهب له على شعره ألفى درهم وفيه يقول

وَلَوْ كَانَتِ الدُّنْيَا لَهُ بِجَمِيعِهَا   لَأَتْلَفَ مَا فِيهَا وَدُنْيَا مَعَ الدُّنْيَا

قال دعبل وكان مختلق الشعر

CXXIV

الوليد بن كعب   Ḥamāsah, p. 666   Ṭawīl

بَكَتْ دَارُ بِشْرٍ شَجْوَهَا إِذْ تَبَدَّلَتْ   هِلَالَ بْنَ مَرْزُوقٍ بِبِشْرِ بْنِ غَالِبِ

قال دعبل بن على هى للوليد بن كعب قالها لما مات بشر بن غالب واشترى داره هلال بن مرزوق

CXXV

يحيى بن نوفل   ʿUmdah, I, 93 n.e.   1-3 Kamil, p. 335   Ḫafīf

واما من لا يمدح فأحرى ان لا يهجوا احدا على ان منهم لم يقل قط الا الهجوا أو شبيها به كيحيى بن نوفل ذكره دعبل فى طبقاته

وقال آخر من المحدثين وهو يحيى بن نوفل انشده دعبل

كُنْتُ ضَيْفًا بِبَرْمَنَايَا لِعَبْدِ   اللَّهِ وَالضَّيْفُ حَقُّهُ مَعْلُومُ

فَانْبَرَى يَمْدَحُ الصِّيَامَ إِلَى أَنْ   صُمْتُ يَوْمًا مَا كُنْتُ فِيهِ أَصُومُ

ثُمَّ أَنْشَا يَسْتَهِلُّ بِزُخْرُفِهِ النَّوْ   دَ مُلِحًّا كَمَا يُلِحُّ الْغَرِيمُ

CXXVI

Fihrist, p. 44   يزيد بن عبد الله ابو زياد الكلابي

قال دعبل قدم بغداد ايام المهدي حين اصابت الناس المجاعة ونزل قطيعة العباس بن محمد

فأقام بها أربعين سنة وبها مات وكان شاعرا من بني عامر بن كلاب

CXXVII

Tarīh Baghdād, XIV, 262; Ibn Hallikān, II, 436   يعقوب بن داود بن عمر

وذكره دعبل بن علي في شعراء اهل بغداد

A I

Ibn ʿAsāk, <u>Tar.</u>, IV, 279   Ṭawīl

الحسن بن هانى ابو نواس

وقال دعبل الشاعر كان له خاتمان خاتم فضة من عقيق مربع عليه مكتوب

تعاظمني ذنبي فلمّا عدلته   بعفوك ربى كان عفوك أعظما

والآخر حديد صيني مكتوب عليه لا اله الا الله مخلصا فأوصى عند موته ان تقلع و تغسل و

تجعل في فمه

A II

<u>Aǵ.</u>, V, 24-25   Wāfir

ابراهيم الموصلى

اخبرني الحسن بن علي قال حدثنا احمد بن زهير قال قال دعبل بن علي لما ولى الرشيد الخلافة

وجلس للشرب بعد فراغه من احكام الأمور ودخل عليه المغنين كان اول من غنّاه ابراهيم

الموصلي شعره فيه وهو

إذا ظُلَمُ البلادِ تَحَلَّلَتْنَا   فَهَارُونُ الإمامُ لَهَا ضِيَاءُ

بِهارون آسْتَقَامَ آلعَدْلُ فِينَا   وَغَاضَ الجورُ وَآنْفَسَحَ الرجَاءُ

رَأَيْتُ الناسَ قَدْ سكنوا اليه   كما سَكَنَتْ إلَى الحَرَمِ الظِبَاءُ

تَبِعْتَ مِنَ الرسول سَبِيلَ حَقٍّ   فَشأنُكَ فِي آلأمور بِهِ آقْتِدَاءُ

فقال له الخادم من خلف الستارة احسنت يا ابراهيم في شعرك وغنائك وأمر له بعشرين

ألف درهم

A III

Ag, XIV, 51

علي بن آدم

اخبرني احمد بن عبيد الله بن عمار قال حدثني محمد بن داود بن الجراح قال حدثنا احمد بن ابي خيثمة قال قال دعبل بن علي كان بالكوفة رجل يقال له علي بن آدم وكان يهوى جارية لبعض اهلها فتعاظم امره وببعث الجارية فمات جزعا عليها وبلغها خبره فماتت ....

اخبرني محمد بن خلف بن المرزباني قال حدثني ابو بكر العمري قال حدثني دعبل بن علي قال كان بالكوفة رجل من بني اسد يقال له علي بن آدم يهوى جارية لبعض نساء بني عبس فباعتها لرجل من بني هاشم فخرج بها عن الكوفة فمات علي بن آدم جزعا عليها بعد ثلاثة ايام من خروجها وبلغها خبره فماتت فعمل اهل الكوفة لها اخبارا هي مشهورة عندهم

A IV

Mu'jam, p. 403

منقذ بن عبد الله القريعي من شعراء خراسان

قال دعبل له اشعار كثيرة جياد

WORKS CITED

(The abbreviations below correspond to those used in annotating the Arabic text. A different system of transliteration is used in the English text.)

Abbott Abbott, N. *Two Queens of Baghdad.* Chicago, 1946.

Abhandlungen Goldziher, I. *Abhandlungen zur arabischen Philologie.* Leiden, 1896-99.

Abriss Rescher, O. *Abriss der arabischen Litteraturgeschichte.* 2 vols. Stuttgart, 1925-33.

Abū'l-Fidā' *Abilfedae Annales Moslemici.* Edited by J. Reiski. 2 vols. Leipzig, 1778.

Adab Ibn Qutaibah. *Adab al-Kātib.* Edited by M. Grünert. Leiden, 1900.

Ag Abū'l-Faraj. *Kitāb al-Aghānī.* 21 vols. Cairo, 1285/1868.

Ahbār as-Sūlī. *Akhbār ar-Raḍī wa'l-Muttaqī.* Translated by M. Canard. Algiers, 1946-50.

Ahlwardt Ahlwardt, W. *Verzeichniss der arabischen Handschriften der königlichen Bibliothek zu Berlin.* 10 vols. Berlin, 1887-99.

Ahsan Mā Sami'tu ath-Tha'ālibī. *Ahsan Mā Sami'tu.* Cairo, 1324/1906.

Amālī al-Qālī. *Amālī.* 4 vols. Cairo, 1324/1906; N.E., Cairo, 1344/1926.

As'ār as-Sūlī. *Ash'ār Awlād al-Khulafā'.* Edited by J. Heyworth-Dunne. London, 1936.

A'yān al-'Āmilī. *A'yān ash-Shī'ah.* 35 vols. Damascus, 1354-70/1935-50.

Azdī al-Azdī. *Kitāb Badā'i' al-Bidā'ah.* Cairo, 1278/1861.

Bad' al-Maqdisī. *Kitāb al-Bad' wa't-Ta'rīkh.* Edited by Cl. Huart. 6 vols. Paris, 1899-1919.

Bard al-Akbād ath-Tha'ālibī. *Bard al-Akbād fī l-A'dād in Khams Rasā'il.* Constantinople, 1300/1883.

Basā'ir at-Tauhīdī. *al-Basā'ir wa'dh-Dhakhā'ir.* Cairo, 1373/1953.

Bayān al-Jāhiz. *al-Bayān wa't-Tabyīn.* 4 vols. Cairo, 1368-9/1948-50.

Bidāyah Ibn Kathīr. *al-Bidāyah wa'n-Nihāyah.* 14 vols. Cairo, 1351-58/1932-39.

Blachère Blachère, R. *Histoire de la littérature arabe.* Paris, 1952.

Bräu Bräu, H. "Die alte Einteilung der arabischen Dichter und das 'Amr Buch des Ibn al-Jarrāh," *SBAW*, CCIII (1927), 7-75. Based on *Fātih* 5306 without *isnāds.*

Buldān Yāqūt. *Mu'jam al-Buldān.* 6 vols. Edited by F. Wüstenfeld. Leipzig, 1866-73.

Criticism Von Grunebaum, G. E. "Arabic Literary Criticism in the 10th Century," *JAOS*, LXI (1941), 51-7.

Dalā'il al-Jurjānī. *Dalā'il al-I'jāz fī'Ilm al-Ma'ānī.* Cairo, 1331/1912.

Daulat-Shāh Daulat-Shāh. *Tadkhiratu-sh-Shu'arā'.* Edited by E. G. Browne. London, 1901.

Dīwān al-Ma'ānī Abū Hilāl al-'Askarī. *Dīwān al-Ma'ānī.* Cairo, 1352/1933.

Dīwāns Goldziher, I. "Some Notes on the Dīwāns of the Arabic Tribes," *JRAS* (1897), 325-34.

Durrah al-Harīrī. *Durrat al-Ghawwās.* Edited by H. Thorbecke. Leipzig, 1871.

Duwal adh-Dhahabī. *Duwal al-Islām.* Haidarabad, 1337/1918.

EI *The Encyclopaedia of Islām.* Leiden, 1913-34.

Faraj at-Tanūkhī. *al-Faraj ba'da'sh-Shiddah.* Cairo, 1357/1938.

Faris Faris, N. *The Antiquities of South Arabia.* Princeton, 1938.

Fātih *Deft. K. F. gāmi'.* Istanbul.

Fawāt Ibn Shākir al-Kutubī. *Fawāt al-Wafayāt.* 2 vols. Cairo, 1283/1866.

Fihrist Ibn an-Nadīm. *Kitāb at-Fihrist.* Edited by G. Flügel. Leipzig, 1871-72.

Fiqh ath-Tha'ālibī. *Fiqh at-Lughah.* Cairo, 1325/1907.

Fusūl Ibn al-Mu'tazz. *Fusūl at-Tamāthīl fī-Tabāshīr as-Surūr.* Cairo, 1344/1925.

GAL Brockelmann, C. *Geschichte der arabischen Litteratur.* Weimar, 1897-1902. *Supplements.* Leiden, 1937-1942.

Gaudefroy-Demombynes Gaudefroy-Demombynes, M. *Introduction au Livre de la Poésie et des Poètes.* Paris, 1947.

Gefährte ath-Tha'ālibī. *Der vertraute Gefährte des Einsamen.* Translated by G. Flügel. Vienna, 1829.

Genealogisches Handbuch *Ibn Dureid's genealogisch-etymologisches Handbuch.* Edited by F. Wüstenfeld. Göttingen, 1854.

Gufrān Abū'l-'Alā' al-Ma'arrī. *Risālat al-Ghufrān.* Cairo, 1370/1950.

Hamawī al-Hamawī. *Khizānat al-Adab.* Cairo, 1291/1874.

Hamāsah Abū Tammām. *Hamāsah.* Edited by G. Freytag. Bonn, 1828-51.

Hammer Hammer-Purgstall, J. *Literaturgeschichte der Araber.* 7 vols. Vienna, 1850-56.

Harīrī al-Harīrī. *Les Séances de Harīrī.* Edited by S. de Sacy. Paris, 1847-53.

Hasan Hasan, Ibrāhīm. *Ta'rīkh al-Islām.* 3 vols. Cairo, 1354-65/1935-46.

Hāss ath-Tha'ālibī. *Kitāb Khāss al-Khāss.* Cairo, 1326/1908.

Hizānah 'Abd al-Qādir al-Baghdādī. *Khizānat al-Adab.* 4 vols. Cairo, 1299/1881.

Hodgson Hodgson, M. "How did the early Shī'a become sectarian?" *JAOS,* LXXV (1955), 1-13.

Huber Huber, A. *Über das "meisir" genannte Spiel der heidnischen Araber.* Leipzig, 1883.

Husrī al-Husrī. *Zahr al-Ādāb.* Cairo, 1344/1925.

Husrī, *Dhail* al-Husrī. *Dhail Zahr al-Ādāb.* Cairo, 1353/1935.

Ibn al-Athīr Ibn al-Athīr. *al-Kāmil fi't-Ta'rīkh.* 14 vols. Edited by J. Tornberg. Leiden, 1851-76.

Ibn al-Athīr, *Mathal* Ibn al-Athīr. *al-Mathal as-Sā'ir.* 2 vols. Cairo, 1358/1939.

Ibn al-Mu'tazz, *Tab.* Ibn al-Mu'tazz. *Tabaqāt ash-Shu'arā' al-Muhdathīn.* Edited by A. Eghbal. London, 1939.

Ibn al-Wardī Ibn al-Wardī. *Ta'rīkh.* 2 vols. Cairo, 1285/1868.

Ibn 'Asāk., *Tar.* Ibn 'Asākir. *Tahdhīb Ta'rīkh Ibn 'Asākir.* 7 vols. Damascus, 1329-51/1911-32.

Ibn Badrūn Ibn Badrūn. *Commentaire historique sur le poème d'Ibn-Abdoun.* Edited by R. Dozy. Leiden, 1848.

Ibn Hallikān Ibn Khallikān. *Wafāyat al-A'yān.* 2 vols. Cairo, 1310/1892.

Ibn Hallikān, Slane. *Ibn Khallikān's Biographical Dictionary.* 4 vols. Translated by W. MacG. de Slane. Paris, 1843-71.

Ibn Sa'd Ibn Sa'd. *Kitāb at-Tabaqāt al-Kabīr.* 9 vols. Edited by E. Sachau. Leiden, 1904-40.

Ibn Saj., *Amālī* Ibn ash-Shajarī. *Amālī.* 2 vols. Haidarabad, 1349/1930.

Ibn Saj., *Hamāsah* Ibn ash-Shajarī. *Hamāsah.* Edited by F. Krenkow. Haidarabad, 1345/1926.

Ibn Sharaf. Ibn Sharaf. *Rasā'il al-Intiqād.* Translated by C. Pellat. *Bulletin des Etudes Arabes,* IX (1949-50), 38-48.

Ibn Sharāshub Ibn Sharāshub. *Ma'ālim al-'Ulamā'.* Teheran, 1353/1934.

Ijāz ath-Tha'ālibī. *al-Ijāz wa'l-I'jāz.* Constantinople, 1300/1883.

Iklīl al-Hamdānī. *al-Iklīl.* Edited by N. Faris. Princeton, 1938.

IPO Instituto per l'Oriente.

'Iqd Ibn 'abd Rabbihi. *al-'Iqd al-Farīd.* 3 vols. Cairo, 1293/1876; N.E., Cairo, 1359/1940.

Irshād Yāqūt. *Irshād al-Arīb ilā Ma'rifat al-Adīb.* 7 vols. Edited by D. Margoliouth. Leiden, 1907-27.

Isābah. Ibn Hajar. *al-Isābah.* 4 vols. Cairo, 1358/1939.

JAOS *Journal of the American Oriental Society.*

Jarrett Jarrett, H. *History of the Caliphs.* Calcutta, 1881.

JNES *Journal of Near Eastern Studies.*

Jumahī al-Jumahī. *Tabaqāt ash-Shu'arā'.* Edited by J. Hell. Leiden, 1916.

Kāmil al-Mubarrad. *al-Kāmil.* Edited by W. Wright. Leipzig, 1864-92.

K. 'Amr Ibn al-Jarrāh. *Kitāb Man Ismuhu 'Amr.* Same as *Fātih* 5306, without *isnāds.*

Kashf Hājjī Khalīfah. *Kashf az-Zunūn.* 8 vols. Edited by G. Flügel. London, 1835-58.

Kazimirski Kazimirski, A. *Dictionnaire Arabe-Français.* 2 vols. Paris, 1860.

K. Baghdād Ibn abī Taifūr. *Kitāb Baghdād.* Edited by H. Keller. Leipzig, 1908.

Kināyāt ath-Tha'ālibī. *Kitāb al-Kināyāt.* Cairo, 1326/1908.

Lane Lane, E. W. *An Arabic-English Lexicon.* 8 vols. London, 1863-93.

Latā'if ath-Tha'ālibī. *Kitāb al-Latā'if wa'z-Zarā'if.* Cairo, 1300/1882.

Lisān Ibn Hajar. *Lisān al-Mīzān.* 6 vols. Haidarabad, 1329-31/1911-13.

Literary Theory Von Grunebaum, G. E. *A Tenth Century Document of Arabic Literary Theory and Criticism.* Chicago, 1951.

Löfgren Löfgren, O. "Daghfal und Di'bil als Gewährsmänner der südarabischen Sage,"

Studi Orientalistici in onore di Georgio Levi Della Vida, II (Rome, 1956), 99-101.

Lubāb Usāmah b. Munqidh. *Lubāb al-Adab*. Cairo, 1354/1935.

Ma'ālim Ibn Shith. *Ma'ālim al-Kitābah*. Beirut, 1331/1913.

Mahāsin al-Jāhiz. *Kitāb al-Mahāsin*. Edited by G. Van Vloten. Leiden, 1898.

Mahāsin, Rescher Rescher, O. *Das Kitāb al-Mahāsin aus dem Arabischen Übersetzt*. Stuttgart, 1922.

Majmū'at Yāqūt. "Majmū'at Hikam wa Adāb," *Thalāth Rasā'il*. Constantinople, 1298/1880.

Maqālat al-Ash'arī. *Maqālat al-Islāmiyyīn*. Edited by H. Ritter. Constantinople, 1929-30.

Maqātil Abū'l-Faraj. *Maqātil at-Tālibiyyīn*. Cairo, 1368/1949.

Margoliouth Margoliouth, D. S. *The Table-Talk of a Mesopotamian Judge*. London, 1921.

Marin Marin, E. *The Reign of al-Mu'tasim*. New Haven, 1951.

Mas'ūdī al-Mas'ūdī. *Murūj adh-Dhahab*. 9 vols. Edited by de Meynard and de Courteille. Paris, 1861-77.

Mir'āt al-Yāfi'ī. *Mir'āt al-Janān*. 4 vols. Haidarabad, 1337-39/1918-20.

Mīzān adh-Dhahabī. *Mīzān al-I'tidāl*. 3 vols. Cairo, 1325/1907.

MM *Majmū'at al-Ma'āni*. Constantinople, 1301/1884.

MS Goldziher, I. *Muhammedanische Studien*. 2 vols. Halle, 1888-90.

Muhādarāt ar-Rāghib al-Isfahānī. *Muhādarāt al-Udabā'*. Cairo, 1326/1908.

Mu'jam al-Marzubānī. *Mu'jam ash-Shu'arā'*. Cairo, 1354/1935.

Muntahab al-Jurjānī. *al-Muntakhab min Kināyāt al-Udabā'*. Cairo, 1326/1908.

Muntahal ath-Tha'ālibī. *al-Muntahal*. Alexandria, 1319/1901.

Murtadā as-Sayyid Murtadā. *Amālī*. 4 vols. Cairo, 1325/1907.

Muslim *Dīwān Muslim b. al-Walīd*. Edited by M. J. de Goeje. Leiden, 1875.

Mustatraf al-Ibshaihī. *al-Mustatraf*. Cairo, 1318/1890.

Mu'talif al-Āmidī. *al-Mu'talif wa'l-Mukhtalif*. Cairo, 1354/1935.

Mutī' b. Iyās Von Grunebaum, G. E. "Collected Fragments of Mutī' b. Iyās," *Orientalia* (New Series), XVII (1948), 160-203.

Muwassā al-Washshā. *Kitāb al-Muwashshā*. Edited by R. Brünnow. Leiden, 1886.

Muwassah al-Marzubānī. *Kitāb al-Muwashshah*. Cairo, 1343/1924.

Muwāzanah al-Āmidī. *Kitāb al-Muwāzanah baina Abī Tammām wa'l-Buhturī*. Constantinople, 1287/1870.

Naqd Qudāmah b. Ja'far. *Naqd ash-Shi'r*. Cairo, 1352/1933.

Nathr ath-Tha'ālibī. *Kitāb Nathr an-Nazm*. Cairo, 1317/1899.

Nicholson Nicholson, R. *A Literary History of the Arabs*. Cambridge, 1930.

Nihāyah an-Nuwairī. *Nihāyat al-'Arab*. 14 vols. Cairo, 1342-74/1923-55.

Niswār at-Tanūkhī. *Nishwār al-Muhādarah*. London, 1921-22.

Nujūm at-Taghrībirdī. *an-Nujūm az-Zāhirah*. 10 vols. Cairo, 1348-68/1929-49.

OIP Abbott, N. "Studies in Arabic Literary Papyri," *Oriental Institute Publication*, LXXV, 1957.

Pellat. Pellat, C. *Le Milieu Basrién et la Formation de Gāhiz*. Paris, 1953.

Plagiarism Von Grunebaum, G. E. "The Concept of Plagiarism in Arabic Theory," *JNES*, III (1944), 234-53.

Qānūn Abū Tāhir al-Baghdādī. "Qānūn al-Balāghah," in Muhammad Kurd 'Alī, *Rasā'il al-Bulaghā'*. Cairo, 1363/1916.

Qutāmī al-Qutāmī. *Dīwān*. Edited by J. Barth. Leiden, 1902.

Rasā'il al-Jāhiz. *Rasā'il al-Jāhiz*. Cairo, 1352/1933.

Rifā'ī Rifā'ī, Farīd. *'Asr al-Ma'mūn*. 3 vols. Cairo, 1346/1927.

Rückert Rückert, F. *Hamāsa*. 2 vols. Stuttgart, 1846.

Sadharāt Ibn al-'Imād. *Shadharāt adh-Dhahab*. 8 vols. Cairo, 1350-51/1931-32.

Salm al-Hāsir Von Grunebaum, G. E. "Collected Fragments of Salm al-Hāsir," *Orientalia* (New Series), XIX (1950), 53-80.

SBAW *Sitzungsberichte der AK. der Wiss. im Wien*.

Sinā'atain Abū Hilāl al-'Askarī. *Kitāb as-Sinā'atain*. Constantinople, 1320/1902.

Si'r Ibn Qutaibah. *Kitāb ash-Shi'r wa'sh-Shu'arā'*. Edited by M. J. de Goeje. Leiden, 1904.

Sūlī, *Abū Tammām* as-Sūlī. *Akhbār Abī Tammām*. Cairo, 1356/1937.

Suyūtī as-Suyūtī. *Ta'rīkh al-Khulafā'*. Cairo, 1305/1888.

Syntax Reckendorf, H. *Arabische Syntax*. Heidelberg, 1921.

Tabarī at-Tabarī. *Annales*. Edited by M. J. de Goeje *et al*. Leiden, 1879-1901.

Ta'rīh Baghdād al-Khātib al-Baghdādi. *Ta'rīkh Baghdād.* 14 vols. Cairo, 1349/1931.
Ta'rīh Guzīda al-Qazwīnī. *Ta'rīkh-i-Guzīda.* 2 vols. London, 1910-13.
T. Qumm al-Qummī. *Ta'rīkh Qumm.* Teheran, 1353/1934.
Tashbīhāt Ibn abī 'Aun. *Kitāb at-Tashbīhāt.* Edited by M. Khan. London, 1950.
Tauhīdī at-Tauhīdī. *Risālah fi's-Sadāqah wa's-Sadīq.* Constantinople, 1301/1884.
Thimār ath-Tha'ālibī. *Kitāb Thimār al-Qulūb.* Cairo, 1326/1908.
Tirāz al-Khafājī. *Tirāz al-Majālis.* Cairo, 1284/1867.
Trabulsi Trabulsi, A. *La Critique Poétique des Arabes.* Damascus, 1956.
'Umdah Ibn Rashīq. *al-'Umdah.* 2 vols. Cairo, 1325/1907; New Edition, Cairo, 1344/1925.
'Uyūn Ibn Qutaibah. *'Uyūn al-Akhbār.* 4 vols. Cairo, 1343-49/1925-30.
Verhältnisse Reckendorf, H. *Die Syntaktischen verhältnisse der Arabischen.* Leiden, 1898.
Von Grunebaum Von Grunebaum, G. E. "Growth and Structure of Arabic Poetry 500-1000 A.D.," *The Arab Heritage.* Princeton, 1944, 121-141.
Vorlesungen Goldziher, I. *Vorlesungen über den Islam.* Heidelberg, 1910.
Wāhidī *Mutanabbii Carmina cum Commentario Wāhidī.* Edited by F. Dieterici. Berlin, 1858.
Waraqah Ibn al-Jarrāh. *al-Waraqah.* Cairo, 1372/1953.
Wasātah 'Alī al-Jurjānī. *Kitāb al-Wasātah baina'l-Mutanabbī wa Khusūmihi.* Saidā, 1331/1912; N. E., Cairo, 1364/1945.
Wright Wright, W. *A Grammar of the Arabic Language.* 2 vols. Cambridge, 1896-98.
Wulāh al-Kindī. *Kitāb al-Wulāh.* Edited by R. Guest. London, 1912.
Yatīmah ath-Tha'ālibī. *Yatīmat ad-Dahr.* 4 vols. Damascus, 1304/1886.
Zahrah Ibn Dā'ūd. *Kitāb az-Zahrah.* Edited by A. R. Nykl. Chicago, 1932.
Zambaur Zambaur, E. *Manuel de généalogie et de chronologie pour l'histoire de l'Islam.* Hanover, 1927.
Zuhr Amīn, Ahmad. *Zuhr al-Islām.* Cairo, 1364/1945.

INDEX

PERSONAL NAMES

'Abd al-Ilāh, 100
'Abd Allāh b. Budail, 3
'Abd Allāh b. Tāhir, 4, 95, 114
'Abīd, 126
'Abū 'Abbād, 104
Abū Bakr, 1, 4
Abū Dil' as-Sindī, 131
Abū Dulaf al-'Ijlī, 112
Abū Hiffān, 6, 114
Abū 'Imrān, 108
Abū 'Īsā, 106
Abū Ja'far, 93
Abū Khālid, 104
Abū'l-'Alā'al-Ma'arrī, 5, 119
Abū'l-'Atāhiyah, 2
Abū'l-Faraj, 7, 130
Abū'l-Ghatammash al-Hanafī, 109
Abū'l-Khandaq al-Asadī, 103
Abū'l-'Udhāfir, 131
Abū Muhammad al-Yazīdī, 119
Abū Muqātil, 119
Abū Nadīr b. Humaid, 109
Abū Nahshal b. Humaid, 96, 109
Abū Nuwās, 2, 5, 7, 122
Abū Sa'd, 5, 101, 103, 108, 113, 122
Abū Shaikh, 131
Abū Tammām, 5, 6, 8, 96, 110, 118, 132
Abū 'Umar, 105
Abū 'Umar, 105
Abū Ziyād al-Kilābī, 131
adh-Dhahabī, 8
Ahmad b. abī Du'ād, 93, 103, 121, 132
Ahmad b. abī Khālid, 104, 109, 117
Ahmad b. abī Tāhir, 7, 94
Ahmad b. al-Anbarī, 7
Ahmad b. 'Alī ar-Ridā, 120
Ahmad b. Muhammad at-Tā'ī, 105
al-'Abbās, 97
al-'Abbās b. Ja'far, 4, 102
al-'Āmidī, 128, 130, 131
al-Amīn, 2, 101, 120, 122
al-Asma'ī, 114
al-Bassamī, 117
al-Buhturī, 7
al-Fadl b. al-'Abbās, 97
al-Fadl b. Marwān, 94, 116, 117
al-Fadl b. Sahl, 116
al-Farazdaq, 3, 126
al-Haitham al-Ghanawī, 103
al-Hasan, 118
al-Hasan b. 'Alī, 1
al-Hasan b. 'Alī, 130
al-Husain b. al-Mutair, 114
al-Jumahī, 125, 126, 127, 128, 129
'Alī, 1, 4, 5, 98
'Alī, Di'bil's father, 120
'Ali ar-Ridā, 4, 5, 6, 105, 120
'Alī b. abī Umayyah, 131
'Alī b. al-Jahm, 5, 116
'Alī b. 'Īsā, 93
'Alī b. Mansūr, 130
'Alī Zain al-'Ābidīn, 98
al-Kumait, 3, 5, 6, 122
al-Mahdī, 3, 131
al-Malāwī, 119
al-Ma'mūn, 1, 2, 3, 4, 5, 7, 95, 102, 104, 108, 114, 120
al-Marzubānī, 128, 130, 131
al-Mumazziq, 131
al-Mustahill b. al-Kumait, 131
al-Muttalib, Abū Qāsim, 4, 93, 95, 97, 115, 119, 122, 123
al-Mutanabbī, 93
al-Mu'tasim, 1, 5, 6, 94, 101, 112
al-Mutawakkil, 5, 6, 101, 110
al-Qasrī, Khālid b. 'Abd Allāh, 122
al-Qutāmī, 118
al-Walīd b. Yazīd, 122
al-Wāthiq, 3, 5, 94, 101
'Āmir, 115
'Amr, 97
'Amr b. abī Bakr al-'Aduwī, 132
'Amr b. abī'l-Habar, 121
'Amr b. al-Hasan b. Hānī, 132
'Amr b. Huwayy, 120, 130, 132
'Amr b. Kulthum, 118
'Amr b. Mabradah, 132
'Amr b. Mas'adah, 109
'Amr b. Zaid, 132
ar-Raqāshī, 100, 119
Ash'ath, 111
Ashnās, 94
as-Sarī b. al-Hakam, 97
as-Sayyid al-Himyarī, 4
as-Sayyid Murtadā, 130
as-Sūlī, 7, 94, 130
Ath'ath, 100
'Atiyyah, 115
Aun b. Muhammad al-Kindī, 130
az-Zutātī, 99

Bakr b. an-Nattāh, 3
Banū 'Abbās, 94, 106
Banū 'Abd al-Madān, 121
Banū 'Amr, 108
Banū Ahban, 96
Banū Mu'ait, 106
Banū Nahshal, 92
Banū Qahtān, 93
Baqiyyah, 104
Barmak, 115
Bashshār b. Burd, 2, 7
Budail b. Warqā', 3
Būrān, 1

Chosroe, 118
Daulat-Shah, 7
Dhiryāb, 121
Dhū Ru'ain, 121
Dīk al-Jinn, 4, 5, 6
Dīnār, 118

Faraj, 121
Fātimah, 1
Fazārah, 114

Gabriel, 98
Ghassān b. 'Abbād, 93

Haitham b. Dā'ūd, 130
Haitham b. 'Uthmān, 104
Hammād ar-Rāwiyah, 3, 126
Hamzah, 98
Harb, 106
Hārūn ar-Rashīd, 3, 4, 5, 106, 120, 123
Harūn b. 'Abd Allāh al-Muhallibī, 130
Hātim at-Tā'ī, 103
Hunain, 110
Huwayy b. 'Amr, 120

Ibn abī Ishāq, 126
Ibn abī Khaithamah, 130, 131
Ibn abī Subaih, 131
Ibn al-Jarrāh, 129, 130, 131
Ibn al-Kalbī, 7
Ibn al-Mu'tazz, 125, 129, 131
Ibn an-Nadīm, 138
Ibn 'Asākir, 8, 130, 131
Ibn az-Zayyāt, 101, 110, 132
Ibn Hajar al-'Asqalānī, 129, 130
Ibn 'Imrān, 92
Ibn Mihrawaihi, 130
Ibn Nahīk, 115
Ibn Qaz'ah, 119
Ibn Qutaibah, 125, 127, 128, 129, 130
Ibn Rashīq, 7, 131
Ibn Sa'd, 125
Ibn Sharaq al-Qairawānī, 8
Ibn Simt, 122
Ibn Tabātabā, 2
Ibrāhīm, the "Slain at Bākhamrā," 1
Ibrāhīm an-Nazzām, 119
Ibrāhīm b. al-'Abbās as-Sūlī, 4, 5, 109
Ibrāhīm b. al-Mahdī, Ibn Shiklah, 5, 6, 110, 113
Imru'u'l-Qais, 128
'Īsā, 111
Ismā'īl b. Ja'far, 105

Ja'far b. Yahyā al-Barmakī, 123
Ja'far as-Sādiq, 99
Ja'far b. Muhammad, 100

Khālid b. Barmak, 1
Kuthayyir, 4

Lailā, 94
Ma'bad, 110
Mālik b. Tauq, 6, 108, 118
Māriq, 113
Marwān, 106
Marwān b. Muhammad, 122
Mihrān, 121
Mihrawaihi, 5, 7
Mu'ādh b. Sa'īd, 124
Muhammad, 1, 3, 4, 5, 96, 98, 110, 129
Muhammad, the "Pure Soul," 1
Muhammad b. abī Umayyah, 100
Muhammad b. Khalaf, 130
Muhammad b. Mūsā al-Birbirī, 130
Muhammad b. Umayyah, 131
Mukhāriq, 113
Muqaddis b. Saifī, 112
Muslim b. al-Walīd, Abū Makhlid, 3, 5, 7, 111, 114, 116

Nabateans, 102
Nasr, 107
Nasr b. Mansūr, 117
Nūh, 95

Qudāmah b. Ja'far, 114
Rajā', 118
Razīn, Di'bil's brother, 106
Razīn, Di'bil's grandfather, 3
Razīn al-'Arūdī, 123
Ruzaiq, 3

Sa'īd, 92
Sa'īd b. Yahyā al-Umawī, 131
Sālih, 115
Sālih b. 'Atiyyah, 103, 118
Salīm, 111
Shamr, 122

Tāhir b. al-Husain, 102, 104, 112, 118
Talhah at-Talhāt, 118
Tālib, 131
Tālūt, 131
Tarafah, 126
Tauq, 114, 118
Tubb'as, 103

'Ubaid Allāh, vizier of al-Mutawakkil, 120
'Umair b. Ma'n, 105
'Umar, 4

Wasīf, 94
Yahyā, 108
Yahyā b. Aktham, 110, 118
Yahyā b. Khālid al-Barmakī, 123
Yahyā b. Khāqān, 120
Yāqūt, 6
Yazīd b. al-Walīd, 122

Zaid b. Mūsā, 2, 105
Ziryāb, 114
Ziyād, 98
Zulzul, 113
Zutt, 110

PLACE NAMES

'Abarah, 98
Ahwāz, 105
'Ailah, 122
Anqarah, 97
'Arafah, 98
Aswān, 4, 119

Badr, 98
Baghdād, 1, 2, 5, 98, 110, 123, 129
Bahrain, 126
Bākhamrā, 98
Balqa'ah, 123
Basrah, 105, 126, 129
Batyāthā, 100
Byzantium, 106

China, 103, 122
Dair Hizkil, 104

Egypt, 4, 115
Fadak, 114
Fakhkh, 98

Ghumdān, 103
Ghurbah, 98

Hijāz, 98, 129
Homs, 111
Hunain, 98

India, 103
Irāq, 1, 115

Janad, 103
Jibāl, 116
Jurat, 97
Juzājān, 98

Karbalā, 5, 98
Kaskar, 105
Khaffān, 112
Khaibar, 98

Khazar, 106
Khurāsān, 4, 95, 100, 104
Kūfah, 2, 3, 98, 122

Madīnah, 98, 122, 126
Makkah, 3, 126
Ma'rib, 103
Marv, 103, 122
Minā, 98
Mosul, 115
Mukharrim, 118

Nadad, 103
Najaf, 5

Persia, 2
Qairawān, 103
Qarqisīyā, 3
Qumm, 100, 115

Sāmmarā, 1, 105, 123
Samaraqand, 122
Sawād, 102
Siminjān, 4
Sughd, 103
Syria, 1

Taibah, 98
Tā'if, 126
Tubbat, 122
Tūs, 106, 120

Valley of Khabr, 102
Yamāmah, 129
Yemen, 103
Zafār al-Mulk, 103

TRIBAL NAMES

'Ād, 101
Azd, 97

Bakr, 105
Dabbah, 97

Fazārah, 108
Himyar, 97
Hudhail, 124

'Ijl, 121
Iyād, 92, 103

Jadīs, 101
Jarīsh, 97
Jurhum, 101

Ka'b, 119
Khuzā'ah, 3, 7, 118, 119, 122, 123
Kilāb, 99
Kindah, 97

Lihyān, 120
Ma'ad, 103
Makhzūm, 5, 121
Mudar, 104, 105

Nizār, 122
Nā'it, 110

Qahtān, 92
Qais, 103
Qais 'Ailān, 99
Quraish, 118

Rabī'ah, 104
Taghlib, 108
Tamīm, 108
Tayy, 105, 118

'Ukl, 114
Umayyah, 1, 2, 106, 120
Yamān, 105

POETS REFERRED TO BY DI'BIL

'Abba'ah al-Basrī, 150
'Abbād al-Mukharriq, 150
'Abd al-Khāliq, 151-2
'Abd Allāh b. abī Umayyah, 151
'Abd Allāh b. 'Amr b. abī Subaih, 153-4
'Abd Allāh b. Ayyūb, 152
'Abd Allāh b. az-Zabīr al-Asadī, 152
'Abd Allāh b. Sabrah, 153
'Abd al-Quddūs, 151
Abū 'Abd Allāh b. Humaid, 142
Abū 'd-Dil' as-Sindī, 147
Abū Dhu'aib an-Numairī, 143
Abū Khālid al-Ghanawī, 142
Abū'l-Aswad ad-Du'alī, 160
Abū'l-Janūb, 141
Abū'l-Muhawwis al-Asadī, 176
Abū'l-Munayyib al-Kalbī, 175
Abū Nahshal b. Humaid, 142
Abū Nasr b. Humaid, 142
Abū Qais b. Sumayy al-Kindī, 166
Abū'r-Rumh al-Khuzā'ī, 144
Abū'sh-Shamaqmaq, 146
Abū's-Salt Maulā banī Sulaim, 146
Abū's-Simt, 141
Abū't-Tamahān al-Qainī, 148-9
Abū Ziyād al-Kilabī, 131
Ahmad b. abī Du'ād, 135
Ahmad b. Ishāq al-Khāriqī, 135
Ahmad b. Muhammad b. Fadālah, 136
Ahmad b. Saif, Abū'l-Jahm, 136
Ahmad b. Umayyah b. abī Umayyah, 136
Ahram b. Humaid, 142
al-'Abbās b. al-Akhnaf, 150-1
al-Fadl b. al-Abbās, 165-6
al-Hārith b. Qais al-Kindī, 141
al-Hasan b. Hāni', Abū Nuwās, 179
al-Hasan b. Rajā', 141-2
al-Husain b. ar-Rawwās, Abū Nīqah, 161
'Alī b. abī Umayyah, 155
'Alī b. Ādam, 180
'Alī b. Razīn al-Khuza'ī, 156
al-Kumait b. Zaid, 167-8
al-Mufaddal b. al-Muhallib, 172-3
al-Mufaddal b. Qudāmah, 172
al-Mumazziq, Abū 'Abbād, 174-5
al-Mundhir b. Harām, 175
al-Mustahill b. al-Kumait, 171-2
al-Qalāh al-Anbarī, 166
al-Walīd b. Ka'b, 177
'Āmir b. 'Umārah, Abū'l-Haidhām, 150
'Amr al-Khariqi, 158
'Amr ar-Rahhāl, 159
'Amr b. 'abd ar-Rahmān al-Bāhilī, 161
'Amr b. abī Bakr, 156
'Amr b. abī'l-Habar, 157
'Amr b. al-'Ās b. Wā'il, 160-1
'Amr b. 'Āmir, 161
'Amr b. Duwairah, 159
'Amr b. Hassān b. Hāni', 157
'Amr b. Humail al-Hudhailī, 163
'Amr b. Huwayy as-Siksikī, 157-8
'Amr b. Mabradah, 162
'Amr b. Nasr al-Qisāfī, 162-3
'Amr b. Qurād az-Ziyādī, 162
'Amr b. Shazbī b. Bishr, 160
'Amr b. Yathribī ad-Dabbī, 162
'Amr b. Zaid b. Hilāl, 160
Anas b. Zunaim, 138
an-Nu'mān b. Nadlah al-Ansārī, 175-6
'Aqīl b. 'Ullafah, 155

'Attāb b. 'Abd Allāh, 154
at-Tirimmāh b. Hakīm, 148
Aus b. Tha'labah, 138

Bakr b. Khārijah, 139
Bishr b. Rabī'ah, 139

Dhū'l-Isba' al-Kalbī, 137
Ghusain b. Barrāq, 164-5

Hājib al-Fīl, 141
Hārūn ar-Rashīd, 176
Humaid b. 'Abd al-Humaid, 142

Ibn abī 'Āsim ash-Shāmī, 149
Ibrāhīm al-Mausilī, 179
Ibrāhīm b. al-'Abbās as-Sūlī, 135
Ibrāhīm b. Hishām al-Ghassānī, 135
Imru'u'l-Qais, 137, 138
Ismā'īl al-Qarātisī, 137
Iyād ath-Thumalī, 163-4

Jamīl al-'Udhrī, 140
Jarīr b. Yazīd b. Khālid, 137

Ka'b b. Mālik, 167
Kathīr b. Kathīr, 166-7

Khalaf al-Ahmar, 143
Khālid b. Ghallāb, 176
Kulthum b. 'Amr al-'Attābī, 167

Mālik b. 'Auf b. Sa'd, 168
Mālik b. ash-Shar'abī, 168
Masrūq b. Hajar b. Sa'īd, 172
Mas'ūd b. 'Ulayyah, 172
Miknaf Abū Sulmā al-Mazinī, 173-4
Mirdās b. Hadhām al-Asadī, 171
Muhalhil b. Rabī'ah, 175
Muhammad b. 'Abd Allāh b. Kunāsah, 170
Muhammad b. 'Abd Allāh, Ibn az-Zayyāt, 170
Muhammad b. abī'l-Hārith, 169
Muhammad b. abī Muhammad al-Yazīdī, 169
Muhammad b. abī Umayyah al-Kātib, 169
Muhammad b. Ismā'īl b. Yasār, 168
Muhammad b. Makhlad, 170
Muhammad b. Umayyah b. abī Umayyah, 168-9
Mukhāriq b. Shihāb b. Qais, 171
Mukhārish al-Umawī, 171

Munqidh b. 'Abd Allāh, 180
Murrah b. 'Amr, 171

Qais b. Mashkūh, 166
Rabī'ah b. Maqrūm, 143
Rib'ī adh-Dhuhalī, 143-4

Sālim b. Musāfi', 144
Shabīb b. al-Barsā', 145-6
Shuwais Abū Far'ūn, 146
Siyān al-Kufī, 145

Tālib, 147
Tālūt, 147
Thābit Qutnah, 139-40

'Umair b. Dābi' b. al-Hārith, 163
'Uthmān b. 'Āmir b. 'Amr, 155
'Uwaimir b. 'Amr, Abū Qilābah, 163
'Uyainah b. Asmā', 164

Ward b. Sa'd, Abū'l-'Udhāfir, 177
Yahyā b. Naufal, 177
Ya'qūb b. Dā'ūd, 178
Yazīd b. 'Abd Allāh, 178
Zurzur ar-Rafā', 144

www.ingramcontent.com/pod-product-compliance
Lightning Source LLC
Chambersburg PA
CBHW081225170426
43198CB00017B/2713